Integrating Aboriginal Perspectives into the School Curriculum

Purposes, Possibilities, and Challenges

From improved critical thinking to increased self-esteem and school retention, there are many benefits to bringing Aboriginal viewpoints into public school classrooms. In this comprehensive study, Yatta Kanu explores educational frameworks that can be effectively implemented to maximize Indigenous students' engagement, learning, and academic achievement.

Based on six years of empirical research, *Integrating Aboriginal Perspectives into the School Curriculum* offers insights from youths, instructors, and school administrators, highlighting specific elements that make a difference in achieving educational success for Aboriginal students. The work draws on a wide range of disciplines, from cognitive psychology to civics, and its findings are applicable among diverse cultural groups and in a variety of classroom settings.

Kanu combines theoretical analysis and practical recommendations to emphasize the need for fresh thinking and creative experimentation in developing curricula and policy. Amid global calls to improve outcomes for Indigenous students, this work is a timely and valuable addition to the literature on Aboriginal education.

YATTA KANU is a professor in the Faculty of Education at the University of Manitoba.

YATTA KANU

Integrating Aboriginal Perspectives into the School Curriculum

Purposes, Possibilities, and Challenges

UNIVERSITY OF TORONTO PRESS
Toronto Buffalo London

© University of Toronto Press Incorporated 2011
Toronto Buffalo London
www.utppublishing.com
Printed in Canada

ISBN 978-1-4426-4244-7 (cloth)
ISBN 978-1-4426-1132-0 (paper)

Printed on acid-free, 100% post-consumer recycled paper with vegetable-based inks.

Library and Archives Canada Cataloguing in Publication

Kanu, Yatta, 1952–
Integrating Aboriginal perspectives into the school curriculum :
purposes, possibilities and challenges / Yatta Kanu.

Includes bibliographical references and index.
ISBN 978-1-4426-4244-7 (bound). – ISBN 978-1-4426-1132-0 (pbk.)

1. Native peoples – Education – Canada.   2. Native peoples – Study and
teaching – Canada.   3. Critical pedagogy.   4. Curriculum change.
I. Title.

E96.2.K36 2011   371.829'97071   C2010-906501-8

This book has been published with the help of a grant from the
Canadian Federation for the Humanities and Social Sciences, through
the Aid to Scholarly Publications Program, using funds provided by the
Social Sciences and Humanities Research Council of Canada.

University of Toronto Press acknowledges the financial assistance to its
publishing program of the Canada Council for the Arts and the Ontario
Arts Council.

 Canada Council Conseil des Arts    ONTARIO ARTS COUNCIL
for the Arts du Canada   CONSEIL DES ARTS DE L'ONTARIO

University of Toronto Press acknowledges the financial support for its
publishing activities of the Government of Canada through the Canada
Book Fund.

Contents

Preface

If the experiences in our public schools have the power to change the stories of children's lives, what happens to those who don't hear the stories of
their own people? And if children do learn stories about their lives, what
happens when their teachers and texts regard those stories as inferior, representing wrong values, and representing inadequate means for survival?
What happens to children whose public education is rooted in an alien
culture? What do they learn to value, what do they learn to reject, and
what do they learn about survival when they don't ever hear or read about
the suffering, loss, and endurance of their people? How do they establish
positive identities about themselves when voices within their culture are
ignored, twisted, and suppressed, and when voices outside their culture
decide who these young people are and who they should become? What
happens to the relationships among children from differing cultures within classrooms?

                                                          Dorothea Susag, 2006

Susag's provocative questions call attention to forms of curricular
knowledge/relations that exclude the social recognition seen as necessary for individuals to flourish as human beings and that can hold the
hope of a more peaceful and just future for the world. In a real sense,
the questions underlie the urgent call for the inclusion of Aboriginal
perspectives in schools and classrooms, one of the most advocated but
still under-researched responses to the challenge of providing social
recognition and justice for Aboriginal students in the Canadian public
school system. This book has emerged from research studies conducted
from 2002 to 2007 in which I investigated the integration of Aboriginal

cultural knowledge and/or perspectives into the school curriculum in a large urban centre in western Canada. My interest in this project is not based on birth or on common cultural and historical experiences with Aboriginal peoples in Canada. Rather, two personal experiences brought me to the project: my experience of colonial education, which began in my native country, Sierra Leone (a former British colony in West Africa) and my experience as a teacher educator at a Canadian university.

The colonial education I received in Sierra Leone and, later, my postgraduate studies in Britain and Canada exposed me, firsthand, to the subjugation or misrepresentation of the rich historical and cultural knowledge and traditions of not only African peoples but also those of other racial and ethnic minorities. I know all too well the struggle for identity, the erosion of self-confidence, and the resistance to Eurocentric forms of education that such subjugation and misrepresentation can produce in those who suffer them. Fundamentally, I believe that education should enable students to draw on repertoires such as their cultural knowledge, traditions, and aspirations to examine the assumptions and beliefs underlying the knowledge, perspectives, and interactions and/ or relations they experience in school and, through critical analysis and reflection, imagine and work toward the future (and the present) they desire. Any education/curriculum focusing on democratic empowerment must have this kind of critical literacy as its foundation. Critical literacy enhances the ability to mould one's world through naming and constructing modes of preferred social and personal life. I believe that cultural capital – that stock of cultural knowledge and awareness which an individual possesses about his or her own history that makes it possible to act as an autonomous human being – plays an important role in this process. By autonomous I mean having freedom to act and contribute to collective and collaborative social life. Without a sense of one's roots it is hard to act in ways that are in the interest of one's self and one's group. However, I am acutely aware that some students' cultural socialization processes are excluded from their schooling experiences, thereby denying them full and equal access to the education they need in order to take up the fight for social justice and a better future. This knowledge and awareness have undergirded my work since 1993 on increasing educational access and equity for minority students in the K–12 system, specifically exploring educational institutions, processes, and practices as sites of capital to which students have unequal access. Informed by sociocultural theories of cognition and learning which make an intricate connection between children's cultural socialization patterns and their thinking, communication, learning, and motivational styles, and given the near-absence of minority cultural knowledge and perspectives from school curricula and among a large number of public school teachers in Canada, my work has focused on the integration of minority cultural knowledge and perspectives into the school curriculum and teacher education programs.

As a teacher educator at a large Canadian university in the province of Manitoba, which has one of the fastest growing populations of Aboriginal youth, I am aware of the lack of knowledge and understanding of Aboriginal cultures and issues among most teacher candidates who come to my faculty and among many practising teachers in the public school system where the vast majority of Aboriginal students attend school. I know firsthand how this lack of understanding compromises teachers' interactions with, and hence the education of, Aboriginal students. For over a decade, I have visited many public schools and classrooms as a faculty advisor to teacher candidates on their teaching practicum. Consistently during these visits, I have noticed that most teachers lack the pedagogical tools and the cultural knowledge to hold Aboriginal students to the same high standards and expectations as their White mainstream counterparts. For example, an Aboriginal student would walk into a class late but would not be held accountable by the teacher candidate or the regular class teacher as other students are. Aboriginal students are not asked questions in class at the same frequency as White students, and on the rare occasion that Aboriginal students volunteer answers, their answers are not probed to the same extent as other students. Asked to explain this differential treatment of Aboriginal students, teacher candidates would often tell me about their fear of pushing Aboriginal students too hard in class because 'doing so may not be appropriate' or 'their lateness may be due to personal issues I do not understand or want to get into.' Responses such as these confirm the results of a Students Awareness Survey administered in 1999 by the Coalition for the Advancement of Aboriginal Studies (CAAS) among postsecondary students across Canada which showed that very few Canadian students feel they have adequate knowledge about Aboriginal peoples or the issues affecting their lives. These experiences set me thinking about curriculum research that advances mainstream educators' understanding of Aboriginal students and how this understanding could inform and shape the education of Aboriginal students in Canada's public schools. In the process, educators would also come to better understand their own identities and reframe their epistemic and ontological assumptions in light of Aboriginal knowledge and ontologies.

Choosing the integration of Aboriginal perspectives into curriculum and pedagogy as a beginning point for the advancement of such understanding, I pondered questions such as the following: Recognizing the rich diversity within and among Aboriginal groups, are there elements of Aboriginal culture sufficiently common among Aboriginal groups which teachers can include in their classrooms not only as part of the cultural heritage and legitimate knowledge of Aboriginal peoples but also as a tool for enhancing classroom learning for Aboriginal students? If there is such cultural knowledge, how can it be effectively integrated into the school curriculum and the instructional repertoires of teachers and teacher educators, the majority of whom have little or no background knowledge of Aboriginal cultures or Aboriginal students? Will such integration increase academic achievement, class attendance, and retention in school among Aboriginal students? If so, what are the critical elements of the integration processes that account for such success? How can these elements be captured and capitalized on in pre-service teacher education and in the professional development of practising teachers? Considering the pivotal role of teachers in any change in the classroom, what are the views of teachers on the integration of Aboriginal perspectives into the school curriculum? And, what are the learning opportunities, prospects, and challenges entailing the integration of Aboriginal perspectives? The search for answers to these questions led me, with research assistance from two Aboriginal graduate students, to the three ethnographic studies comprising the research reported in this book. I strongly believed that answers to these important questions would not only throw light on some of the salient issues arising from the popular call for the integration of Aboriginal perspectives into school curricula and classrooms but also would provide much-needed direction for those charged with the responsibility of implementing this reform in schools. This belief and my interest in increasing educational access and equity for Aboriginal students in the public school system provided the impetus for this research.

I hope this brief description of my personal location in this research, and my lived experiences and desires that brought me to it, will provide readers with a context within which they can understand why and how I have conducted the studies and reported on the findings. As a social researcher, I do not subscribe to the positivistic notion that the researcher has no position of personal interest. Who I am, what I believe, and the experiences I have had inevitably have an impact on the research that I do. As Patricia Hill Collins (1991) points out in her work on Black feminist thought, *who* makes knowledge claims is as important as *what* those knowledge claims are. Like her, I believe that individuals' commitments to ideological or value positions are important in understanding knowledge claims.

This self-reflexive consciousness allowed me, throughout my data collection, to continually ask myself whether I was recording what was really there or only what I wanted to see. Dei and colleagues (1997) remind us that the integrity of an ethnography relies on our ability as researchers to relay the uncompromised truths of others without appropriating their voices or inferring our own biases: 'Ethnography, then, must accept the self-defined truths of its subjects in order to validate its claim to represent who they "really" are' (p. 221). Therefore, the task of investigating and understanding the integration of Aboriginal perspectives necessitated a methodological and intellectual process that allowed me to establish proper relations between the original data and the account that I have produced. In this case, the process revealed correspondence between the transformative political and social goals of the Aboriginal populations affected by chronic underachievement of Aboriginal students and my own goals as a social researcher attempting to provide a means of educational and social change dedicated to improving schooling for racial and ethnic minorities like Aboriginal students.

REFERENCES

Coalition for the Advancement of Aboriginal Studies (1999). Student awareness survey. Retrieved from: www.crr.ca/index2.php?option+com_content+do-pdf=1+id=252

Collins, P.H. (1993). It's in our hands: Breaking the silence on gender in African-American studies. In L. Castenell Jr. & W. Pinar (Eds.), *Understanding curriculum as racial text: Representations of identity and difference in education*, pp. 55–82. New York: State University of New York Press.

Dei, G.S., Mazzuca, J., McIsaac, E., & Zine, J. (1997). *Reconstructing dropout: A critical ethnography of the dynamics of Black students' disengagement from school*. Toronto: University of Toronto Press.

Susag, D. (2006). Indian Education for all: Through our own eyes. *Phi Delta Kappan*, November 2006 Special Edition, 201–3.

Acknowledgments

The author gratefully acknowledges the contributions of the following organizations and people: The Social Sciences and Humanities Research Council of Canada (SSHRC) for funding the research studies comprising this book; the Aboriginal Education Directorate and Aboriginal education resource centres in Winnipeg for advice and access to Aboriginal education resources; the Aboriginal and non-Aboriginal students and teachers whose voices and viewpoints, as research participants, have framed and informed my recommendations and suggestions for effective school and classroom practices in the integration of Aboriginal perspectives; the undergraduate and graduate students who read and provided valuable feedback on the accessibility of the book for its primary audience – students in faculties of education; and Linda Marynuk and Leone Simard, Aboriginal graduate research assistants, for their cultural advice and invaluable assistance with data collection and other aspects of the research studies.

Three of the chapters in this work appeared in earlier versions (as preliminary data) in the following journals, to whose editors and publishers I am profoundly grateful. Chapter 3 appeared in 2002 (*Alberta Journal of Educational Research*, 48(2), 98–121); Chapter 6 in 2006 (*Journal of Advanced Academics*, 18(1), 116–45); and Chapter 7 in 2005 (*Alberta Journal of Educational Research*, 51(1), 1–20).

Integrating Aboriginal Perspectives into the School Curriculum

Purposes, Possibilities, and Challenges

1 Introduction: Integrating Aboriginal Perspectives into School Curricula: Why Does It Matter?

In a recent paper on embedding Indigenous perspectives in university teaching and learning in Australia, Juliana McLaughlin and Sue Whatman (2008) argued that providing a literature base that signifies the importance of embedding Indigenous knowledge/perspectives in the curriculum provides not only a rationale for this important and timely undertaking but also the theoretical and conceptual platform for realistic curriculum reform. This introductory chapter draws on a broad range of literature to provide such rationale and context, including barely explored ideas on why the integration of Aboriginal perspectives matters so much. These views, which reflect my own, are rooted in emerging ideas about human learning and development as psychosocial and cultural processes, intimate and cultural citizenship, collective intelligence in a knowledge economy, and the functioning power of the school curriculum in shaping students' identities and social and economic circumstances.

The Call to Integrate Aboriginal Perspectives

Recent years have seen more and more calls from places like New Zealand, Australia, Canada, Alaska, Hawaii, and the Pacific nations to decolonize Aboriginal education and improve the educational attainment of Aboriginal students by including Aboriginal cultural knowledge/perspectives into school curricula and other schooling processes. These calls are part of a larger effort to reflect critically on the impact of colonization on Aboriginal peoples, in particular internal colonization, whereby carefully selected mechanisms are employed by dominant groups to subordinate or regulate Aboriginal populations. These mechanisms include the subjugation of Indigenous knowledge/perspectives and the use of colonial ideology to cultivate psychological subordination in Indigenous peoples. Because culture has always been a crucial site of struggle in the colonization and decolonization of 'the Other' and because formal education plays a pivotal role in the promotion and validation of the cultural knowledge of dominant groups as 'official knowledge' for all students, Aboriginal scholarly effort has focused on two things: (a) challenging the dominance of Western European culture in defining and shaping school knowledge and (b) reclaiming Aboriginal knowledge, which has been devalued and delegitimated in formal education. Among Aboriginal peoples, reclamation of the knowledge of Aboriginal peoples in education is seen not only as a strategy of resistance and commitment to redressing colonial processes of knowledge generation and its implications of imperialism and knowledge/power relations (Battiste, 2000) but also as a means of expanding the general knowledge base of education (Thaman, 2003), especially in the current information age when capital is invested with knowledge which in turn is invested with cultural values.

Multiple critical sites of struggle in assisting the reclamation of Aboriginal knowledge in education have been identified in the literature. Three such sites are: the need to decolonize research (Smith, 1999; 2005; Mutua & Swadener, 2004); the strategic reinvestment in theoretical tools that challenge the status quo and assist the positive transformation of Indigenous communities and peoples (Smith, 2003); and the engagement of state socialization apparatuses such as the school to position and legitimate Indigenous knowledge as relevant and significant in the hierarchy of valued knowledges (see Canadian Council on Learning, 2007; Friesen & Friesen, 2002). The research studies on which this book is based were undertaken in an effort to explore the third site, namely, the engagement of the school in promoting Aboriginal interests by integrating Aboriginal cultural knowledge and perspectives into public school curricula.

Internationally, the disproportionately lower rates of academic success among Indigenous Aboriginal students have been consistently explained in terms of the discontinuity between the cultural patterns of these students and the processes, environments, and requirements of the schools (see, e.g., the report of the Canadian Royal Commission on Aboriginal Peoples, 1996; the Australian report by the National Aboriginal Education Committee, cited in McConaghy, 2000; and Montana's Indian Education for All project [Starnes, 2006]). Particularly in the case of Aboriginal students who move from their home communities to attend urban /metropolitan public schools where the vast majority of the teachers are non-Aboriginal and belong to the dominant Western European cultures of their countries, the lack of Aboriginal cultural knowledge in school curricula and among teachers, and the conflict between teachers' and students' culturally determined interactional styles have been identified as crucial factors in failure in school, prompting calls for the inclusion of Aboriginal perspectives across school curricula and teacher education programs. The assumption is that the integration of Aboriginal cultural socialization processes, especially if based on an understanding of the Aboriginal communities where Aboriginal students live their lives and how they are culturally socialized to participate in routine practices in these settings, will create links between the home and school cultures and motivate Aboriginal students to learn in school. In turn, this may close the educational achievement gap between Aboriginal students and their non-Aboriginal counterparts in the public school system (Battiste, 1998; McAlpine, 2001; Royal Commission on Aboriginal Peoples [RCAP], 1996). As the next section shows, a burgeoning collection of research that views learning and development as psychosocial and cultural practices supports this assumption.

The Centrality of Cultural Mediation in Learning and Development

Why does it matter that we undertake research that helps us better understand cultural socialization and its mediating influence on, and consequences for, student learning? It matters because social-cultural and cultural-historical psychology begins with the assumption of an intimate connection between the special environments that human beings inhabit and human psychological processes. In their work, James Wertsch and Michael Cole have explicated this link by explaining that the special quality of the human environment is that it is suffused with the achievements of prior generations in reified form. This idea is also found in the writings of cultural historical psychologists from many national traditions. John Dewey, for example, wrote that from birth to death we live in a world of persons and things which is in large measure what it is because of what has been done and transmitted from previous human activities. When this fact is ignored, experience is treated as if it were something which goes on exclusively inside an individual's body and mind. According to Dewey, experience does not occur in a vacuum; there are resources outside an individual which give rise to experience (Dewey, 1938/1963). The early writings of Russian cultural psychologists also emphasize the cultural medium. They argue that the special mental quality of human beings is their need and ability to mediate their actions through artifacts previously shaped by prior human practice, and to arrange for the rediscovery and appropriation of these forms of mediation by subsequent generations (Cole and Wertsch, 2001). In this regard, Vygotsky wrote: 'the central fact about human psychology is the fact of cultural mediation' (1981, p.166).

From the perspective of the centrality of cultural mediation in mind and mental development, the mind develops through an interweaving of biology and the appropriation of the cultural heritage. Higher mental functions are by definition culturally mediated, involving an indirect action in which previously used artifacts are incorporated as an aspect of current action (Cole and Wertsch, 2001). This perspective has several implications for learning and cognition. First, cultural artifacts do not simply serve to facilitate mental processes; they fundamentally shape and transform them. Second, because artifacts are themselves culturally, historically, and institutionally situated, all psychological functions begin and, and to a large extent, remain culturally, historically, and institutionally situated; there is no universally appropriate form of cultural mediation. A third implication is that context and action are not independent of each other. As Cole and Wertsch put it, 'objects and contexts arise together as part of a single bio social cultural process of development.'

These implications suggest that mind can no longer be seen as located solely inside the head. Rather, higher psychological functions include the biological individual, the cultural mediational artifacts, and the culturally structured social and natural environments of which individuals are a part. The position of Dewey, Vygotsky, Cole and Wertsch, and others on the centrality of cultural artifacts in human mental processes has great resonance in recent movements in cognitive science, and the position undergirds much of the emerging science on distributed cognition and situated learning.

This primacy of cultural mediation in learning and development invites us as educators to provide opportunities for our most disadvantaged groups to draw on their cultural capital – what they bring from prior cultural socialization in their homes and communities – to support and enhance classroom learning for them. Understanding how individuals or groups historically engage in shared practices in their cultural communities may account for dispositions they may have in new circumstances such as classroom learning (see Kanu, 2007a).

The Effort to Reconnect Aboriginal Education to Its Cultural Roots

The strong link between prior cultural socialization and student learning suggests that schools should be held even more accountable for the educational success of marginalized students, such as Aboriginal students, whose home cultures have been excluded or only sparsely included in schooling processes.

Beginning with the Hawthorne report (1966/7) and its claim that 97 per cent of Indian [sic] children dropped out of the public school system, research and other reports have consistently pointed out that public education in Canada has continued to fail Aboriginal youth. They leave the school system without the requisite skills to participate in the economic life of their communities and Canadian society, without the language and cultural knowledge of their people, with their identities and self-worth eroded, and without realizing the Aboriginal vision of culturally and linguistically competent youths ready to assume the responsibilities of their nations (Royal Commission on Aboriginal Peoples, 1996). Because this failure has been largely explained in terms of the discontinuity between the home cultures of Aboriginal students and the processes and environments of the formal school system, the efforts of Aboriginal educators and communities are currently directed at restoring continuity between the home culture and the school. Significant strides have been made in this area. For example, the assumption of local leadership of band-controlled schools by First Nations Tribal Councils and locally elected school committees, instruction for all subjects conducted in the students' (Aboriginal) first language (rather than English or French), the teaching of Aboriginal languages in schools, the staffing of schools with Aboriginal teachers, the inclusion of Aboriginal elders as teachers, and the development of curricula grounded in the values, histories, and traditions of Aboriginal peoples, are all attempts to reduce the cultural discontinuity experienced by Aboriginal students in the formal education system. Provincial governments and school boards have also put many initiatives in place to create positive learning environments for Aboriginal students. For instance, schools have hired Aboriginal teachers and Aboriginal support staff, and curricula have been reviewed to eliminate obvious racism (RCAP, 1996; Wotherspoon, 2006).

What are the overall results of these efforts? According to the Royal Commission on Aboriginal Peoples, gains have been modest and much more needs to be done. Most of the success has been noticed in band-controlled schools that are located on reserves and that serve homogeneous groups of students in terms of linguistic and cultural heritage (Haig-Brown et al., 1997). These schools often experience greater autonomy in responding to Aboriginal students' needs than schools in urban and rural settings where control remains in the hands of 'paternalistic' bureaucracies (Corson, 1992). In provincial schools where the majority of Aboriginal students outside of the territories attend school (DIAND, 1994), parents and Aboriginal community members have little direct access to decision making; no special effort is made to make them feel part of the life of the school; and the vast majority of teachers in these schools belong to the dominant mainstream Euro-Canadian culture. The lack of Aboriginal cultural knowledge among these teachers is generally seen as resulting in pedagogical and interaction patterns that have produced negative learning experiences for Aboriginal students.

Since the 1960s, Aboriginal people have responded by lobbying for programs that would bring Aboriginal teachers into public school classrooms. However, although there are many more Aboriginal teachers in Aboriginal and non-Aboriginal school systems and many more Aboriginal teacher education programs today, the numbers remain far too low, relative to current and projected needs (Canadian Council on Learning, 2007). For the foreseeable future, therefore, efforts need to be made to infuse the preparation of teachers from the mainstream culture with the history, language, and pedagogical traditions of Aboriginal peoples. This strategy is particularly important in provinces like Manitoba, where it is reported that close to 20 per cent of children and youth are Aboriginal, that Winnipeg has the second highest concentration of Aboriginal persons in an urban area in Canada, and that Aboriginal youths are more likely to live in low socioeconomic areas and have poorer educational outcomes than non-Aboriginal youths (Brownell et al., 2006; Canadian Education Statistics Council, 2003; Peters, 2005).

Most research on culture and the teaching and/or learning of Indigenous students has focused on the identification of key features of the methodology of education in Indigenous cultures (Alonge, 1982; Cajete, 1994; Ezeife, 1999; Kanu, 1997), learning style preferences and their relation to school success (Browne, 1990; Osborne, 1985; Pepper & Henry, 1986; Ryan, 1992; Shade, 1989), and materials and practices from Indigenous traditional settings that support the teaching and/or learning of Indigenous students (Ezeife, 2001; 1999; Haig-Brown et al, 1997; Kirkness, 1998). Although some of these studies have been criticized on several grounds (for example, analysis of research on learning style preferences among Aboriginal groups has included the criticism that data are collected and interpreted within an essentialist framework that treats social groups as homogeneous entities; see McCarthy, 1998), they are valuable for their documentation of evidence that patterns do exist in how members of different cultural groups approach learning tasks. Thus, these studies provide important directions for helping teachers to develop appropriate cross-cultural teaching and assessment processes.

Researchers (e.g., Kennedy, 1997) have pointed out the need for further research exploration of these directions for practical and theoretical insights relating to teaching Indigenous students. As Kennedy elaborates, awareness of knowledge about how Indigenous students learn is not synonymous with the ability of teachers to translate that knowledge into meaningful learning opportunities. Ezeife (2001), therefore, suggests the integration (meaning *consistent infusion*) of such knowledge throughout the regular school curricula and evaluating the effect on school success for Aboriginal students. Canadian studies on this kind of integration and appraisal are sparse; therefore, the research studies discussed in this book are timely and important. They provide educators and curriculum developers/leaders with theoretical and practical understandings of how to effectively integrate Aboriginal perspectives and pedagogical practices into existing provincial curricula, thereby increasing the opportunities for educational access for Aboriginal students. Education not only increases the human potential of Aboriginal students, it also leads to the development of a larger pool of Aboriginal employment and a critical mass with potential economic clout (Winnipeg Chamber of Commerce, cited in Binda, 2001a).

Beyond economic benefits, the integration of Aboriginal cultural knowledge and perspectives into regular school programs (as opposed to current calls for separate Aboriginal school divisions) has the potential for promoting better intercultural understanding among all students, positive intergroup relations, solidarity and community building, and overall, an enhanced social climate. By providing knowledge about effective ways of integrating Aboriginal perspectives into the teaching of the regular school curriculum, this book also makes a significant contribution to educators' understanding of how to reconnect the education of Aboriginal students to their cultural roots, a particularly important consideration given the ongoing concern among

Aboriginal communities over the 'de-culturation' (loss of culture and hence identity) of indigenous students in the public school system (see, e.g., Cajete, 1994; Hill, 2001).

Integration for Intimate and Cultural Citizenship

Contemporary critical discourses of citizenship also provide conceptual resources for building the case for the integration of Aboriginal perspectives into schooling processes. In a democracy, citizenship not only confers membership and identity, it also involves rights of participation. Critical discourses of citizenship draw attention to issues of membership, identity, engagement, and participation in productive ways in society. These discourses challenge civic republican and liberal notions of citizenship which, respectively, value commitment to one's political community (local, state, and national), and autonomy and individual liberty within certain constraints imposed to promote the liberty and rights of others. They attempt to broaden the agendas of human freedom by focusing especially on exclusion based on race, gender, culture, ethnicity, nationality, sexuality, and socioeconomic class. Two critical citizenship discourses of relevance to the integration of Aboriginal perspectives into schooling processes are 'intimate citizenship' (Plummer, 2003) and 'cultural citizenship' (Abowitz & Harnish, 2006), particularly useful because they challenge us to rethink the relationship between citizenship, the nation state, and social difference.

Ken Plummer's idea of intimate citizenship extends citizenship beyond its traditional focus on rights and a firm division between public and private. It draws on insights from psychoanalysis and the sociology of emotion to challenge us to consider more carefully the resources and types of relationships entailed in active, participatory citizenship. As Plummer (2003) describes it, intimate citizenship concerns itself with: 'The decisions people have to make *over the control (or not) over* one's body, feelings, relationships; *access (or not) to* representations, relationships, and public spaces, etc.; and *socially grounded choices (or not) about* identities, gender experiences, erotic experiences. It does not imply one model, one pattern or one way' (p. 14, original emphasis).

Intimate citizenship thus extends to the political arena issues that have traditionally been seen as issues of private choice and personal morality, thereby giving weight to the conditions that underpin the successful exercise of rights and responsibilities. In highlighting an aspect of social theory neglected by other theories of citizenship, Plummer has drawn our attention to the prerequisites of citizenship that are rooted in the sociology of emotion. As Faulks (2006) explains, 'The exercise of effective citizenship presumes a series of underpinning emotions such as trust, confidence, and security; similarly, negative emotions of fear, envy, and shame will seriously undermine the capacity of citizens to exercise their rights and responsibilities' (p. 130). Psychological processes such as personal emotions and self-awareness are, therefore, central to civic participation in a successful democracy. For this reason, Andrew Samuels (2001), writing from the perspective of psychoanalysis, has contended that in order to reinvigorate politics and civic participation, there is need to close the gap between subjective, emotional experiences of politics /public spaces on the one hand and public policy on the other. As he explains, politics and civic participation are not purely rational, objective activities that are divorced from feelings and perceptions of one's place in society; an understanding of the emotions undergirding people's political beliefs and prejudices is important for improving communication across ethnic, class, and ideological boundaries. Political institutions, therefore, need to find ways of encouraging individuals to articulate their own private responses, and to connect with these responses. Samuels describes this pathway as representing 'the last untapped fount of new energies ... in the political and social realm' (p. 167). Intimate citizenship suggests, then, that the social bonds between citizens are likely to be stronger if we seek to actively develop relationships that are based on mutual caring and mutual respect.

Historical analysis shows that intimate citizenship, as explicated above, has not been fully experienced by Aboriginal peoples in Canada even after the 1996 report of the Royal Commission on Aboriginal Peoples and its recommendation of a renewed relationship based on the principles of recognition, the redistribution of material resources and social goods such as rights and respect, and the elimination of domination and institutional constraints on self-development and self-determination. Experiences of assimilationist models of citizenship, racism, discrimination, unequal organization of social structures and decision-making bodies, and, until relatively recently, the lack of Aboriginal voice in the determination of Aboriginal affairs have produced negative emotions that have seriously undermined Aboriginal peoples' capacity to exercise their rights and responsibilities and participate in Canadian society productively and meaningfully.

It is important to emphasize the institutionalized nature of many of the social injustices suffered by Aboriginal peoples. Unlike overt, singular acts of discrimination or oppression, 'institutionalized forms are built into the taken-for-granted norms, rules, skills, and values of social institutions and, because of their naturalized status, frequently remain unchallenged' (Schon, cited in North, 2006, p. 150). Hence, 'the complex ways in which individual identities and capacities are ... the products of social processes and relations' (Young, 1990, p. 27) are overlooked or even denied.

Examining how this dynamic plays out in formal education has led to a unique focus on issues of cultural imperialism in schooling, the privileging and normalization of dominant values and beliefs in the public school system, the exclusion of Aboriginal and other ethnic minority values, and the under-funding of schools serving Aboriginal populations. Numerous reports and research studies have drawn attention to what Schissel and Wotherspoon (2003, p. 2) have called 'the dark side of education' for Aboriginal peoples, implicating schools in processes that have 'badly damaged' the lives of the majority of Aboriginal peoples, and severely curtailing the exercise of successful citizenship for them. Cultural practices and belief systems that provide emotional strength, security, and spiritual sustenance for Aboriginal peoples are ignored in formal education – thereby divorcing the education of Aboriginal students from their emotional roots and provoking the call for Aboriginal cultures to be integrated into conventional education, and to be respected and held in high esteem (Battiste, 2000; Friesen & Friesen, 2002; Kirkness & Bowman, 1983).

The need to improve educational opportunities and meaningful inclusion for ethnic minorities like Aboriginal students has invoked discourses of 'cultural citizenship.' Cultural citizenship discourses interrogate how ethnic, language, and other cultural groups have found citizenship 'to be a role and identity purchased at a high price' (Rosaldo, cited in Abowitz & Harnish, 2006, p. 667). This is because 'citizenship identities can require assimilation and thus prove inhospitable and harmful to cultural identities that are of great importance to individuals and groups' (p. 667). Cultural citizenship is fraught with struggle over culture, representation, minority rights, and a host of other issues pertaining to inclusion. It is an idea of citizenship that emphasizes the role of conflict but 'conflict that produces new cultural and political forms' and 'speaks a language of rights and agency' (p. 670). Abowitz and Harnish have observed that if culture is what provides meaning for people, then culture cannot realistically or productively be segregated from citizenship as a practice or status. In dominant culture societies, however, full citizenship and cultural visibility appear to be inversely related. 'When one increases the other decreases, and too many people have had to choose between trying to belong to their cultural community and their national community' (p. 670).

James Banks, a leading voice in the discourse of cultural citizenship, posits that citizenship education in a multicultural, democratic society must incorporate the voices, experiences, and perspectives of ethnic minority and low-income students. He writes: 'Our goal should not be merely to educate students of color or White mainstream students to fit into the existing workforce, social structures, and society. Such an education would be inimical to students from different cultural groups because it would force them to experience self-alienation ... This kind of unidimensional and assimilationist education would also create problems for the citizenship and national identity of youths of color' (1990, p. 211).

From the perspectives of intimate and cultural citizenship, the case for the integration of Aboriginal perspectives into the school curriculum and other schooling processes cannot be stated any more clearly.

Increasing/Broadening Our Knowledge Base in a Knowledge Society

The emergence of the knowledge society gives renewed invigoration to the importance of Indigenous/Aboriginal knowledge in the preparation of young people for a world of creativity, flexibility, and change. The knowledge society is a learning society where continuous innovation depends on the capacity of workers to learn from one another. As Hargreaves (2003) writes, 'Knowledge operates not just by sponsoring know-what, know-why, or know-how. It also operates by know-who. 'Know-who' involves information about who knows what and who knows what to do. But it also involves the social ability to cooperate and communicate with different kinds of people and experts' (p. 26).

Brown and Lauder have argued that successful knowledge economies depend on their societies' ability to create and pool what they call 'collective intelligence': 'Collective intelligence involves a transformation in the way we think about human capacity. It suggests that all are capable rather than a few; that intelligence is multiple rather than a matter of solving puzzles with only one right answer; and that our human qualities for imagination and emotional engagement are as important as our ability to become technical experts' (cited in Hargreaves, 2003, p. 27).

Important, then, for education systems in knowledge societies is the understanding that intelligence is not singular, fixed, or the property of one cultural group. Rather, as Hargreaves points out, intelligence is multiple, infinite, and shared. The key, he argues, is grasping the methods and dispositions for accessing explicit and tacit knowledge from others. In this regard, there is growing interest in the traditional knowledge of Aboriginal peoples as a different way of knowing that is not based on European models and thought processes grounded in rational, scientific or bureaucratic principles (Schissel & Wotherspoon, 2003). Although they may differ in forms and manifestations across diverse Aboriginal groups, the central dimension of indigenous Aboriginal knowledge is that they encompass established forms of local knowledge or ways of knowing that have developed from the long-term occupancy of Aboriginal places by Aboriginal peoples. The RCAP (1996) describes indigenous Aboriginal knowledge as 'a distinct system of knowledge with its own philosophical and value base ... . It includes ecological teachings, medical knowledge, common attitudes towards Mother Earth and the Circle of Life, and a sense of kinship with all creatures' (pp. 526–7).

Much can be learned, for example, from how First Nations people view themselves not as having dominion over the Earth but as an integral part in the family of the Earth. Traditional Aboriginal ecological knowledge, based on detailed, local, long-term observation, is now one of the new frontiers of knowledge, making great contributions to scientific understanding of marine ecosystems, for example. The Haudenosaunee Environmental Task Force's recommendations on strategies for addressing the environmental concerns of the Haudenosaunee has been singled out for recognition by the United Nations Environmental Program and the U.S. Environmental Protection Agency (Canadian Council on Learning, 2007). In drought-stricken Australia farmers have recently begun utilizing Australian Aborigines' traditional knowledge of the flora and fauna of the land to predict weather conditions and make decisions about crop planting. And increasingly, in the 'race' for knowledge to cure various diseases, we are noticing a convergence of Indigenous knowledge and Western science, where in ethnobotany, for example, botanists and biologists are working closely with Indigenous communities to collect and document plants and medicinal remedies. Ethnobotanists are talking to experts in Aboriginal communities where they are also observing practices and developing word banks and other resources in order to identify medicinal properties that can be reproduced in laboratories and later commercialized.

It is unfortunate that the gatekeepers of Western intellectual traditions have repeatedly dismissed traditional Aboriginal knowledge as inconsequential and unfounded. Such Eurocentrism does nothing but decrease Canada's 'funds of knowledge' (Gonzalez et al., 2005) at a time when, as a knowledge society, it should be drawing on its pool of collective intelligence for more success in a competitive global environment. As Bobby Starnes recently wrote in justification of 'Indian Education for All' in the state of Montana in the United States, 'Our collective and individual ignorance makes us ethnocentric and stupid … We need to know more in order to create new solutions to old problems. For example, if instruction related to evolution were excluded from the nation's Biology curriculum, students' understanding of how the world works would be severely limited. And their poorly developed understandings would constrain their thinking and performance in scientific endeavors, thus limiting scientific discovery and progress' (2006, p. 188). Elsewhere (Kanu, 2007b) I have written that we are what we know (i.e., our own epistemologies, values, philosophies, and so on); but we are also what we don't know (i.e., others' epistemologies, values, philosophies, and so on). Refusal to access the knowledge and wisdom of others produces self-fragmentation in us. A fragmented self lacks full access both to itself and to the world, thereby impairing capacity for informed action. For example, there are factual truths in Canadian history that we all need to know, not only to deepen our own intellectual understanding and awareness of ourselves as a people but also to be able to make appropriate, informed, political decisions for our nation and for our lives. For instance, because of our lack of understanding of the relationships between Canada's Aboriginal peoples and the Canadian federal government, many of us stereotype Aboriginal peoples as receiving special privileges that other Canadians do not get. Because we may not know that Aboriginal peoples signed treaties with the federal government that granted Aboriginal peoples certain rights in exchange for the cession of millions of acres of Aboriginal land (for example, the constitutional and treaty right to formal education for successive generations of First Nations peoples), we look upon these so-called privileges not as treaty or constitutional obligations but as Aboriginal people getting something free at the expense of other Canadians. In short, our ignorance leads us to look at policies divorced from historical contexts. To the extent that Aboriginal knowledge and perspectives, and indeed the knowledge and perspectives of other ethnic minorities, are integrated into the education of all Canadians we can expand our understanding of the world beyond a predominantly Eurocentric lens. A more complete understanding could help us 'reframe taken-for-granted notions that limit our thinking, innovation, and problem solving' (Starnes, 2006, p. 189).

Raising Essential Curriculum Questions

All of the reasons discussed in the foregoing sections, and many others brought forward by the participants in the studies from which this book emerged, provide important justifications for integrating Aboriginal perspectives into the organization and delivery of formal schooling in Canada – in particular the school curriculum, which has been described as 'lying at the heart of the efforts to understand and improve the educational attainment and status of Aboriginal people' (Schissel & Wotherspoon, 2003, p. 119). Curriculum is frequently cited in the research literature as the major cause of early school dropout (or push-out) among many Aboriginal and other ethnic minority students, largely because of its omission of the histories, languages and cultural values of these students and its commission of education that is unjust and unequal (see, e.g., Dei et al., 1997; Gaskell & Kelly, 1996; Tanner et al., 1995). Dei and colleagues (2006, p. 63) have referred to the curriculum as 'the wholeness of education.' Curriculum is not just the subject matter or the topics selected for directing learning. It also includes the instructional practices employed to deliver learning and the surveillance strategies utilized to ensure that the desired subject matter is learned in a particular way. Curriculum includes the stipulated rules, regulations, and procedures that structure the character and everyday practices of the school. To the extent that the requirements for school success involve mastering the school curriculum and exhibiting 'good' school behaviours, the curriculum is often interpreted as designed to deprive certain students of their identities – ethnic minority students, for example. Steele (1992) explains this identity-transforming role of the curriculum in relation to Black students in the American public school system: 'One factor is the basic assimilationist offer that schools make to Blacks. You can be valued and rewarded in school (and society), the schools say to these students, but you must first master the culture and ways of the American mainstream, and since that mainstream (as it is represented in school) is essentially White, this means you must give up many particulars of being black – styles of speech and appearance, value priorities, preferences, at least in mainstream settings. This is asking a lot' (p. 71).

This sentiment is echoed in Dei and colleagues's (1997) study of school dropout among Black high school students in Toronto, Canada. They reported that many of the dropouts interviewed attributed their decision to quit school to their schools' attempt to deny their identity and reconstruct them according to dominant norms. This is how Michelle, one of the interviewees in that study expressed it: 'Why did I drop out of school? Personally, I believe high school especially, it's a processing plant. You walk in there in grade 9 and you are about to be processed and in the end you will come out as a product, for lack of a better word ... the atmosphere lacks respect. It lacks principles, morals, values. I think it invades everything about one's character, totally breaks it down, to then reconstruct another character' (1997, p. 146).

This interpretation of the school curriculum becomes clearer when we consider that what counts as curriculum is socially determined and, therefore, representative of power relations between different groups in society. As Beyer and Apple (1998) remind us, the arguments behind particular curricula carry more than the intention that students gain particular academic skills; they are also imbued with ideas about distinct social outcomes – notions of the body of knowledge, skills, values, attitudes, and dispositions students should gain in order to live in a particular social order. This explains why the school curriculum is seen as a battleground for competing ideologies and why the debates over what schools should do are so vociferous. It is also the reason why critical perspectives on curriculum – for example, multicultural, post-structural, feminist, and anti-colonial perspectives – urge educators to shift their focus from merely technical questions dealing with how to organize, teach, and evaluate curriculum efficiently, to substantive questions that interrogate and contest the curriculum. As curriculum reconceptualists like Pinar and colleagues (1995) have noted, we already know a lot about the procedural aspects of creating and implementing curricula; now we should focus on understanding how the key players experience the 'educational play' we have written, and to what effect.

While no list can comprehensively cover or do justice to the complex issues deserving consideration in curriculum for democratic educational practices, Beyer and Apple (1998) provide some flavour of the substantive and complex questions worth interrogating if we are to understand and contest the curriculum. These questions are:

- *Epistemological:* What should count as knowledge and as knowing?
- *Political:* Who should control the selection and distribution of knowledge and through what institutions?
- *Economic:* How is the control of knowledge linked to the existing and unequal distribution of power, goods, and services in society?
- *Ideological:* What knowledge is considered to be of most worth? Whose knowledge is it?
- *Technical:* How shall curricular knowledge be made accessible to students?
- *Aesthetic:* How do we link curricular knowledge to the biographies (lives, personal experiences, and histories) of students?
- *Ethical:* How shall we treat others responsibly and justly in education? What ideas of moral conduct and community serve as the underpinning of the ways students and teachers are treated?

Once we begin to interrogate the curriculum through these questions, we begin to see education as 'integrally connected to the cultural, political, and economic institutions of the larger society – institutions that may be strikingly unequal by race, gender, and class' (Beyer & Apple, 1998, pp. 4–5). Knowledge taught in the school becomes illuminated as predominantly consisting of the knowledge, values, and desires of particular interest and power groups, thereby severely restricting what counts as worthwhile knowledge. Formal schooling emerges as the institutional vehicle through which dominant knowledge and values are distributed as official school knowledge (Apple, 1993; Aronowitz, 1993) and schools are revealed as institutions that largely embody and reproduce societal inequalities, although they may alleviate some of these inequalities. For these reasons, our sensitivity and concern with curriculum must include the connections between educational institutions and differential cultural, political, and economic power. They are questions that beckon us toward curriculum reconceptualization that takes into account issues of social justice and thicker forms of democracy in education.

Vigilance regarding the curriculum is particularly urged in contemporary educational contexts of neoliberal rationality, in which the market becomes the defining feature for both private and public institutions. In such contexts, citizens are expected to be autonomous individuals sufficiently liberated from their locations in history, culture, and community to be able to 'manage' their own lives and make rational decisions that would supposedly lead to 'personal profits' based on fair and equal competition in a global economy. Canada, like many other industrialized countries, is experiencing a strong neoliberalization of its economy and the inevitable cultural tensions that this process heightens in terms of knowledge and power, particularly for Aboriginal peoples and other cultural minority groups. Curriculum questions, in such a context, concern the broader implications of the economic, political, cultural, and social changes engendered by this change.

Recognition of the functioning power of the curriculum in shaping identity, representation, and social and economic circumstances lies behind the drive by Aboriginal peoples to have their perspectives integrated not only into school curricula but also the organization and delivery of formal schooling as a whole. In this regard, schools under Aboriginal control have made some headway, with impressive results. For example, Simard (1994) reported some gains in terms of students graduating from the grade 12 program into postsecondary institutions when curricula and teaching strategies were developed that aimed at integrating the cultural and academic worlds of students at Children of the Earth, an all-Aboriginal high school in Winnipeg. Ezeife (2001) reported overwhelming enthusiasm and interest in learning among Cree pre-service teachers in an Aboriginal-focused teacher education program when he required them to identify and integrate environmental phenomena, materials, and practices from traditional Cree settings into the teaching of Science to Cree students in Pukatawagan, Northern Manitoba. In a study conducted by Schissel and Wotherspoon (2003) in alternative schools with unique programs addressing Aboriginal youths in northern Saskatchewan, Aboriginal students expressed high levels of satisfaction with nourishment of their self-esteem and the traditional cultural and spiritual teachings they received, which translated into higher academic achievement and retention of these students in school. Most recently, the Society for the Advancement of Excellence in Education (SAEE, 2007), a non-profit Canadian education research agency, released the results of another study it commissioned on Aboriginal education in ten schools scattered across north, central, and eastern Canada, in which considerable increases were reported in academic achievement and sense of identity and self-worth when Aboriginal cultures were integrated into the schools and in appropriate areas of the school curricula.

While these success stories of integration are encouraging, studies on integration and its impact *outside* of predominantly Aboriginal communities, in public schools with Aboriginal and non-Aboriginal students and dominant culture teachers, are needed. Furthermore, Binda (2001b) reports that, despite these successes, 'Provincial Learning Assessments across Canada show that among Aboriginal students, scholastic achievement is horrible in its own right, as well as in comparison with mainstream Canadian students' (p. 5). For example, in 1998, the average score in Grade 12 Mathematics for Manitoba First Nations students was 14.4 per cent compared to 61.2 per cent for mainstream Canadian students, and 34.6 per cent for English Language Arts compared to 67.1 per cent for mainstream Canadian students (p.5). More recently, Rubenstein and Clifton (2004) have reported anecdotal evidence suggesting that many Aboriginal parents, including community leaders and other influential persons, have withdrawn their children from Aboriginal band-controlled schools because of poor academic results and sent them to nearby schools outside of Aboriginal jurisdiction and with higher academic standards. These statistics and reports were confirmed by the Auditor General of Canada's report (November 2004) that Canada's $1.7-billion a year Native education system is failing Native children, the third such report in as many years, and that it will take 28 years for the proportion of Aboriginal high school graduates to reach parity with non-Aboriginals.

Some have attributed the underperformance of Aboriginal controlled schools to the poor management by Aboriginal community leaders of the fiscal transfers from the federal government to finance Aboriginal education (see, for example, Minnis, 2006); others say that educational underachievement in band-controlled schools is the result of the reduction of funding by the federal government through policies such as the 'Debt Recovery Plan' by which Indian and Northern Affairs Canada (INAC) recovers the costs of paying for an external third-party management of First Nations' financial administration, and 'First Nations Deficit' by which debt or deficit from previous years is deducted from the First Nations' budget in subsequent years, including funds allocated to education (see Carr-Stewart, 2006). Regardless of where the blame lies for First Nations' educational underachievement, it is an alarming situation that calls for a concerted effort that focuses on the improvement of teaching not only in band-controlled jurisdictions but also urban areas with high Aboriginal student populations and dominant culture teachers so that Aboriginal students, who have the same rights as all Canadians to preserve their culture as much as they desire, are not faced with a choice between assimilating and dropping out of school.

This book is a response to the call for the integration of Aboriginal cultural knowledge and perspectives into the curricula of Canadian public schools. The research studies from which the book emerged were conducted from 2002 to 2007 in an urban setting, and undertaken to investigate five specific questions that are salient to the call for the integration of Aboriginal perspectives:

1. What specific aspects of Aboriginal cultural knowledge can teachers integrate not only as part of the cultural heritage and legitimate knowledge of Aboriginal peoples but also as tools for enhancing and supporting classroom learning for urban Aboriginal students?
2. What are the most effective ways of integrating such cultural knowledge into the school curriculum?
3. How does such integration have an impact on academic achievement, class attendance/participation, and retention in school among urban Aboriginal students?
4. What are the critical elements of the integration processes that affect academic achievement, class attendance/participation, and retention in school among this group of students?
5. What are teachers' perceptions of the integration of Aboriginal perspectives into the school curriculum?

With its focus on explaining how teachers can usefully integrate Aboriginal perspectives into the teaching of the existing curricula of urban public schools, the book significantly informs stakeholders' (e.g., pre-service teachers, practising teachers, teacher educators, curriculum development leaders, and policy makers) understanding of the integration process and what it takes to implement integration successfully in schools. One caveat, however, is that because the studies were conducted among participants in an urban context, the conclusions and suggestions derived apply mainly to urban situations.

Additionally, the book is an important contribution to the effort to improve cross-cultural teaching and teacher education in urban areas, especially in light of Kleinfeld's (1995) study of Alaskan Native students, which suggested that, although ethnic membership contributed to Native student learning in important ways, what differentiated effective teachers of Indian and Native Alaskan students was their instructional style.

Organization of the Book

The book is divided into eight chapters. This introductory chapter has contexualized the call for the integration of Aboriginal perspectives by addressing a question that is salient to the project: Why does integration matter? In answering this question the chapter has moved beyond the familiar rationale of academic underachievement among Aboriginal students, and examined this question from new perspectives previously unexplored in discussions about Aboriginal education. These perspectives are: emerging notions about learning and development as psychosocial and cultural processes, intimate and cultural citizenship, collective intelligence in a knowledge society, and the functioning power of the school curriculum in shaping identity and social and economic circumstances.

Chapter 2 discusses distinct but overlapping theoretical frameworks undergirding the studies from which the book originated and that served as lenses for the analyses and interpretations of the research data. Sociocultural theories of learning and cognition, macrostructural theories/explanations of ethnic minority school success/failure, critical race theory, and racism and anti-racism discursive frameworks were utilized to make sense of the data and understand the issues surrounding the integration of Aboriginal perspectives.

Chapter 3 presents the rarely heard voices of Aboriginal learners as particular groups of Aboriginal students (Cree, Ojibway, Dene, Dakota, and Métis) identify nine aspects and several sub-aspects of their home and community cultures that influence/mediate how they learn in the formal school system. Briefly, these cultural aspects included storytelling, providing learning scaffolds, learning by observing and emulating, use of problem-solving circles, spirituality, community support, infusion of Aboriginal content, and teacher warmth and respect. Based on the first of our three studies in which the cultural-historical approach was utilized to inquire into the influence of cultural participation on classroom learning, these aspects of Aboriginal cultural socialization, along with other Aboriginal beliefs, practices, and issues reported in the literature as important among diverse Aboriginal groups, provided the material for the integration processes that occurred in the social studies classrooms where our second set of studies were conducted. Much is learned in this chapter about how schools can draw on the cultural socialization of Aboriginal students to support and increase classroom learning for these students.

Chapters 4, 5, and 6 are derived from the second set of studies, which investigated effective ways of integrating Aboriginal perspectives into the school curriculum, the impact of such integration on school success among urban Aboriginal students, and the critical elements of instruction that account for that success. Chapter 4 describes the integration processes in detail. Beginning with descriptions of the researchers' working definition of the term 'Aboriginal perspectives' and the guiding principles undergirding the integration processes, the chapter goes on to present integration not as the creation of completely new curricula but as consistently adding meaningful and inclusive layers to what teachers are currently doing in their classrooms. This layering occurs at five specific levels or teaching moments:

1. Identifying student learning outcomes
2. Selecting curriculum content and learning resources
3. Selecting activities or student learning experiences
4. Identifying assessment methods and strategies
5. Embracing integration as a philosophical underpinning of the curriculum where integration ceases to be an occasional add-on activity in the classroom and becomes an integral part of daily curriculum implementation.

These moments depict integration as a 'habit of mind' where teachers' planning processes at all five levels include the ongoing question of how the curriculum content, learning experiences, patterns of classroom interactions, and assessment practices relate to the Aboriginal students in their classrooms. Specifics about what and how Aboriginal perspectives were integrated at each level are discussed.

Chapter 5 discusses the effects of the integration processes on academic achievement, class attendance/participation, and retention in school among the Aboriginal students. Although not a direct focus of the research, the views of some non-Aboriginal students on how the integration of Aboriginal perspectives impacted their learning are also presented. The learning opportunities and the challenges entailing integration are discussed. A major finding discussed in this chapter is that although the integration of Aboriginal cultural knowledge/perspectives results in positive outcomes (such as higher test scores, better conceptual understanding/higher level thinking, improved self-confidence, and, among Aboriginal students from socioeconomically stable homes, increased motivation to attend class) cultural integration *alone* is insufficient to reverse academic achievement trends among Aboriginal students. A multipronged approach that also takes into account macro-structural variables affecting schooling – for example, the poor socioeconomic conditions of many Aboriginal families, structural racism, and insufficient educational financing of schools serving some Aboriginal communities – is also called for. As U.S. social critic Nancy Fraser (1997) aptly put it in *Justice Interruptus*, what we need are remedies that combine a politics of (cultural) recognition with a politics of redistribution of wealth. In other words, recognition and redistribution are mutually irreducible dimensions of justice.

Previous studies have reported gains when Aboriginal perspectives are included in school curricula and other schooling processes. However, there is a dearth of available knowledge about the specific elements of such inclusion that account for the gains and can inform teachers' understanding of how best to teach Aboriginal students in the public high school system, where the highest dropout rate occurs among Aboriginal students. Chapter 6 addresses this knowledge gap by discussing some critical elements of instruction that produced positive effects on the academic achievement, class attendance, and participation of some of the Aboriginal students in our research. Prominent among these elements are teachers' sense of efficacy (the belief that they are able to engage in courses of action that will improve educational outcomes for their students), teachers' knowledge/attitude/expectations, and teachers' personal and instructional style, all of which confirm Kleinfeld's (1995) research finding that instructional style was a defining attribute of effective teachers of Native (Indian) Alaskan students.

A crucial omission thus far from the discourses and discussions surrounding the integration of Aboriginal perspectives into school curricula is the voices of teachers – the very people who are mandated to implement this curriculum reform in classrooms. In studies of curriculum reform/innovation involving change in experienced teachers' practices (e.g., an innovation such as the integration of Aboriginal perspectives into the teaching of existing school curricula) teachers' attitudes, beliefs, and perceptions about the change have been identified as a critical factor that can make or break the innovation. Based on our third research study, Chapter 7 presents Manitoba teachers' perceptions of the integration of Aboriginal cultural knowledge and perspectives into the school curriculum. Although, in general teachers perceived the integration of Aboriginal perspectives as timely and important, their low sense of efficacy, the lack of classroom-ready Aboriginal learning resources, school administrators' lukewarm support for integration, and teachers' own sociopolitical investments in the educational status quo were among the factors that teachers perceived as impediments to the integration of Aboriginal perspectives. Studies in other Canadian jurisdictions (e.g., Aikenhead and Huntley's [1999] study of science teachers in Saskatchewan) suggest that some of these perceptions are not idiosyncratic to Manitoba.

Chapter 8, the Conclusion, discusses the implications of the research studies for policy, practice, and further research. Appropriately titled 'Lessons in implementation,' it draws on the lessons learned from the research studies first to theorize curriculum futures that would sustain the integration of Aboriginal perspectives and then to make policy and practical recommendations for the successful integration of Aboriginal perspectives in classrooms.

Together, these chapters make significant contributions to the ongoing effort to understand the integration of Aboriginal perspectives into school curricula and teachers' pedagogies. The book offers theoretical and practical insights about this timely topic – insights that have application for Canadian and international audiences concerned with this aspect of Aboriginal education. These audiences are primarily undergraduate college and university students in curriculum/methods courses and courses in cross-cultural education, teacher educators, and public school teachers grappling with how best to meet the challenge of integrating Aboriginal perspectives into their curricula. As well, researchers will benefit from the detailed qualitative analyses of the data reported. The book is also suitable as a supplementary reading in graduate level courses such as 'Curriculum Inquiry,' 'Culture and Curriculum,' and 'Curriculum Design and Development for Cross-cultural Teaching.' Curriculum development leaders spearheading integration efforts in their schools, curriculum consultants facilitating and coordinating curriculum change efforts in Aboriginal education, and educational policy makers seeking research input for informing curriculum policy in Aboriginal education may also find this book useful. The book is an attempt to address a common but still unanswered question often posed by each of these audiences: How can we utilize the potent power of the school curriculum to improve the educational status and attainment of Aboriginal students? Theoretical and practical tools for answering this question are provided in this book. Learning opportunities and challenges entailing the integration of Aboriginal perspectives are reported in the voices of two important but often ignored constituencies – Aboriginal students and public school teachers whose narratives I have given an elevat-ed presence, mindful of Spivak's (1990) words: 'We cannot but nar-rate, but when a narrative is constructed something is left out' (pp. 18–19). Even when participants' words are quoted directly, I chose which words to include and which to leave out. This work, therefore, remains my interpretation of the participants' voices and what I saw in the research field. I hope that the intellectual and methodological process I have used to arrive at these interpretations maintains some correspondence between the social and transformational goals of disenchanted Aboriginal students and my own goals as a researcher attempting to throw light on their educational plight.

To enhance the book's utility in college and university curriculum courses, each chapter concludes with questions that invite opinions, discussion, and critical reflection about its content. Chapter summaries provide a quick review of the main topics presented and the reference list at the end of each chapter also serves as recommended readings for further exploration of the issues and topics raised. A list of web and print resources is included as an appendix, making this book a valuable reference to help teachers meet the challenges of integrating Aboriginal perspectives into their curricula.

Curriculum is one of the most influential tools that we can use to effect serious change in schools today. Parents, students, schools, and society look to it as a primary force in shaping a student's identity, expectations, and life-long trajectory. It should, therefore, come as no surprise that curriculum has been accorded pride of place in the effort to increase school success for Aboriginal students by returning their education to its cultural roots. *Integrating Aboriginal Perspectives into the School Curriculum: Purposes, Possibilities, and Challenges* provides the intellectual and practical tools teachers, curriculum developers, and policy makers need in order to undertake this important work.

To Generalize or Not to Generalize

Some readers may ask whether research studies focused almost exclu-sive in Manitoba with a relatively low number of participants (a total of 84 Aboriginal students and 18 teachers from six inner-city high schools) has wider applicability in different schools, different regions, and dif-ferent groups of Aboriginal students outside of Manitoba. This is an age-old question and, indeed, the persistent criticism regarding the transferability or generalizability of the findings of a particular qualitative study to contexts or participants beyond the specific research setting and subjects involved. Perhaps it ought to be reiterated that the goal of qualitative research is to understand and describe a social phenomenon, and its findings are not generalizable in the traditional (quantitative/probabilistic /statistical) sense of the word. Indeed, considering that all observations are defined by the specific contexts in which they occur, most qualitative/naturalistic researchers maintain that no true generalization is possible. Nevertheless, in anticipation of this concern/question, I have attempted to address the transferability / generalizability issue through the following processes:

1. Because transferability in a qualitative study depends on similarities between the sending and the receiving contexts, I have provided sufficiently detailed or thick descriptions of data – derived from prolonged observations at the research sites and in-depth interviews with research participants – to allow judgments about transferability to be made by the reader.
2. In selecting elements of Aboriginal culture for integration we targeted not only cultural elements that are specific to Aboriginal groups in Manitoba but also those identified in the literature as common or general among diverse Aboriginal groups in Canada and elsewhere.
3. We purposely selected three different classroom contexts in three schools and students from different Aboriginal groups for our studies of integration. The teachers we interviewed for the 'Teachers' perceptions study' (reported in Chapter 7) came from three different inner-city schools and were different from one another , in important ways, in their perception of and commitment to the integration of Aboriginal perspectives. These selections were intended to maximize the range of information that could be obtained from these contexts and populations.
4. In my data analyses, I drew upon a wide range of studies to establish the representativeness and the non-idiosyncratic nature of our research findings. These studies were mainly about Indigenous/ Aboriginal education in diverse contexts – for example, in the United States, Australia, New Zealand, and Canada.

Thus, I was able to derive statements of general processes that appeared in one setting (Manitoba) where I attempted to understand the integration of Aboriginal perspectives into the school curriculum.

While the book copiously informs the reader about the approaches to integration attempted in our research, local cultural and contextual adaptations and consultations will always be a necessary complement for the teacher attempting integration. As one of the anonymous reviewers of the manuscript acknowledged, if there is anything true about Aboriginal education, it is that generalizations often do not work anyway. Although Aboriginal peoples and cultures share certain similarities, they also have significant local variations. Hence the obligation (and the power) to successfully transfer the processes described in this book belongs to the reader or the researcher who would apply these processes to their own contexts (e.g., through the concept of relatability).

On Terminology

This section provides clarification on how certain terms have been used in this book.

The word *Aboriginal* means the indigenous peoples of a particular country. Aboriginal peoples in Canada comprise the First Nations/ Indians, Inuit, and Métis – the three main groups recognized by the Constitution Act of 1982. Each of these groups is separate and distinct, with a unique history and culture. The term 'First Nations,' which has been used since the 1970s instead of 'Indian,' describes all Aboriginal peoples in Canada who are not Inuit or Métis. Different First Nations communities have different languages, cultures, and traditions depending largely on where they are located. What makes the First Nations distinct is that they possess a unique relationship with the Canadian Federal government by virtue of the Royal Proclamation of 1763. This document is important because it:

- Recognized that Indian people had rights to the land
- Established a treaty making process whereby land rights could be surrendered only to the Crown
- Established the relationship between the Crown and Indian people
- Recognized the existence of Aboriginal rights which include rights to land, to hunt, fish, and gather, self-government, cultural integrity, and other rights

The term Inuit applies to Aboriginal peoples who live in Canada's North. What sets them apart from First Nations peoples is that many

Inuit groups have not signed treaties and therefore have retained not only their Aboriginal rights but also much of their traditional political power in their traditional lands.

The Métis are mixed blood peoples and descendants of marriage between early French and English fur traders and First Nations women. They have not signed treaties with the Crown and, as Indigenous peoples, they have Aboriginal rights. According to the Supreme Court of Canada (in *R.v.Powley*) three criteria define who is Métis:

- Self-identification
- Ancestral connection to the Métis community, and
- Community acceptance

The Métis retain the Aboriginal right to define their own identity.

As used in the research studies discussed in the book, the term *Aboriginal* refers to individuals who reported themselves as First Nations and Métis groups during the studies. These groups were Ojibway, Cree, Dene/Saltaux, Dakota, and Métis. This clarification is important because Aboriginal peoples constitute diverse groups with unique cultural identities, traditions, and life circumstances. They are also marked by considerable social differentiations, which may have implications for their educational attainment and status (see Schissel & Wotherspoon, 2003 for an in-depth description of these differentiations). Although Aboriginal peoples are not a homogeneous group, there are commonalities in their educational experiences and cultural socialization patterns as indigenous people, which provide a basis for speaking about Aboriginal peoples in the collective when discussing culture and Aboriginal student learning in the public school system – for example, the belief in the wisdom of elders as keepers of knowledge whose role is vital to the education of Aboriginal youth. Nonetheless, the themes and issues reported in this book are discussed mainly in reference to the particular Aboriginal groups that participated in our research studies. In certain documents, Aboriginal peoples are also referred to as Indigenous, First Nations, Indians, and Natives; where appropriate, these terms are used interchangeably in this book.

'*Non-Aboriginal*' refers to those students who are other than Aboriginal. It is recognized that this reference implies multiple social locations and diversity of students, but the term is useful for centring Aboriginal students and their experiences. Where appropriate, particular students have been identified by their ethnicity.

As used in the book, the term *'culture'* is defined as those shared beliefs, values, and meanings which inform the educator about a learner's culturally determined learning and thought processes. As the process of production of meanings on which different groups draw to make sense of their world, culture is dynamic and always socially and historically situated (Kanu, 2001).

'Aboriginal perspectives' refers to curriculum materials, instructional methods/styles, and interaction patterns that Aboriginal peoples see as accurately reflecting their experiences, histories, cultures, traditional knowledges, standpoints, and values. These perspectives would develop positive self-identity for Aboriginal students and help non-Aboriginal students develop understanding and respect for Aboriginal histories, cultures, and contemporary lifestyles (Manitoba Education and Youth, 2003). Our understanding of this term is also informed by McLaughlin and Whatman's (2008) view that to integrate an Aboriginal perspective is to constantly critique one's cultural and intellectual positioning vis-à vis curriculum, unsettle Western authoritative discourses about learning and knowledge, champion the struggle against colonial forms of knowledge and pedagogical practices, and develop a commitment to reclaim Indigenous knowledge and values in a search for cultural continuity and social justice.

Summary

This introductory chapter has contextualized the call for the integration of Aboriginal cultural knowledge/perspectives into the school curriculum by providing pressing reasons for taking up this democratic challenge. These reasons stretch beyond statistical and other reports on Aboriginal educational underachievement, into recent ideas about learning and development as psychosocial and cultural processes; the relationships between citizenship, the nation state, and social difference; and collective intelligence in a knowledge society. The role of the school curriculum in shaping the identity and the social and economic circumstances of students was also explored as a lens through which to examine the call for the integration of Aboriginal perspectives into the organization and delivery of public schooling. Five questions of salience to the call for integration, investigated in the research studies discussed in this book, were described. The contents of each chapter of the book, and the meanings of certain terms used in the book were also described.

QUESTIONS FOR DISCUSSION

1. The inclusion of minority cultural perspectives in the classroom has been criticized on the grounds that there are ethnic minority groups who are different from the mainstream culture of the public school and yet succeed without culturally responsive curricula and pedagogy. Do you think that closing the cultural gap between the home and the school is a necessary condition for improving ethnic minority school achievement? Suggest other ways of improving school achievement for Aboriginal students.

2. This chapter lists five research questions, each of which focuses on an issue salient to the integration of Aboriginal perspectives into the school curriculum. Add three questions of your own to this list and present arguments why your questions are important and relevant for research on the inclusion of Aboriginal perspectives in schools and classrooms.

3. Citing specific examples, discuss Schon's statement that 'institutionalized forms of discrimination and oppression are built into the taken-for-granted norms, rules, skills, and values of social institutions, and, because of their naturalized status, frequently remain unchallenged.'

4. Should governments spend resources on preparing all public school teachers or only Aboriginal teachers to serve the needs of Aboriginal students? What are the consequences of preparing each group of teachers?

5. Discuss the statement that the treatment of the minorities in the wider society is reflected in their treatment in education.

6. Why should teachers, curriculum workers, and curriculum leaders concern themselves with Beyer and Apple's seven curriculum questions listed in this chapter? What are the implications of these questions for implementing the integration of Aboriginal perspectives into curricula and classrooms?

REFERENCES/RECOMMENDED READINGS

Abowitz, K.K., & Harnish, J. (2006). Contemporary discourses of citizenship. *Review of Educational Research, 76*(4), 653–90.

Aikenhead, G.S., & Huntley, B. (1999). Teachers' views on Aboriginal students learning Western and Aboriginal science. *Canadian Journal for Native Education, 23,* 159–75.

Alonge, E.I. (1982). The relevance of traditional methods in modern education: A quest for relevant science education in Africa. *Journal of the Science Teachers' Association of Nigeria, 21*(1), 34–44.

Apple, M.W. (1993). *Official knowledge: Democratic education in a conservative age.* New York: Routledge.

Aronowitz, S. (1992). *The politics of identity.* New York: Routledge.

Auditor General of Canada (2004). Chapter 5. Indian and Northern Affairs Canada: Education program and post-secondary student support. Report of the Auditor General. Retrieved December 2007, from: www.oag-bvg.gc.ca/domino/reports.nsf/html/20041105ce.html

Banks, J.A. (1990). Citizenship education for a pluralistic democratic society. *The Social Studies, 8*(5), 210–14.

Battiste, M. (1998). Enabling the autumn seed: Toward a decolonized approach to Aboriginal knowledge, language, and education. *Canadian Journal of Native Education, 22*(1), 16–27.

– (Ed.) (2000). Reclaiming indigenous voice and vision. Vancouver: UBC Press.

Beyer, L.E., & Apple, M.W. (Eds.). (1998). *The curriculum: Problems, politics, and possibilities.* New York: State University of New York Press.

Binda, K.P. (2001a). Native diaspora and urban education: Intractable problems. In K.P. Binda with Sharilyn Caillou (Eds.), *Aboriginal education in Canada: A study in decolonization,* pp. 179–94. Mississauga: Canadian Educators Press.

– (2001b). Aboriginal education in comparative and global perspectives: What have research and practice done for Aboriginal education in Canada? *Canadian and International Education, 30*(1), 1–16.

Browne, B.D. (1990). Learning styles and Native Americans. *Canadian Journal of Native Education, 17*(1), 23–35.

Brownell, M., Roos, N., & Fransoo, R. (2006). Is the class half empty? A population-based perspective on socio-economic status and educational outcomes. *Institute for Research on Public Policy (IRPP) Choices, 12*(5), 3–30.

Cajete, G.A. (1994). *Look to the mountain: An ecology of Native education.* Skyland, NC: Kivaki Press.

Canadian Council on Learning (February, 2007). *Lessons in learning: The cultural divide in science education for Aboriginal learners.* Retrieved February 2007, from: http://www.ccl-cca.ca/CCL/Reports/LessonsInLearning/LinL20070116 Ab sci edu.htm

Canadian Education Statistics Council (2003). *Education indicators in Canada:*

Report of the Pan-Canadian Education Indicators Program. Toronto: Canadian Education Statistics Council.

Carr-Stewart, S. (2006). First Nations education: Financial accountability and educational attainment. *Canadian Journal of Education, 29*(4), 998–1018.

Cole, M., & Wertsch, J.V. (2001). *Beyond the individual-social antinomy in discussions about Piaget and Vygotsky.* Retrieved 12 September 2008, from: http://www.massey.ac.nz/~alock/virtual/colevyg.htm

Corson, D.J. (1992). Minority cultural values and discourse norms in majority culture classrooms. *Canadian Modern Languages Review, 48,* 472–96

Dei, G.S., Asgharzadeh, A., Bahardor, S.E., & Shajahan, R.A. (2006). *Schooling and difference in Africa: Democratic challenges in a contemporary context.* Toronto: University of Toronto Press.

Dei, G.S., Mazzuca, J., McIsaac, E., & Zine, J. (1997). *Reconstructing dropout: A critical ethnography of the dynamics of Black students disengagement from school.* Toronto: University of Toronto Press.

Department of Indian Affairs & Northern Development (DIAND)(1994). *Basic department data, 1994.* Ottawa: Supply and Services.

Dewey, J. (1938/1963). *Experience and education.* New York: Macmillan.

Ezeife, A.N. (1999). The use of the environment in science teaching: An African and Aboriginal viewpoint. *The Manitoba Science Teacher, 41*(2), 19–23.

– (2001). Integrating the learner's schema, culture, and environment into the science classroom: Some cases involving traditional and Aboriginal societies. *Canadian and International Education, 30*(1), 17–44.

Faulks, K. (2006). Rethinking citizenship in England: Some lessons from contemporary social and political theory. *Education, Citizenship and Social Justice, 1*(2), 123–40.

Fraser, N. (1997). *Justice interruptus: Critical reflections on the post-socialist condition.* New York: Routledge.

Friesen, J.W. & Friesen, V.L. (2002). *Aboriginal education in Canada: A plea for integration.* Calgary: Detselig.

Gaskell, J., & Kelly, D. (Eds.)(1996). *Debating dropouts.* New York: Teachers College Press.

Gonzalez, N., Moll, L., & Amanti, C. (2005). *Funds of knowledge: Theorizing practices in households, communities, and classrooms.* Mahwah, NJ: Erlbaum.

Haig-Brown, C., Hodgson-Smith, K.L., Regnier, R., & Archibald, J. (1997). *Making the spirit dance within: Joe Duquette high school and an Aboriginal community.* Toronto: Lorimer.

Hargeaves, A. (2003). *Teaching in the knowledge society: Education in the age of insecurity.* New York: Teachers College Press.

Hawthorne, H.B. (1966/7). *A survey of the contemporary Indian of Canada: A report on economic, political, and educational needs and policies,* Vol. 1. Ottawa: Indian Affairs Branch.

Hill, D. (2001). Prior learning assessment and recognition: Applications for an Aboriginal model of holistic learning. Presentation made at Joe Duquette High School, Saskatoon, 16 Nov.

Kanu, Y. (2001). The influence of culture on Aboriginal student learning. Paper presented at Western Canada Student Teaching Conference (WestCAST). Vancouver, British Columbia, 16 Feb. Kanu, Y. (1997). Understanding development education through action research: Cross-cultural reflections. In T. Carson & D. Sumara (Eds.), *Action research as a living practice,* pp. 167–85. New York: Peter Lang.

– (2005). Tensions and dilemmas of cross-cultural transfer of knowledge: Post-structural/postcolonial reflections on an innovative teacher education in Pakistan. *International Journal of Educational Development, 25,* 493–513.

– (2007a). The culture-learning connection: A cultural-historical approach to understanding learning and development. In J. L. Kincheloe & R. A. Horn (Eds.), *The Praeger handbook of education and psychology,* Vol. 1, pp. 385–99. Westport: Praeger.

– (2007b). Tradition and educational reconstruction in Africa in postcolonial and global times: The case of Sierra Leone. *African Studies Quarterly,* 9 (3), 1–23.

Kennedy, D.M. (1997). Prompt action wins changes to Bill 160. *Professionally Speaking: The Magazine of the Ontario College of Teachers.*

Kirkness, V.J. (1998). Our people's education: Cut the shackles, cut the crap, cut the mustard. *Canadian Journal of Native Education,* 22(1), 10–15.

Kirkness, V.J. & Bowman, S.S. (1983). *First Nations and schools: Triumphs and struggles.* Toronto: Canadian Education Association.

Kleinfeld, J. (1995). Effective teachers of Eskimo and Indian students. In L. Roberts & R.A. Clifton (Eds.), *Cross-currents: Contemporary Canadian educational issues,* pp. 68–96. Toronto: Nelson Canada.

Manitoba Education and Youth (2003). Integrating Aboriginal perspectives into curricula: A resource for curriculum developers, teachers, and administrators. Winnipeg: Author.

McAlpine, L. (2001). Teacher training for the new wilderness: Quantum leaps. In K.P. Binda & S. Caillou (Eds.), *Aboriginal education in Canada: A study in decolonization.* Mississauga: Canadian Educators Press.

McCarthy, C. (1998). *The uses of culture: Education and the limits of ethnic affiliation.* London: Routledge.

McConaghy, C. (2000). *Rethinking indigenous education: Culturalism, colonialism and the politics of knowing.* Flaxton, Queensland: Post Pressed.

McLaughlin, J., & Whatman, S. (2008). Embedding Indigenous perspectives in university teaching and learning: Lessons learnt and possibilities for reforming/decolonizing curriculum. In R.W. Heber (Ed.), *Indigenous education: Asia/Pacific,* pp. 123–46. Regina: Indigenous Studies Research Centre, First Nations University of Canada.

Minnis, J. (2006). First Nations education and rentier economics: Parallels with the Gulf states. *Canadian Journal of Education, 29*(4), 975–97.

Mutua, K., & Swadener, B.B. (2004). *Decolonizing research in cross-cultural settings: Critical personal narratives.* New York: State University of New York Press.

North, C. (2006). More than words: Delving into the substantive meanings of 'social justice in education. *Review of Educational Research, 76*(4), 507–35.

Osborne, B. (1985). Research into Native North Americans' cognition: 1973–1982. *Journal of American Indian Education, 24*(9), 9–25.

Pepper, F., & Henry, S. (1986). Social and cultural effects on Indian learning style: Classroom implications. *Canadian Journal of Native Education, 13*(1), 54–61.

Peters, E.J. (2005). First Nations and Metis people and diversities in people in Canada. Paper presented at 'The Art of State III: Diversity and Canada's Future' Institute for Research on Public Policy. Montebello, Quebec, 13–15 October.

Pinar, W.F., Reynolds, W.M., Slattery, P., & Taubman, P.M. (1995). *Understanding curriculum.* New York: Peter Lang.

Plummer, K. (2003). *Intimate citizenship: Private decisions and public dialogues.* Washington, DC: University of Washington Press.

Royal Commission on Aboriginal Peoples (1996). *Gathering strength: Report of the Royal Commission on Aboriginal Peoples,* Vol. 3. Ottawa: Canada Communication Group.

Rubenstein, H., & Clifton, R.A. (2004). The challenge of Aboriginal education. *Fraser Forum,* June, 24–5.

Ryan, J. (1992). Aboriginal learning styles: A critical review. *Language, culture, and curriculum, 5*(3), 161–83.

Samuels, A. (2001). *Politics on the couch: Citizenship and the internal life.* London: Profile Books.

Schissel, B., & Wotherspoon, T. (2003). *The legacy of school for Aboriginal people: Education, oppression, and emancipation.* Don Mills: Oxford University Press.

Shade, B.J. (1989). The influence of perceptual development on cognitive style: Cross-ethnic comparisons. *Early Child Development and Care, 51,* 137–55.

Simard, L. (1994). Curriculum adaptation: Just do it. In K.P. Binda (Ed.), *Critical issues in First Nations education,* pp. 78–86. Brandon, MB: BUNTEP, Brandon University

Smith, G.H. (2003). Indigenous struggle for the transformation of schooling. Keynote address to the Alaskan Federation of Natives Convention, Anchorage, Alaska, October 2003.

Smith, L.T. (1999). *Decolonizing methodologies: Research and indigenous peoples.* London: Zed Books.

– (2005). On tricky ground: Researching the native in the age of uncertainty. In N. Denzin & Y. Lincoln (Eds.), *The handbook of qualitative research,* 3rd edition, pp. 85–108. New York: Sage.

Society for the Advancement of Excellence in Education (SAEE) (2007). *Sharing our success: More case studies in Aboriginal schooling* (Authors: George Fulford et al). Retrieved March 2008 from: www.saee.ca/publications/A_035_HHH_EXECSUM.php

Spivak, G. (1990). Gayatri Spivak on the politics of the subaltern. *Socialist Review, 20*(3), 85–97.

Starnes, B.A. (2006). Montana's Indian education for all: Toward an education worthy of American ideals. *Phi Delta Kappan, 88*(3), 184–92.

Steele, C. (1992, April). Race and the schooling of Black Americans. *The Atlantic Monthly,* pp. 68–75.

Susag, D. (2006). Why Indian Education for all? Through our own eyes. *Phi Delta Kappan, 88*(3), 201.

Tanner, J., Krahn, H., & Harnagel, T.F. (1995). *Fractured transitions from school to work: Revisiting the dropout problem.* Toronto: Oxford University Press.

Thaman, K.H. (2003). Decolonizing Pacific studies: Indigenous perspectives, knowledge and wisdom in higher education. *The Contemporary Pacific, 15*(2), 1–17.

Vygotsky, L.S. (1981). The genesis of higher mental functions. In J.V. Wertsch (Ed.), *The concept of activity in Soviet psychology,* pp. 144–88. Armonk, NY: Sharpe.

Winzer, M.A., & Mazurek, K. (1998). *Special education in multicultural contexts.* New York: Prentice Hall.

Wotherspoon, T. (2006). Teachers' work in Canadian Aboriginal communities. *Comparative Education Review, 50*(4), 672–94.

Young, I.M. (1990). *Justice and the politics of difference.* Princeton: Princeton University Press.

2 Understanding the Integration of Aboriginal Perspectives through Theory

The previous chapter provided a number of compelling reasons why Aboriginal perspectives must be integrated into school curricula, pointing out in particular the socialcultural, socioeconomic, and personal development benefits that would accrue from such integration – benefits that are currently missing because of the disparities in schooling that many Aboriginal peoples face in comparison with other Canadians and in relation to Aboriginal aspirations. Different scholars and education analysts have utilized different theoretical lenses for analyzing and making sense of these disparities. This chapter discusses the theoretical and conceptual frameworks that were used in our research studies to make sense of the issues surrounding Aboriginal educational performance and the integration of Aboriginal perspectives into the curriculum.

Although some may question the relevance of a separate chapter on theoretical perspectives in this book, I strongly believe in the importance of researchers disclosing and discussing the theoretical and conceptual frameworks informing their research because very few researchers now claim that they enter the research field unencumbered by ideas about the phenomena they seek to understand. As I stated in the preface to this book and as Benz and Shapiro (1998) before me contend 'Research is always carried out by an individual with a life world ... a personality and personal experiences, a social context and various personal and practical challenges and conflicts all of which affect the research – from the choice of research question or topic through the method used, to the reporting of the project's outcome' (p. 4).

Indeed as Yin (1994, p. 28) wrote in connection with case study research 'The complete research design embodies a theory of what is being studied.'

In the next section I elaborate on the role of the theoretical/conceptual framework in qualitative research, followed by discussions of the theoretical/conceptual frameworks of my research.

The Role of Theory in Understanding Phenomena

A theory is primarily a tool that we use systematically to explain or understand a given problem or phenomenon – why things are the way they are and how they came to be that way. Regardless of what we are trying to explain, 'we rely on theories to help us organize and make sense of the facts at our disposal, to guide our search for new facts, evidence or counter-evidence, and to create linkages among the various pieces of information at our disposal' (Schissel & Wotherspoon, 2003, p. 17). Due to the complexities inherent in certain phenomena or because there are alternative frameworks through which issues are defined and examined, there are usually different and competing theories about phenomena. Each theory could provide a reasoned and sensible explanation of the phenomenon being studied. Theory, then, can be construed as a set of conceptual tools that shapes both our understanding and our actions. It illuminates some aspects of social and natural phenomena for consideration and leaves others in the background. According to Moss and colleagues (2006) we represent different theories as conceptual tools that enable and constrain what we can understand about the social world and these theories shape or are shaped by the contexts in which they are used.

Some scholars (e.g., Gay & Airasian, 2003) treat theory as nearly invisible (by barely mentioning or discussing it) or relegate the role of theory to particular methodologies in qualitative research (e.g., Gall, Borg & Gall, 2003; Yin, 1994). Others, however, contend that theory plays a key role in framing and conducting almost every aspect of a study. Merriam (1998), for example, emphasizes the place of the theoretical framework in qualitative research by referring to it as 'the structure, the scaffolding, the frame of your study' (p. 45), contending that we would be lost in conducting our research if we had no theoretical framework to guide us. The theoretical framework, according to Merriam, is derived from the concepts, terms, definitions, models, and theories of a particular literature base and disciplinary orientation and affects every aspect of a study – from framing the research problem and purpose, to determining what to look for, and how to make sense of the data. The entire process is 'theory-laden' (p. 46).

In a similar vein, Miles and Huberman (1994) write, 'any researcher, no matter how unstructured or inductive, comes to fieldwork with *some orienting ideas*' (p. 17). Like Merriam, Miles and Huberman argue that without some rudimentary conceptual framework, there would be no way to make reasoned decisions about what data to collect or determine what is important from among a universe of possibilities. The conceptual framework 'can be rudimentary or elaborate, theory driven or commonsensical, descriptive or casual' (p.18) but it is always there, implicit or explicit, and it delineates the main things to be studied and the personal relationships among them. Schram, too, associates the conceptual context of a study with theory, arguing that the researcher's perspective, fundamental beliefs, assumptions, and purposes for undertaking the study constitute 'premises about the world and how it can be understood and studied' (2003, p. 29), and plays a pervasive role in directing the study and what is seen as legitimate and important to document.

With theory playing such a pervasive role in the qualitative research process, it behooves us as researchers to disclose and discuss the theoretical perspectives informing our research, for to adopt a particular theory for explaining and understanding a phenomenon is to travel into that theory and be able to perceive reality as portrayed in it. Research after all, is not a neutral act.

Theoretical Frameworks for Understanding School Performance of Minority Students

Scholars have employed various theoretical perspectives on Aboriginal education, indicating the diverse understandings and interpretations brought to this phenomenon. Perspectives have included liberal-individualist theories which place the responsibility for success or failure on the individual; structural theories which focus on the analysis of the larger social, economic, and political contexts of Aboriginal schooling; and cultural perspectives that emphasize cultural differences between racial minorities and the dominant culture (see Schissel & Wotherspoon, 2003, for a fuller discussion of these perspectives). Below, I summarize the main theoretical perspectives that I selected from among the plethora of perspectives in the literature to inform and guide the research questions, research procedures, and my analyses and interpretations of the data we collected for the studies from which this book emerged. Specifically, sociocultural theories of learning and cognition, macro-structural theories of ethnic minority school success/failure, theories of racism and anti-racism, and critical race theory are presented as the frameworks I used to make sense of the studies we conducted. These selections are informed by Aboriginal/Indigenous perspectives (e.g., Aboriginal voices on culturally responsive curriculum and pedagogical practices and indigenous perspectives on appropriate conceptual frameworks for understanding integration) and by broader analyses of the larger contexts in which Aboriginal education takes place.

Sociocultural Theories of Learning and Cognition

Sociocultural theories of learning and cognition link the development of children's thinking, communication patterns, and learning and motivational styles with the culture into which they are socialized, and argue that an intricate connection exists between culture and student learning (e.g., Ramirez & Castenada, 1974; Vygotsky, 1981; Wertsch, 1991; Winzer & Mazurek, 1998). According to Wertsch, for example, all forms of cognition are socially situated within the contexts of small groups and within the broader social and institutional settings; cultural mediation constitutes one way by which cognitive processes become contextualized. Vygotsky (1981) asserts that various semiotic systems are used to negotiate meaning between individuals and to mediate higher mental functions. These systems develop in specific ways within different cultures and act as negotiators of meaning and as agents that transform mental functions (see Chapter 1 of this book). Winzer and Mazurek (1998) echo these claims in their argument that children's conceptual framework – that is, their learning and thinking processes – are deeply embedded in their own cultures, and that difficulties in classroom learning and interactions arise when there is a conflict, mismatch or discontinuity between a child's culture and all the intricate subsets of that culture, and the culture of the teacher and the classroom, setting up that child for failure if the school or the teacher is not sensitive to the special needs of that child. Cultural socialization, therefore, influences how students learn, particularly how they mediate, negotiate and respond to curriculum materials, instructional strategies, learning tasks, and communication patterns in the classroom.

Cultural discontinuity theory, most popular in terms of influencing research and political activism, has influenced some Indigenous leaders to advocate strongly for separate or 'special' school programs for Aboriginal children. Others, however, have criticized any idea of separate or special programs in favour of the notion of cultural diversity and cultural sensitivity which values and incorporates Indigenous learning styles and pedagogical orientations in classroom processes. The assumption is that making the curriculum and the classroom processes culturally responsive will mean higher rates of successful school outcomes (and eventually success in the labour market) for Indigenous students whose home cultures are different from the cultural environments of the school. Incorporation, or the 'Both Ways' approach to Indigenous education, as this latter movement has come to be known in North America, Australia, and New Zealand, has received significant endorsement both as an anti-colonial strategy by which marginalized Indigenous voices can 'make the voyage in' (Said, cited in McConaghy, 2000) and as a model for the development of Indigenous education (see, e.g., Lipka, 2002).

My criticism of the cultural learning style theory is that despite its immense relevance for understanding school under-performance among cultural minority students, it does not sufficiently help us understand how individual learning relates to the practices of cultural communities. Furthermore, the cultural learning style approach can hinder effective assistance to student learning by producing overgeneralizations within which a single way of teaching and learning may be used with a particular group without accounting for individuals' past experiences with certain practices or without providing instruction that both extends those practices and introduces new and even unfamiliar ways of doing things. The cultural learning styles approach also creates a false dichotomy between contexts and actions, viewing individuals as though their characteristics were unrelated to the cultural contexts in which they and their families have participated in recent generations.

Confronted with these limitations but still drawn to the cultural discontinuity theory for my analysis, I turned to the more recently emerging *cultural historical* theory of learning which helps us understand how patterns/regularities in the engagement of shared and dynamic practices of different communities contribute to human learning and development. Rather than viewing an individual's learning style as a static, essentialized trait that is independent of tasks and contexts, constant over time and setting, and attributable to ethnic group membership, a cultural historical approach focuses on individuals' histories of engagement in activities in their cultural communities. A central and distinguishing feature of the cultural historical theory is that the structure and development of human psychological processes emerge through participation in culturally mediated practical activities involving cultural practices in contexts (Gutierrez & Rogoff, 2003). The cultural historical theory also recognizes that individuals participate in the practices of their cultural communities in varying and overlapping ways which change over their lifetime and according to changes in the community's organization and relationships with other communities. Undoubtedly, there are patterns and regularities in the ways groups draw on cultural artifacts to function and participate in the everyday practices of their respective communities; however, as Gutierrez and Rogoff (2003) have argued, the emergent goals and practices of participants are in constant tension with the relatively stable characteristics of these environments. It is this tension and conflict that account for and contribute to the variation and ongoing change in an individual's and community's practices. Researchers and practitioners can examine people's usual ways of doing things and characterize the commonalities of experience of people who share cultural backgrounds.

To be able to characterize learners' repertoires of cultural practices and help them extend these practices or use them in new ways in the classroom, the researcher and practitioner will have to understand both the community and the individual practices, and the nature and forms of cultural tools/artifacts used (e.g., social relations, belief systems, customary approaches to performing specific tasks). To facilitate this type of understanding, cultural historical theorists suggest prolonged observations in multiple situations in communities, assuming various vantage points so as to understand not only the complexity of human activity but also the participant's familiarity of experience with cultural practices (see, e.g., Demmert & Towner, 2003). The relevance of the cultural historical approach to understanding Aboriginal education is that it builds on the cultural learning style theory to help us understand more clearly the links between individual Aboriginal student learning and participation in their cultural communities, and how teachers can draw on those links to facilitate or enhance classroom learning for Aboriginal students.

Macro-structural Theories/Explanations of Minority School Performance

Macro-structural theorists (notably Marxist anthropologist, John Ogbu, 1981; 1982; Ogbu & Simons, 1998), on the other hand, have explained minority students' school performance largely in terms of macro-structural conditions such as lack of access to educational resources, racism and other forms of discrimination against minorities, structural pover-ty among many minority groups, and the generally low status minori-ties have been accorded in dominant culture societies – all of which produce structural inequalities and inequities that cause school failure. Ogbu (1982), without disputing the importance of prior cultural sociali-zation in school learning, has criticized the cultural discontinuity the-ory for its failure to explain the school success of immigrant minority students who experience cultural discontinuities between their home and schools at least as severe as those experienced by Native students, Blacks, Chicanos/Chicanas, and Puerto Ricans who have consistently experienced school failure in the United States. Ogbu attributes the fail-ure of these groups to what he calls their 'caste-like minority status' within the larger society. Castelike minorities, according to Ogbu, are those who have been incorporated into the society involuntarily and permanently (e.g., Aboriginals/Natives after European colonization of their land and Blacks who were forcibly brought to America as slaves). They face a job and status ceiling and tend to formulate their collective economic and social problems in terms of the discriminations they face as minorities. These include: instrumental discrimination (for exam-ple, in employment and wages), relational discrimination (for exam-ple, social and residential segregation), and symbolic discrimination (for example, denigration of minority cultures and languages) (Ogbu & Simons, 1998). In education, these discriminations take three forms, all of which affect school performance. The first form is the overall edu-cational policies and practices toward the minorities in the dominant culture society, for example, inequalities in school funding, educational resources, and staffing of minority schools. The second is the treatment/mistreatment of minority students in schools and classrooms in terms of levels of teacher expectations, teacher-student interaction patterns, and grouping/tracking, for example. The third form is the reward, or lack thereof, that society gives to minorities for school accomplishments and credentials, especially in employment and wages. Ogbu (1983), Dei and colleagues (1997), Valencia (1991), Low (1982), and Wilson (1991) to name a few, are among the numerous scholars and researchers who have used these discriminations to explain, to various extents, the low school achievement of African-American, African-Canadian, Chicano, Chinese-American, and Canadian Aboriginal (specifically Sioux Indi-an) students respectively.

However, if this theory/explanation of minority under-performance holds, then all minorities would not do well in school because all are faced with such discriminations. How, then, does the theory account for the success of many minority students, especially those belonging to voluntary immigrant groups? Ogbu and Simons (1998) suggest that the clue to the differences among minorities in school performance may lie in the differences in their 'community forces.' 'Community forces' is essentially a study of how the minorities have perceived and responded to these discriminations and how these perceptions and responses have affected their schooling. In a U.S. study, Ogbu and Simons (1998) hypothesize four factors as constituting community forces: a frame of reference for minority school comparison (e.g., comparison with schools 'back home' or schools in White suburbs); beliefs about the instrumental value of schooling (e.g., role of school credentials in getting ahead); relational interpretations of schooling (e.g., degree of trust of schools and school personnel); and symbolic beliefs about schooling (e.g., whether learning the school curriculum, the dominant language, etc. is considered harmful to minority language and cultural identity). Ogbu and Simons argue that different minority groups tend to interpret and respond to these factors differently. Creating a heuristic classification of minority groups in the United States, the authors posit that although voluntary immigrant minorities, for example, tend to look favourably on U.S. schools compared to their school situations 'back home' and are willing to accept less than equal treatment in order to improve their chances of economic success in the United States, involuntary minorities (like Native-Americans and African-Americans) tend to compare their school situations negatively with those of the White middle class and resent the fact that Whites have more opportunities. Involuntary minorities do not have the 'back home' educational situation to compare things with, and they see no justification for their inferior schooling situation – except discrimination. They tend to be more critical of the curriculum and other schooling practices and are more mistrustful of teachers and the school than are voluntary immigrants. Based on their parents' negative experiences of discrimination in the job market, involuntary minority students do not believe that either the United States or Canada is a land of opportunity where anyone who works hard and has a good education will succeed. When they compare their situation with their White counterparts, Native and Black students do not believe that they are fully rewarded or accepted on the basis of their hard work and education.

Furthermore, Ogbu and Simons (1998) contend that voluntary minority communities and parents are unequivocal in their support for their children learning English and the rest of the school curriculum, seeing these as requirements for success in school and in the job market. Kanu's (2008) study of educational needs and barriers for African refugee students in Canada found similar support among the African parents who participated in the study.

Involuntary minority communities and parents, in contrast, have ambivalent attitudes toward these requirements and pass on these attitudes to their children. Their endorsement of the abstract ideology that Standard English and the other school requirements are needed for success in the dominant White society is contradicted by their concrete experience of the failure of schooling to lead to economic rewards for them. In addition, they see school as a White institution whose requirements for success are designed by White society to deprive minorities of their cultural and linguistic identities and impose White culture on them. This is the defining reason why involuntary minority parents and community leaders are so vocal in their demand for their perspectives, world-views, histories, knowledge, and experiences to be included in the curriculum and other schooling processes.

Ogbu and Simons are careful to point out that the beliefs and responses of the different minority groups discussed above are dominant patterns observed among these groups and do not apply to all individuals in the group, because there are both individual and sub-group variations in attitudes and behaviours towards school. A strong example of such variation is Peggy Wilson's (1991) study of the factors having an impact on the academic performance of Sioux Indian high school students in Canada. Wilson revealed that poor academic performance and eventual dropout among these students were a consequence of macro-structural factors, the trauma of transition into high schools in urban centres away from their homes and communities, and school personnel's lack of understanding of cultural conflicts rather than ambivalent or oppositional attitudes of these students towards the schools. Wilson even rejects Ogbu's 'caste-like' characteristic of job and status ceiling as applicable to the students in her study, arguing that the students did not perceive 'failure in school as failure in society or terminal failure' and that 'in many instances these students can and will go back to settings where they can perform positively and regain strong positive self-concepts' (p. 380). Wilson's findings are important both for revealing the limitations of Ogbu's 'caste-like' status theory for some contexts and for suggesting that changes can be made in the macro-structure to provide positive schooling experiences for Aboriginal students. For example, the trauma of transition suffered by Aboriginal students can be prevented by providing well-resourced high schools in Aboriginal communities so that Aboriginal students do not have to move away to urban centres for secondary education. Nevertheless, ample evidence suggests that, where they are present, the beliefs and responses posited by Ogbu and Simon do affect minority attitudes and behaviours towards school. For example, the ambivalence of involuntary minority parents and communities is reflected in the attitudes and behaviours of students who profess a belief in the importance of 'getting a good education' but nevertheless engage in behaviours that contradict this belief. In addition, because of the inferior status accorded them by the dominant culture, involuntary minorities define their cultures not merely as different from the dominant culture but in opposition to it and may therefore resist achievement in school which they see as representing dominant cultural values. In other words, as Ledlow (1992) explains and as Dei and colleagues (1997) assert in their study of school dropout among Black students in high schools in Toronto, Canada, the cultural discontinuity argument that minority students experience school failure merely because of cultural differences between their homes and the schools denies the historical and larger structural contexts in which those differences are embedded. In explaining minority school failure, therefore, Ogbu (1981) recommends looking beyond the micro-ethnography of the classroom, the home and the playground, toward an ecological framework. He writes: 'The ecological framework suggests that these classroom events are built up by forces originating in other settings and that how they influence classroom teaching and learning must be studied if we are ever to understand why a disproportionate number of minority children do poorly in school, and if we are ever going to design an effective policy to improve minority school performance' (Ogbu, 1981, p. 23).

The compelling arguments put forward by both the cultural discontinuity theorists and the macro-structural theorists suggest a synthesis of these opposing viewpoints where, in examining causes and remedies for school under-performance among minority students (e.g., Aboriginal students) cultural differences and macro-structural determinants of school performance are taken into account. It was such a synthesized framework that guided my investigation of the integration of Aboriginal cultural knowledge/perspectives into the curriculum and to what effect.

Racism, Antiracism, and Critical Race Theories

Race is a complex, dynamic, and changing construct that must be explored as an autonomous concept in the effort to understand minority education. Race is not a biological given but a cultural invention, a culturally and historically specific way of categorizing and treating human beings in order to maintain social, political, and economic privilege. Race has been and remains a powerful ideology for legitimizing social and economic inequality between groups with different ancestries, national origins, and histories. 'Indeed, the concept of race is also a major system of social identity, affecting one's own self-perception and how one is perceived and treated by others' (Mukhopadhyay & Henze, 2003, p. 673). Not only does race and racial classification determine how we are treated and how we treat others, it also profoundly structures our access to resources and rights, making the study of racism fundamental to any effort to understand educational disparities and to bring about social change.

There are many theories of racism that can be useful for understanding Aboriginal education – for example, racism as individual pathology, institutional or structural racism, racism as ideology, racism as discursive formation, etc. Two traditions of understanding racism on which I drew as theoretical frameworks for my research are (a) postcolonial theory of racialized othering (Rizvi, 1993) selected because of its capacity to subsume the various theories of racism to explore the specific characteristics of racisms within colonial contexts, and (b) critical race theory (Ladson-Billings & Tate, 1995) which details how the intersection of race and rights could be used to better understand inequities in racialized societies.

Of central importance in the postcolonial theory of racialized othering are issues of representation and positionality. According to Rizvi (1993), one of the most significant ways in which racism works is in regulating our representations of ourselves and others. He writes: 'Popular racism ... is an ideology that works through certain cultural practices of representation, which makes it possible to sustain particular racist constructions of social difference' (p. 131). Representation includes practices such as inaccurate characterizations of the 'other' and their truth, knowledge, and histories in the curriculum; photographic illustrations and images which become representations of identity especially when reprinted in textbooks; erasures and omissions; token mentioning; and invisibility which Susan Edgerton (1993, p. 64) describes in these words: '... you are hidden in the open ... but they wouldn't see you because they don't expect you to know anything since they believe they've taken care of that.' Representation is important not only because it reflects identity at a particular historical moment, but also because it creates that identity. As Pinar and colleagues (1995, p. 346) note, 'We teach ourselves when we teach textbooks. The identities we represent to children are those we wish (as a nation) to become and to avoid as well as those we are and have been.' It is no surprise, then, that representations of difference have produced such contentious curriculum politics.

An interrelated concept in postcolonial theory of racism is 'positionality,' represented in acts of centering and marginalizing. Here, racism is frequently manifested as processes of exclusion, subordination, marginalization, bias, and discriminations. The biggest problem in education is not knowing these forms of racism, highlighting the need for an understanding of critical race theory (CRT) of education.

Ladson-Billings and Tate (1995) posit at least five elements of CRT of import to education: (1) the centrality of race and racism and their intersectionality with other forms of subordination; (2) the challenge to dominant ideologies (e.g., neutrality, colour blindness, and meritocracy); (3) the commitment to social justice and working toward eliminating racial oppression and all forms of oppression; (4) a transdisciplinary perspective that values and includes diverse epistemologies; and (5) the centrality of experiential knowledge of people of colour. CRT focuses on the effects of race and racism and on challenging the hegemonic hold of White supremacy on the 'meritocratic' system, the intent being to bring about change in the form of social justice (DeCuir & Dixson, 2004). Radical multiculturalists crucially draw on CRT and on an antiracism discursive framework to analyze and explain minority student underachievement and to make proposals for meaningful educational reform.

Two tenets of CRT were of particular relevance to my data analysis: *interest convergence* and *critique of liberalism*. Interest convergence refers to those concessions which dominant culture Whites offer to the extent that such concessions do not constitute a major disruption to the self-interests of Whites and their 'normal' way of life. Critique of liberalism challenges two liberal ideas – that of *colour blindness* in the dispensation of the law, rights and opportunities, and that of *incremental change* where gains for marginalized groups come at a slow pace 'palatable for those in power who are less likely to be affected by oppressive and marginalizing conditions' (DeCuir & Dixson, 2004, p. 29). Critical race theorists and radical multiculturalists have mounted vigorous challenges to the ideas of colour blindness and incremental change on the ground that they ignore race-based policies that promote societal inequity.

Indigenous scholars (e.g., McLaughlin & Whatman, 2008; Watson, 2005; Williamson & Dalal, 2007) have suggested CRT as an appropriate framework for informing and understanding the issues they consider as crucial for the integration of Indigenous perspectives. Williamson and Dalal (2007) list these issues as:

- the need to problematize the endeavour of embedding Indigenous perspectives
- the requirement that students deconstruct their own cultural situatedness in order to appreciate the ways in which the 'other' is framed
- the hegemonic and appropriating capacities of 'Western' disciplines and the dissonance between Indigenous and Western 'ways of knowing'
- the complexities of interactions at the cultural interface and the difficulties of achieving cross-cultural understandings and acquiring cultural competencies
- the need to reorient curricula by engaging with alternative ways of knowing and alternative skill sets (Williamson & Dalal, 2007, p. 52).

A corollary of CRT is an anti-racism discursive framework which acknowledges the role of the education system in the production and reproduction of exclusions and inequalities based on race, gender, and other markers of difference. An anti-racism discursive framework links these identity issues to schooling processes and highlights the need for an education system that is genuinely inclusive and responsive to the challenges of diversity and difference in public schooling. This means, among other things, school administrators and educators developing a commitment to power sharing with students, parents, and local communities. It also means taking serious account of the rich knowledge, experiences, and voices of marginalized groups and dealing foremost with issues of equity (Dei et al., 1997).

While none of the theories discussed in this chapter, alone, is adequate for understanding the complex nature of Aboriginal educational performance, collectively they help us to better understand the critical role of Aboriginal cultural socialization in the learning and development of Aboriginal students, the impact of the larger social, economic and political contexts on Aboriginal school achievement, and the impact of racist ideologies and racism on Aboriginal education. When we are able to understand and interpret the multiple determinants of Aboriginal school performance, we are more aware of the possibilities for successful intervention. Subsequent chapters will show how these theories were deployed in our research to interpret and illuminate various data/issues pertaining to the integration of Aboriginal perspectives.

Summary

This chapter described the role of theory in understanding phenomena and the importance of theoretical frameworks in qualitative research such as the one reported in this book. It identified the theoretical frameworks which guided and informed the research studies we conducted, specifically discussing socio-cultural theories of learning and cognition, macro-structural theories of minority school performance, and racism/anti-racism and critical race theories as the theoretical frameworks employed.

QUESTIONS FOR DISCUSSION

1. How do the various theories discussed in this chapter inform your understanding of Aboriginal education?
2. What other theories are you aware of that have been useful in helping you understand Aboriginal education?
3. What are the advantages and disadvantages of examining a phenomenon from diverse theoretical perspectives?
4. Discuss the policy implications for Aboriginal education that arise from each of the theoretical perspectives presented in this chapter.

REFERENCES/RECOMMENDED READINGS

Benz, V.M., & Shapiro, J.J. (1998). *Mindful inquiry in social research*. Thousand Oaks: Sage.
Creswell, J.W. (1998). *Qualitative inquiry research and design*. Thousand Oaks: Sage.
Dei, G.S., Mazzuca, J., McIsaac, E., & Zine, J. (1997). *Reconstructing dropout: A*

critical ethnography of the dynamics of Black students disengagement from school. Toronto: University of Toronto Press.

Decuir, J.T., & Dixson, A.D. (2004). 'So when it comes, they aren't surprised that it is there': Using critical race theory as a tool of analysis of race and racism in education. *Educational Researcher, 33*(5), 26–31.

Demmert, W., & Towner, J. (2003). *A review of the research literature on the influences of culturally based education on the academic performance of Native-American students.* Portland, OR: Northwest Regional Educational Lab.

Edgerton, S. (1993). Love in the margins. In L. Castenell Jr. & W. Pinar (Eds.), *Understanding curriculum as racial text: Representations of identity and difference in education,* pp. 55–82. New York: SUNY Press.

Gall, M.D., Borg, W.R., & Gall, J.P. (2003). *Educational research* (7th edition). New York: Longman.

Gay, L.R., & Airasian, P. (2003). *Educational research* (7th edition). Upper Saddle River, NJ: Merrille Prentice Hall.

Gutierrez, K.D., & Rogoff, B. (2003). Cultural ways of learning: Individual traits or repertoires of practice? *Educational Researcher, 32*(5), 19–25.

Kanu, Y. (2008). Educational needs and barriers for African refugee students in Manitoba. *Canadian Journal of Education, 31*(4), 915–40.

Ladson-Billings, G., & Tate, W. (1995). Toward a critical race theory of education. *Teachers College Record, 97*(1) 47–68.

Ledlow, S. (1992). Is cultural discontinuity an adequate explanation for dropping out? *American Indian Education, 31*(3) 21–36.

Lipka, J. (2002). *Schooling for self-determination: Research on the effects of including Native language and culture in schools.* Charleston: ERIC Clearinghouse on Rural Small Schools.

Low, V. (1982). *The unimpressible race: A century of educational struggle by the Chinese in San Francisco.* San Francisco: East-West Publishing.

McConaghy, C. (2000). *Rethinking indigenous education: Culturalism, colonization and the politics of knowing.* Flaxton, Queensland: Post Pressed.

McLaughlin, J., & Whatman, S. (2008). Embedding Indigenous perspectives in university teaching: Lessons learned and possibilities of reforming/decolonizing curriculum. In R.W. Heber (Ed.), *Indigenous education: Asia/Pacific,* pp. 123–45. Brisbane: QUT Publications.

Moss, P.A., Girard, B.J., & Haniford, L.C. (2006). Validity in educational assessment. *Review of Educational Research, 30,* 109–62.

Merriam, S.B. (1998). *Qualitative research and case study application in education.* San Francisco: Jossey Bass.

Miles, M.B., & Huberman, A.M. (1994). *Qualitative data analysis,* 2nd ed. Thousand Oaks: Sage

Mukhopadhyay, C., & Henze, R.C. (2003, May). How real is race? Using anthropology to make sense of human diversity. *Phi Delta Kappan*, pp. 669–78.

Ogbu, J.U. (1981). School ethnography: A multilevel approach. *Anthropology and Education Quarterly, 12*, 3–29.

– (1982). Cultural discontinuity and schooling. *Anthropology and Education Quarterly, 13*, 290–307.

– (1983). Minority status and schooling in plural societies. *Comparative Education Review, 37*(2), 168–90.

Ogbu, J., & Simons, H.D. (1998). Voluntary and involuntary minorities: A cultural-ecological theory of school performance with some implications for education. *Anthropology and Education, 29*(2), 155–88.

Pinar, W., Reynolds, W., Slattery, P., & Taubman, P. (1995). *Understanding curriculum*. New York: Peter Lang.

Ramirez, M., & Castenada, A. (1974). *Cultural democracy, bicognitive development and education*. New York: Academic Press.

Rizvi, F. (1993). Children and the grammar of popular racism. In C. McCarthy & W. Crichlow (Eds.), *Race, identity, and representation in education*, pp. 126–39. New York: Routledge.

Ryan, J. (1996). Restructuring First Nations education: Trust, respect, and governance. *Journal of Canadian Studies, 15*(2), 211–30.

Schissel, B., & Wotherspoon, T. (2003). *The legacy of school for Aboriginal people: Education, oppression, and emancipation*. Don Mills: Oxford University Press.

Schram, T.H. (2003). *Conceptualizing qualitative inquiry*. Columbus, OH: Merrille Prentice Hall.

Valencia, R. (1991). *Chicano school failure and success: Research and policy agenda for the 1990s*. London: Falmer Press.

Vygotsky, L.S. (1981). The genesis of higher mental functions. In J.V. Wertsch (Ed.), *The concept of activity in Soviet psychology*, pp. 144–88. New York: Sharpe.

Watson, N. (2005). Indigenous people in legal education: Staring into a mirror without reflection. *Indigenous Law Bulletin*. Retrieved 8 July 2008 from: www.kirra:austlii.edu.au.au/journals/ILB/2005/1.html.

Wertsch, J.V. (1991). A sociocultural approach to socially shared cognition. In L.S. Resnick, J.M. Levine, & S.D. Teasely (Eds.), *Perspectives on socially shared cognition*, pp. 85–100. Washington, DC: American Psychological Association.

Williamson, J., & Dalal, P. (2007). Indigenizing the curriculum or negotiating the tensions at the cultural interface? Embedding Indigenous perspectives and pedagogies in a university curriculum. *The Australian Journal of Indigenous Education, 36*, 51–8.

Wilson, P. (1991). Trauma of Sioux Indian high school students. *Anthropology and Education Quarterly, 22*(4), 367–83.

Winzer, M., & Mazurek, K. (1998). *Special education in multicultural contexts.* New York: Prentice Hall.

Yin, R. (1994). *Case study research.* Thousand Oaks: Sage.

3 Cultural Mediators of Aboriginal Student Learning in the Formal School System

This chapter presents the rarely heard voices of Aboriginal learners, as particular groups of Aboriginal students identify nine aspects and several sub-aspects of their home and community cultures that influence and mediate how they learn in the formal school system. It is based on the first of our three research studies and draws on cultural-historical theory to inquire into the influence of cultural participation on Aboriginal student learning. The cultural aspects include: story-telling; use of learning scaffolds; learning by observation and emulation; communal concepts of self; clear communication between teacher and student; community support; infusion of Aboriginal content; and teacher warmth, firmness, and respect.

Investigating the Influence of Culture on Learning through a Cultural-Historical Approach

Psychosocial and sociocultural research on learners, learning, cognition, and teaching is often undertaken using the cultural learning styles approach, which attributes individual learning styles/traits categorically to membership in ethnic groups. Based on this attribution, prescriptions are made for creating learning environments that complement the learning styles of different ethnic groups. Undoubtedly, the cultural learning styles approach has made positive contributions towards helping us move away from the 'cultural deficit thesis' which posits that socially disadvantaged communities have remained educationally and economically marginal primarily because of their negative values and moribund attitudes which in turn create the material conditions that reproduce their social disadvantage (see Rahim, 1998). Clearly, this is a thesis that judges cultural practices which differ from those of dominant groups to be less adequate without examining those practices from the perspective of the community's participants. Increasingly, however, the assumption that the dominant culture is inherently superior is being questioned and debunked and, with emerging research challenging educational psychology's traditional assumption that learning and development are purely psychological processes disconnected from the individual's cultural socialization, efforts are now being made to provide training, resources, and support for addressing cultural differences in classrooms. But, as I pointed out in Chapter 2, despite its important contribution, the cultural learning styles approach does not sufficiently help researchers understand how an individual's learning relates to the practices of his or her cultural communities. In light of this shortcoming of the cultural learning styles approach researchers have proposed the use of a 'cultural historical approach' which emphasizes the richness of potential associations between a student's cultural participation and academic learning (see Chapter 2 for a fuller description of the cultural-historical approach).

Using cultural historical theory, I set out to investigate how Aboriginal cultural socialization mediates/influences classroom learning for urban Aboriginal students from low-income backgrounds in Winnipeg, Manitoba in western Canada. As stated earlier, cultural differences between the homes/communities of Aboriginal students and the school environment has been consistently identified in the literature as a major cause of school failure among Aboriginal students in public school systems, provoking calls for the inclusion of Aboriginal cultural perspectives across school curricula, classroom practices, and teacher preparation programs. In response to this call and inspired by a cultural historical framework, I set out to investigate the following questions in this study: (1) What specific aspects of Aboriginal cultural experience/socialization influence and mediate classroom learning for Aboriginal students? (2) Would these cultural experiences be similar and supportive of classroom learning for all students from a particular Aboriginal group or should we base interventions on patterns/regularities discerned in individuals' histories of participation in and familiarity with cultural activities? (3) What are the histories of Aboriginal students' participation and engagement in activities in their cultural communities? (4) What are the patterns and variations of engagement of shared cultural practices among particular groups of Aboriginal students? (5) How does such participation/engagement enhance or impede classroom learning for these students? These questions led me to a one-academic-year study, conducted September 2002 to June 2003 among Aboriginal students in a prairie city, to identify aspects of their cultural socialization (existing knowledge structures) that influenced/ mediated how they received, negotiated and responded to curriculum materials, teaching methods/strategies, and learning tasks in their high school social studies classroom. Knowledge of cultural mediators of Aboriginal student learning is critical to our understanding of how teachers could best adapt classroom materials and processes to the cultural repertoire of Aboriginal students thereby enabling them to continue to have generous and positive access to their cultural heritage while also acquiring knowledge and confidence with the content and codes of the dominant cultures embedded in the curriculum and schooling processes.

Research Methods and Procedures

The use of the cultural historical approach as a theoretical framework for this study necessitated conducting the study at two sites simultaneously. One site was a low-income Aboriginal community, with a mixed population of Ojibway, Cree, Dene, Dakota, and Métis, where my two Aboriginal graduate research assistants (Cree and Ojibway) and I carried out prolonged observations (one visit per week over 38 weeks) of ten Aboriginal students (three Ojibway, three Cree, one Dene, two Sioux, and one Métis of Cree and Scottish ancestry) who volunteered to be observed as they engaged in shared activities in their community. While this sample of students may seem too small to warrant generalization of the research findings, the number has to be interpreted within the context of the nature of the data needed for our particular study as well the research design. According to Merriam (1998) the number of participants in a sample depends on the questions being asked, the data being gathered, the resources available to support the study, and the analytic procedures that may be needed during the ongoing process of the study. Our research goal was an in-depth understanding of the questions we set out to investigate and, through prolonged field observations, in-depth interviews, and rigorous data analysis informed by studies of Indigenous/minority education conducted in diverse contexts, provide readers with rich data from research participants belonging to diverse Aboriginal groups in Manitoba and non-Aboriginal students and teachers. Generalization of the research results, as I wrote in Chapter 1, is achieved through comparability of the sample to similar cases occurring elsewhere and the extent of the reader's relatability to the research findings.

The other research site was an inner-city alternative high school where the ten students attended school. This school was selected because of its high Aboriginal student population (80%) and its interest in working with the Faculty of Education, University of Manitoba, to find teaching methods, processes, and curriculum materials that reach *all* students in the classroom. According to the vice-principal, the school is one of the toughest in the inner city. Each year, over six hundred students register and only three hundred will complete the school year. The majority of the students are teenage parents on welfare. Of the parents in the neighbourhood, 79 per cent are unemployed, and many of the students have experienced little success in their lives and need to be convinced to come to school. In a school like this, school courses are used more to help students to understand and improve the quality of their lives than to transmit purely academic knowledge.

The study was conducted in a Grade 9 social studies classroom with twenty-eight students – twenty-one Aboriginal and seven White – and two teachers. One teacher was Caucasian (ethnically English-Canadian) and had taught Grade 9 Social Studies for 23 years. The other was a Black (African-Canadian) teacher who taught mainly science but provided support through individualized instruction during the teaching of social studies.

Selection of the research participants was done on the basis of their willingness to participate in the study. Because the research involved extensive intrusion into the classroom of the teachers and the lives of the students and the Aboriginal community participating in the study, a great deal of sensitivity was brought to the research process. In line with Archibald's (1993) call for mutual respect in conducting research among Aboriginal peoples, trusting relationships were built between us (the researchers) and the research participants long before the study began. Entry into the school and the social studies classroom was negotiated largely through the help of the vice-principal (a Métis woman), who said during our second meeting that she recognized the importance of a study that was inclusive of Aboriginal voice and that had potential for educational change. She introduced us and our research intent to the teachers and students of the Grade 9 Social Studies class. This introduction was followed by several visits to the classroom, first simply as visitors sitting in on their classes. Our intent was to make the students and the teachers feel comfortable with our presence, and for the teachers to realize that we were not there to be critical of their work or devalue what they were doing. Rather, the intent was for us to work together as educators to find ways of arriving at more inclusive classroom teaching. Entry into the Aboriginal community for our research was negotiated through the ten Aboriginal students and my two Aboriginal graduate research assistants, who were able to convince their parents/relatives and community members that the results of our study would benefit Aboriginal students in the public school system. All participants were first informed orally about the study by the researchers after which, as required by our university's research ethics board, free and informed written consent of the teachers, students, parents, and community leaders was obtained through letters before starting the research. Research participants were given the option to withdraw from the study whenever they wished to do so.

Data collection occurred at the community site and in the Grade 9 Social Studies classroom. A social studies classroom was chosen for the study because a large part of the content of social studies is derived from the social science disciplines; social studies, therefore, offers opportunities for the use of a variety of curriculum materials, teaching strategies and learning tasks that apply across a large number of subject areas. As well, I am a social studies instructor and was more likely to understand the curriculum goals, concepts, and the teaching/learning processes targeted in such a class.

Ethnography offers enhanced opportunities to understand research participants within their own settings, and the flexibility to follow and document events as they arise during the research (Bogdan & Biklen, 2003). Therefore, an ethnographic approach was used for the study. In line with ethnographic methodology, multiple data collection methods were used. These were: site observations, research conversations, students' journals, and focus groups.

Site observations: Our interest was in understanding the valued, shared practices and activities of the Aboriginal groups in the study, the history and patterns of participation/engagement of the ten Aboriginal students in these activities, and the mediating influence of these prior knowledge structures on their classroom learning. We, therefore, spent an enormous amount of time observing activities and interactions in the Aboriginal community and in the Grade 9 Social Studies classroom. In the community, we observed and wrote down field notes on the participation of the ten students and their parents/relatives in activities/ interactions such as: patterns of verbal and non-verbal communication and their intended meanings; approaches to task performance; norms regarding competition and interdependence; extent to which children are left to accomplish things on their own and arrive at their own independent decisions and opinions; how children and adolescents engage in pastimes; ways of responding to persons in authority; and interpersonal relationships and interactions. The intent was for us to be able to characterize the cultural repertoires of our ten student volunteers and their dexterity in moving between approaches appropriate to varying activity settings. Over the one academic year of the study, we would have an account of each participant's and the community's value-laden experience, and be able to speak about the usual/customary/habitual approaches taken in known circumstances.

At the school site, where we also spent 34 weeks, our classroom observations focused on the curriculum materials, teaching and assessment methods/strategies, and learning tasks used in the lessons, and how our ten student participants used their cultural knowledge/ socialization to negotiate and cope with these classroom processes. Data collected from both sites were later used as material for research conversations with the participants.

Research conversations: In the Aboriginal community, we had many informal conversations with our ten research participants and their relatives to help us better understand the practices and/or behaviours we were observing and confirm or disconfirm our own beliefs and hypotheses about issues such as social relations, rules, division of labour, cultural tools and artifacts used, and certain actions and the rationales behind them. More formally we held two sets of research conversations, organized in the form of one-hour circle discussions, with the students in the study. The first set of conversations was intended to get the students' initial responses to our research questions pertaining to: (a) how the curriculum materials and the classroom activities, processes and interactions helped or impeded class participation and conceptual understanding for them; (b) the specific aspects of their prior cultural knowledge and socialization that contributed to enhance or impede class participation and conceptual understanding when these classroom materials and processes were used; (c) their preferred teaching and learning methods in the classroom and how these were similar to or different from the dominant methods through which they learned in their cultural community; and (d) additional questions intended to further illuminate the data collected at the community and classroom sites. The second set of conversations provided us (the researchers) the opportunity to probe specific responses in more detail and explore any new questions and ideas that emerged. These formal conversations were audio-recorded and later transcribed verbatim for analysis.

Students' journals: All of the ten Aboriginal students in the study were asked to maintain a journal where they documented the cultural experiences that influenced/mediated how they received, negotiated, and responded to curriculum materials, teaching strategies, and learning tasks in the social studies classroom.

Focus groups/Talking circle: Our initial plan was to include all twenty-one Aboriginal students in our community observations and research conversations but for practical and resource reasons, we selected a mixture of only ten of them for these intensive and extensive observations. However, the voice of every Aboriginal student in the class was important to us. Therefore, we conducted two focus groups in the form of talking circles among the remaining eleven students, using the same research conversation questions (conversation openers) we had used earlier with our ten participants. These conversations were recorded and transcribed and the data were cross-checked with data from our ten participants.

For data analysis, important sections of the data from these multiple sources were highlighted and summarized. Doing so enabled us to get an overview of what the data offered concerning the research questions as well as see whether the data gave rise to any new questions, points of view, and ideas. All data were read and segmented into meaningful analytical units and coded, using both a priori codes (previously developed based on the research questions and the cultural-historical theoretical framework) and inductive codes generated directly from examining the data. Coded data were organized according to themes emerging from the data. These themes were examined in collaboration with the participants in order to understand what certain data meant and how certain facts could be explained. Data analysis and interpretation, therefore, incorporated both emic and etic perspectives (Jones, 1979). Research narratives were then constructed, based on the data. To address the concern expressed in the RCAP (1996) report that 'Aboriginal people have had almost no opportunity to correct misinformation and to challenge ethnocentric and racist interpretations' (p.235) and to give voice to the Aboriginal students, a key concern in this study, these research narratives were returned to the research participants for comments, changes or/and confirmation before being included in the final report. According to Te Hennepe (1993), 'Returning the text is to move the conversation into an outer circle and ask the people there if, in their opinion, the reconstructed conversation has integrity' (p.236).

Te Hennepe also writes 'the integrity of the speaker's words can be lost as the text writer creates a new telling of what was said' (p. 236). An attempt was made to respect the participants' words/contributions by including them as direct quotes, where appropriate, to enrich the research narratives. Where participants are quoted in the following discussion of the research findings, pseudonyms have been used to protect their identities.

Aboriginal Students' Indentification of Cultural Mediators of Their Learning[1]

Analysis of the data generated from the different research instruments revealed several findings related to the two main concerns of the study: (a) the participants' history of participation in and familiarity with activities in their cultural community, and (b) the curriculum materials and teaching/learning processes and interactions used in the social studies classroom, and the aspects of Aboriginal cultural socialization which enhanced or inhibited Aboriginal student participation and conceptual understanding when these materials, strategies and learning tasks were employed.

The first important finding was that all ten students that we followed for this study showed an impressive level of familiarity with the cultural practices and knowledge structures of their community. To a large extent, they participated easily and consistently in activities with comfort, authority, and knowledge of their culture. Of course, some differences were observed among individual participants, as the discussion will show. However, there were sufficiently common elements among the participants that appeared to conflict with the values, culture, and processes that are dominant in the conventional classroom. These common elements in the data provided the bases for the construction of themes.

Part I of this report presents, in tabular form (Table 3.1), representative samples of the curriculum materials, learning tasks/activities,

Table 3.1: Curriculum materials, teaching methods/learning tasks, and learning goals in a Grade 9 Social Studies class

Curriculum Materials	Teaching Methods/ Learning Tasks	Learning Goals
No prescribed textbooks were used. Materials were selected according to needs and interests of students, but of relevance to successful living in mainstream Canadian society. Materials used included the following:		
Stories with moral messages from the book Chicken Soup for the Soul	Reading of the stories by the teacher; teacher-led discussion of questions on the stories (questions ranged from recall to higher levels of thinking).	To develop students' listening and comprehension skills; to develop higher level thinking; to provide student motivation through the moral lessons in the stories (e.g. perseverance, respect for self and others).
Concepts such as 'stereotyping,' 'discrimination,' 'prejudice,' 'racism,' 'lazy' which depicted some of the lived experiences of many Aboriginal students.	Small group discussion of concepts; two teachers and one teacher aide in the room provided support to students as they worked in groups; sharing of insights through verbal presentations; teacher input through further discussion, examples, probing questions (scaffolding) and notes.	For students to understand the ignorance and discrimination present in stereotyping; for students to recognize their own prejudices; for students to improve their discussion and public speaking skills; to relate curriculum to students' daily lives.
Concepts of more general relevance and application, e.g., 'supply and demand,' 'critical consumer decision-making factors,' 'advertising,' 'motives for purchasing goods and services,' 'human rights.'		
Pictures of accomplished Aboriginal people in respected professions.	Whole class teacher-led discussion through higher level thinking questions which encouraged student participation (expression of ideas and opinions).	To make the curriculum relevant to the Aboriginal students (students see themselves in positive ways in the curriculum); students will be motivated by positive role-models.
'The Canadian Scrapbook: Looking Back on Aboriginal Early Lives.'	Independent and small group worksheet activities; scavenger hunt locating information from pages already identified	For Aboriginal students to understand their rich history; for students to develop research skills.

Table 3.1: Curriculum materials, teaching methods/learning tasks, and learning goals in a Grade 9 Social Studies class *(concluded)*

Curriculum Materials	Teaching Methods/ Learning Tasks	Learning Goals
	by the teacher (scaffolding research work); individualized instruction by teachers; whole class discussion of student responses.	
Teacher's notes on transparencies and other visual aids.	Visual aids were used by the teacher to explain certain concepts. Notes provided lesson summaries for students.	To support student learning through visual examples.

teaching methods/strategies, and learning goals observed in the social studies classroom during the research. Part II discusses the themes which emerged from site observations, participants' journals, focus groups and research conversations with the students about the aspects of their cultural socialization which helped or hindered their learning in the social studies classroom.

Related Themes

Data analysis produced a number of themes relating to how culture influenced/mediated Aboriginal students' learning in the social studies classroom. I have labeled these themes as: Aboriginal approaches to learning, effective communication between the adult/teacher and Aboriginal students, communal concepts of self, relevant curriculum, and the interpersonal style of the teacher.

Theme 1: Indigenous Approaches to Learning

Five indigenous approaches to learning which appeared to be common in the community we observed were also found to have facilitated or hindered class participation and conceptual understanding for the students in our study. These approaches were: learning through stories and anecdotes, learning by observing and emulating, learning through visual sensory modalities, learning through scaffolding, and learning through community support.

Learning through stories and anecdotes: Anecdotes and stories were sometimes observed to be used by adults, especially parents and elders, to convey important messages to the young and to each other in the community we observed. This probably explains why all ten students in the study agreed that the story reading method adopted by their social studies teacher was very effective in helping them understand the concepts and messages contained in each story. In their journals and in our research conversations the students revealed the following cultural reasons for the effectiveness of the storytelling method.

First, in indigenous Aboriginal culture, traditional stories, legends, songs and many other forms of knowledge are passed on among generations by constant re-telling by elders who carry the knowledge of these spoken forms in their memories. As one Ojibway student put it, 'My grandmother knows these stories inside out. My parents also know them and I learn the stories from them all. We all know the songs that go with each story' (Don).

In many indigenous cultures, stories and proverbs are primary ways by which a great deal of indigenous philosophical thought, knowledge, and wisdom has been taught. As there were no written records of the ancient past of many indigenous peoples, all that has been preserved of their knowledge, myths, philosophies, liturgies, and songs has been handed down by word of mouth from generation to generation. Preliterate indigenous cultures in West Africa, for example, were characterized by an oral tradition that found expression in stories, folktales, anecdotes, proverbs, and parables that provoked a great deal of reflection. These oral media preserved, more or less accurately, the history of the people, their general outlook on life, and their conduct and moral values, and they were used especially in rural communities as forms of indigenous knowledge which played an important role in the education of the young. For example, adults would gather youngsters around a fire at night and tell them myths, legends, and stories that not only captured the tribal past but also passed on political and cultural information that helped the youngsters to relate precedents to the present and grasp the prevailing ethical standards of their tribe. Stories that personified animal characters were often told, and these stories, while explaining the peculiar trait of each animal, also transmitted the virtues valued by the society. Among the Mende of Sierra Leone (West

Africa), for example, stories about 'kasiloi' (the spider), always taught youngsters about the unwanted consequences of traits such as greed, egotism, disobedience, or cunning. Typically, a spider story intended to teach a lesson about greed, for example, would begin with a question such as 'Do you know why the spider has such a slender waist?' The narrator, an adult/elder, would then answer the question by narrating an instructional story such as the following:

> Spider was invited to two feasts in two villages at the same time. Not wanting to miss either feast, Spider tied a rope around his waist and gave each end of the rope to each village. He instructed each village to pull him by the rope at precisely the time when the feast began. The harder Spider was pulled in each direction, the smaller his waist became. He screamed and screamed in pain until his neighbour heard his cries and came and untied the rope. Through greed, therefore, Spider lost the feast in each village and never regained his waistline.

The narration of these stories was interspersed with frequent bouts of songs that kept the listeners engaged, interested, and involved in the narration. The role of the listeners(s) was to reflect on the story and deduce the moral message contained in it (see Kanu, 2007).

Cruickshank (1990) and Haig-Brown (1997) affirm the role of oral tradition in Aboriginal culture in their assertion that narratives are often used for teaching about cultural norms and values in Aboriginal communities. According to Armstrong (cited in Kirkness, 1992, p.7) this aspect of 'Aboriginal traditional education is a natural process occurring during everyday activities ... ensuring cultural continuity and survival of the mental, spiritual, emotional, and physical well-being of the cultural unit and of its environment.'

Children develop a sense of morality through stories, anecdotes and legends which they hear from parents and elders, and by observing parents and elders modeling certain behaviours. A Cree student expressed this view succinctly:

> We learn what is right and wrong from these stories. For example, I came to Winnipeg from Oxford House reserve where my grandpa still goes hunting. Many stories of hunting he has told me are about being honest about the number of catches each person had on a group hunting trip (Jon)·

Second, stories and anecdotes offer effective ways for individuals to

express themselves safely (e.g., convey messages of chastisement) without directly preaching the message or specifically moralizing or assign-
ing blame. From an informal conversation with an Ojibway parent in
the community we observed, we learned that Aboriginal peoples' stories are shared with the expectation that the listeners will make their
own meaning, and that they will be challenged to learn something from
the stories. Stories, therefore, contain layers of meaning that listeners
decode according to their readiness to receive certain teachings. Ned, a
Sioux student put it this way: 'You just get the message as you listen to
the story and you loosen up and improve your behaviour, if you want
to ...'

   Stories and anecdotes can, therefore, serve as metaphors for guiding moral choice and self-examination; when reflected upon, they act
as mirrors for seeing things in a particular way. More than any theoretical discussion or philosophical writing, stories and anecdotes throw
light on the concrete reality of lived experience; they serve as important pedagogical devices because they provide experiential case material on which pedagogical reflection is possible. As learners break into
(analyse) a story or anecdote they are able to reflect on the embedded
meanings and implications. Furthermore, these devices bring together
the learners and the community because the elders, as the sources of
the stories and songs and as experts in oratory, are charged with the
responsibility of teaching them to the young. Unfortunately, these valuable pedagogical tools are often excluded from school education, thereby creating a huge disconnect between the school and the community.

Learning by observing and emulating: Another learning approach which
appeared to have a strong basis in the Aboriginal community we
studied was observational learning, which involves observing others
(experts) performing a task or solving a problem. The learner watches
the expert and the processes at stake. If the processes are not manifest or easily observable by the learner, the expert explicates the decision processes and strategies underlying the problem-solving activities
and gives an explanation of when and why particular strategies are
useful. Learners reflect on the learning process by rehearsing the task
mentally and by so doing refine their initial representations (Bandura,
1976). This is thought to be effective because the emphasis in observational learning lies on the rationale behind it as well as the procedure
itself. Learners learn to recognize typical problem situations and which
problem-solving procedures to use in those cases (Eysink et al, 2009).

Probing questions during our research conversations with the students revealed a close link between learning by watching and doing and some traditional child-rearing practices which have survived in many Aboriginal families. From our observations and the research conversations, it appeared that Cree and Ojibway children have developed a learning style characterized by observation and emulation as children and adults in the extended family participate in everyday activities. As their abilities develop, learners do what they are able to do. Joe, a Cree student in the study, elaborated on this approach to learning:

> When they [parents, grandparents, or teachers] actually show you and you see it in action, it's easier for you to grab … You learn as you watch. Sometimes you ask questions and they explain to you.

Kem, an Ojibway student, linked this learning method to preparation for adult responsibility:

> Actually seeing how something is done, instead of reading how it's done, that's hard to remember. When you watch how it is done it automatically clicks in your head. It's like making bannock [an Aboriginal bread], you learn to make it by watching the older people and then making it by yourself.

By contrast, all the students in the study pointed out that the 'talk approach' to much of school instruction actually inhibited classroom learning for them. In an effort to reconcile this claim with the benefits of verbal instruction touted earlier by these participants during our discussion about storytelling, I asked them for clarification. Liz's comment below reflected those made by the rest of the students:

> Do you remember how I said some teachers explain too much information and too fast? That really confuses me. I get lost in the explanation and then I tune out. But Mr.X, he cuts it down to size, right to the chase, works the formula on the board which I watch step by step. I like that…

Joe concurred: 'I get bored with all that talking, period.'

It appears that while verbal instructional methods such as storytelling are an important cultural approach to learning for these students, the verbal saturation which characterizes much of school instruction, especially when this instruction is fast-paced and delivered through a different language, is not conducive to classroom learning for some Aboriginal students. Haig-Brown and colleagues (1997) support this finding with their description of the concise communication style of the Aboriginal mathematics teacher they observed at Joe Duquette High School, an Aboriginal community school:

> His directions are minimal, short, almost abrupt: 'Put your name at the top. Straight multiplication. Maximum, five minutes and there is a table at the top. Five seconds. Start.' There are no words wasted, no wasted time. One might think of the speaker in another class telling the students of his learning that the Cree language is a gift of the creator to be used wisely. (p. 110)

This is an important finding because differences in approaches to learning have far-reaching consequences in the formal education of Aboriginal students, particularly in view of the fact that the formal education system almost always favours those who are highly verbal. The references to 'tuning out' and 'getting bored' are indicative of the emotional and psychological conditions that contribute to student disengagement from what's going on in the classroom. Students like Joe and Liz simply 'fade out' of the school system when they feel they can no longer conform to its demands and impositions.

Community support encourages learning: Learning through verbalization was also disparaged by the students for another reason – the felt lack of support in a mixed classroom, compared to the family and community support we observed in the field. All but one Ojibway student pointed out that the teaching/learning method they found most uncomfortable was when they were called upon to make a verbal presentation in front of the class. Three of the students, who had left their reserves less than a year earlier to attend high school in Winnipeg, said they were not used to speaking English all the time and had difficulty pronouncing some English words correctly. Others revealed that they were intimidated by the direct criticism which this method entailed in the formal (Western) school system. Jon's comment on this point is instructive:

> It's like they are looking out for the mistakes you make and they pounce on you. Even the teachers sometimes make you feel dumb by the questions they ask after you have presented in class.

I probed further to see how learning would be different in their community and Ned said:

> In the (Aboriginal) community, if you don't have the right answer you are not criticized directly and you ask for some help because you know the people that are around you, so you feel secure. Also, in the community you are doing it for the community or their approval, so everyone is supportive and pitches in to help or encourage you. In school, although you know the teacher and the other class members but you are on your own. You are doing it for your own education as an individual. As far as school is concerned, I don't look forward to sharing my responses.

These comments are consistent with our observations and informal conversations with two relatives of the student participants about parenting and social interaction in some Aboriginal cultures as entailing 'non-interference' (meaning guiding without directly criticizing, or controlling the behaviour of others, the goal being for children to make their own decisions). The comments are also consistent with Collier (1993) who, based on his research on teaching Aboriginal students, made a suggestion to 'never put Native students on the spot (by) asking them directly by name to answer a question in public' (p. 114). Native American Walter Flemming (2006) elaborated on this point in reference to the myth that giving the Native-American child centre stage will enhance his or her self-confidence and show off their knowledge: 'Traditional Native-Indian cultures sometimes teach that a child not attempt to outshine his or her peers' (p. 215). For the Aboriginal students in our study, silence seemed to be the best defence mechanism and tool of resistance in a mixed classroom where they felt they were among White strangers whom they have come to believe are constantly critical of them rather than being supportive. Chris's comment spoke to this form of resistance:

> Yeah, that's why in my former school I preferred to remain silent in class ... It's just that I didn't really know and trust people in the school. At home and in my community, I know and trust people, so I just blabber away without fear of making mistakes or being criticized. But when school starts, I don't speak, so they leave me alone.

Te Hennepe (1993), in her study of the experiences of First Nations students in university anthropology classrooms, quotes one of her interviewees, Mary, on how Native students deal with the breakdowns and spiritual disembodiment that occur when the expected respect and authority of their voices are violated in the formal learning process:

> Mary: 'When a Native student goes into a classroom, part of you is removed and sort of your Indian spirit is put apart from you, so you are separated so you can deal with the mainstream societal values. You try to talk about native matters that are in the text without using the eyes of your Indian spirit ... When you look at it with your wholeness all that emotional stuff wells up. You try to see it through their eyes. When you leave the room your spirit is back. This is how I deal with the pain. Remove yourself from from your body. Your spirit is up there waiting for you. You are up there and looking at yourself. You look back and you see compliance. You comply.' (p. 257)

Some researchers have explained the classroom silence of Native students in terms of 'interference theory,' which states that Native children in non-school contexts 'talk a mile a minute,' and that their silence in class derives from the culture of the classroom because the instructor and the context may require a different language to learn material that is foreign (Whyte, 1986). Whyte writes: 'The problem (of classroom silence) lies not with the child but rather is an educational problem of designing a learning setting which is right for the children – in which children feel comfortable and secure enough to participate' (p. 297). I endorse Whyte's statement wholeheartedly. With skillful understanding of how to bring out examples of learning and critical thinking from students and with knowledge of how to create learning environments that are respectful and non-threatening, teachers can enhance the class participation and quality of learning for their Aboriginal students. This requires teachers to inform themselves about prevailing pedagogical norms in the communities from which their Aboriginal students originate and use this understanding to the advantage of these students. This type of cultural understanding is imperative for teachers, because when students' cultural realities are ignored or marginalized, the students themselves feel relegated to the margins of social acceptance and they come to see the school as unresponsive or excluding.

The sole Ojibway student who said he was not uncomfortable with verbal classroom presentations is a clear indication that, as Ogbu and Simons (1998) emphasized, membership in a certain group does not predict behaviour; it only makes certain types of behaviour more probable. This shows that culture is not a unified monolithic whole, and while there may be distinctive learning patterns among cultures, variations do exist among individuals within groups.

Learning through scaffolding: When students spoke about the type of support they needed in order to best learn in social studies classes, it was frequently about the need for some form of scaffolding or temporary framework of support, at least until they were able to develop the skills to learn independently. Forms of scaffolding identified by the students included: specific direction and guidance from the teacher through clear and concise explanations; explicit steps to follow in the performance of a given task; direct feedback from the teacher; and concrete examples, preferably from the students' cultural and experiential backgrounds. Data from the classroom observations showed that the two teachers and the occasional teacher aide in the classroom provided some of these structures to enhance learning by Aboriginal students. These five forms of scaffolding appear to have direct foundations in child-rearing practices among the Aboriginal community we observed, where we learned that children are socialized to accomplish tasks largely through support, direct guidance, and feedback from parents and other significant adults. Don compared this cultural approach to what obtained in his classroom:

'Mrs B., Mr X. and Ms T. always go round when we are working on our own, to explain more clearly about what we are to do. It helps a lot, just like at home.'

Consistently missing in the classroom, however, but clearly desired by the students, were concrete examples from their cultural and experiential backgrounds – a topic which took our focus groups and research conversations into the need for Aboriginal teachers and school counselors in the school. For these students, Aboriginal teachers were not only equipped to draw on their firsthand knowledge of Aboriginal communities to provide needed learning scaffolds, they were also seen as role models to be emulated and compatriots who are able to provide a social perspective more congruent with that of Aboriginal students, based on similar experiences and struggles. Furthermore, the presence of Aboriginal teachers and counselors would help Aboriginal students feel a sense of belonging and connectedness to the school. Justification for Aboriginal teachers and counselors, therefore, ranged from pedagogical reasons to issues of identity, representation, and belonging. Janelle captured all these sentiments in her comment:

I really do like Mrs B. (her White social studies teacher). She is a good teacher. The problem is that the information she teaches about Aboriginal people is all second hand. It's not based in concrete experience. Now Mr D. (the Aboriginal guidance counselor); he has been 'there' and he has turned his life around, so he understands that when I am absent from school for a few days, it's not because I want to drop out. I am just chilling out due to personal issues going on in my life. He does not put all the blame on me, he understands. So he explains my situation to the other [non-Aboriginal] teachers and so I get the chance to do 'catch-up' work.

Even students who said that the teacher's cultural and ethnic background was not a factor as long he or she was a 'good teacher' and 'not racist' admitted that they could learn a lot more from Aboriginal teachers than just academic material. Manny put it this way:

It's not just learning inside the classroom. You also learn from teachers outside the classroom – from their struggles and experiences and their advice and how they made it through the system. White teachers, no matter how good they are as role models, simply do not have the same impact.

Learning through visual sensory modalities: Eight of the ten students in the study pointed out that they were better able to understand and retain concepts when presented through visual images (a Cree and an Ojibway student did not agree with this claim). Ned, for example, said:

Mrs B. can explain something verbally over and over and many of us still ask her for further clarification. But when we see it in pictures or on transparency, when the overhead comes on, it is different, probably because it is bright. It does grab your attention and then you see the material as she is talking about it. It's like a different way of learning.

Liz agreed:

For me too. I understand better when I actually see an image or picture of something, which the teacher is talking about.

Rich added,

She [Mrs B.] gets our attention better with things we actually get to see. Most of the students stop fooling around when the transparency comes on, for example. That's why many of us also like to learn on the computer. We actually see the images in front of us and then understanding becomes less difficult.

Although these findings are consistent with Grossman's (1995) assertion that Native American and Alaskan Native youth tend to be visual learners, the claims to elevated visual abilities need to be established by further research. Psychological research is still inconclusive about whether visualization abilities are higher among Aboriginals than among comparative groups. For example, Berry (1966) in several studies found that Canadian Inuit indeed scored considerably higher on various spatial and visual tests than comparative groups from West Africa and Scotland, but Mackinon (1972, cited in Kleinfeld & Nelson 1991) failed to replicate this finding in a small study of Canadian Inuit students. Berry (1969), however, theorized that the ecological demands of a particular environment, along with the cultural group's adaptation to that environment, may press for the development of a particular pattern of cognitive abilities.

Kleinfeld (1971), in a study conducted in the United States, also found that Inuit village students exceeded urban students of the same ages on a modified version of the Memory for Designs Test. However, as the students in our study were neither Inuit nor living in villages, further research is needed to develop a theoretical basis for their claims to elevated visual abilities. Furthermore, of three studies found by Kleinfeld and Nelson (1991) investigating the proposition that adapting instruction to Native groups' learning styles would increase achievement, two did not show that Native groups learn more with visually based instruction. Another study found support for the proposition in one site but not in another, and the visually based instruction was even more effective for Caucasian students (Kleinfeld and Nelson, 1991). These findings called into question the idea that instruction was effective because it was 'culturally adapted,' and established the need for further research into the hypothesis that instruction adapted to Native groups' visual learning style will increase learning.

Theme 2: Effective Oral Interaction Assists Learning

This theme emerged as we examined certain data through the lens of cultural and socio-economic class differences in patterns of oral interactions between parents and children. In studies conducted on linguistic interactions among different cultural and socio-economic groups, researchers (e.g., Corson, 1992; Heath, 1983) observed that white middle-class parents tended to use discussion, playfulness, questions, and indirect statements when instructing their children (e.g., 'Is that your coat on the floor?', meaning pick up your coat from the floor) whereas working-class Whites and African-American parents tended to be more overtly directive (e.g., 'Pick up your coat from the floor and hang it in the closet').

Our research suggests that some Aboriginal parents also communicate with their children mainly through the use of overt directives. Two of the students, for example, said:

> They (parents) tell me directly what they expect me to do rather than making suggestions; they do not leave it up to me to figure out what they mean … In class if they [the teachers] want me to read chapter 4 for a test, they should tell me directly to read chapter 4 instead of saying to us 'You might want to read chapter 4.' (Liz)

> Mr X. (the African-Canadian teacher) tells you straight what he requires from you. He is more demanding. I like that. (Don)

Because teachers in Canadian classrooms are mainly white and come from middle class backgrounds, some Aboriginal students may not always understand what is required of them if the teachers use indirect statements. Clarity is important to school success because students are judged by what they produce in class and on tests. Such product, based as it is on the specific codes of a dominant culture (English or French in the case of Canada), is more readily produced when the directives on how to produce it are made explicit. In this regard, Delpit (1995) has urged teachers to help non-dominant culture students succeed academically by making explicit the way in which language and communication style signal cultural capital. Our study strongly suggests that effective parents and teachers of Aboriginal students offer clarity about what they demand, and that they provide structures which help learners to produce it. I am not suggesting here that Aboriginal students are incapable of learning through discussions or questions and indirect statements. Instead, I am drawing attention to the fact that teachers must be assisted to recognize and attend to the particular strengths and needs that non-dominant cultural groups may have in relation to unfamiliar instructional strategies such as discussion in the classroom, while also questioning the role of schooling in the perpetuation of such linguistic inequities.

Theme 3: Concepts of Self Mediate Learning

This theme refers to notions of the self, how the self is constructed and understood, and how this construction mediates the learning process in different cultures. The self, a classed, gendered, and raced subject position related to *difference* and which may be referred to in terms of identity or subjectivity, is constructed discursively. Gee (2006) defines discourse as:

> A socially accepted association among ways of using language, of think-
> ing and of acting that may be used to identify oneself as a member of a
> socially meaningful group or 'social network' … Think of a discourse {as}
> an 'identity kit' which comes complete with the appropriate costume and
> instructions on how to act and talk so as to take on a particular role that
> others will recognize. (p. 29)

Butler writes, 'We do not take on roles to act out as in a performance; we become subjects through repetition' (in Youngblood, 2004, p. 680). Subjectivity, then, is discursively produced through language.

Bearing in mind that any ontological boundaries of the self are primarily theoretical (most theorists propound hybrid concepts of what constitutes the self), our research revealed that the Aboriginal students in this study understood and described notions of the self largely in terms of interdependence, communality, and interaction with the world around them more so than, say, Caucasian groups, who tend to treat the self as a relatively self-contained agent. Because they viewed themselves less as a separate psychological unit and more as a part-function of the cultural forces from which they emerged, the students identified a cultural model of learning that is grounded in Aboriginal cultural values such as cooperation, collaboration, group effort, and group rewards. In school, these values would lend themselves well to group work and cooperative tasks and it was, therefore, not surprising that eight of the ten students disclosed that they thrived better as learners in cooperative/collaborative/group work situations. However, they also pointed out that because group work and cooperative learning tasks in school were not usually organized effectively for productive work, group work had actually hindered rather than promoted learning for them. Several of the students elaborated on this point, as the following quotations demonstrate:

> You see, it's different in school than in the (Aboriginal) community. In the community everybody participates equally or almost. You have a bunch of people who carry their share of the task and they know it is for the good of the community. So everyone does their part and you learn from each other. In school no one in the group cares, really. Group members do not share their opinions or ideas. (Don)

> And they make a lot of noise during group work. (Liz)

> Yes, and if you have someone smarter than the other people in the group, then they are going to rely on that one person for all the ideas. (Mike)

> So I think what we need is better group work organization from them (the teachers). I like group work because you can talk to others. You can discuss your ideas if you don't understand something, like in the community … But in class that does not happen in groups. (Ned)

Our findings suggest that communal work is integral to life and each day in the Aboriginal community we observed. As Haig-Brown and colleagues (1997) confirm, Aboriginal community members do work together, each taking on the responsibilities appropriate to their knowledge and abilities. Caution, however, is needed in interpreting this finding as specific only to Aboriginal students. In a study conducted into the learning styles of different cultural groups in the United States, Cox and Ramirez (1981) found that many minority culture students were more group-oriented, more sensitive to social environments, and more positively responsive to adult modeling than are European-American students.

What is clear from the finding is that attention needs to be paid to the contextual barriers that interfere with the deployment of cultural tools such as the cooperative, collaborative, communal, and supportive aspects of Aboriginal cultural socialization which enhance student learning. Teachers do not generally seem to acknowledge group identity, insisting that all students are individuals with individual differences, thereby denying that group membership is an important part of some students' identities.

Theme 4: Relevant Curriculum

Like education in many other indigenous societies, Aboriginal education appears to be for an immediate introduction to the community and preparation for adulthood. It is largely informal and emphasizes work orientation, social responsibility, and community participation. These aims are interwoven with the content and learning processes which are derived from the needs and purposes of the community and its patterns of work, which probably explains the 'observation and emulation' approach to learning discussed earlier. Because education is for entering adulthood, the work and ways of adults provide the material for this education. 'Curriculum' is, therefore, relevant and closely linked with productive activity.

Unfortunately, the school curriculum is far removed from this indigenous view of education. Not only does the school curriculum pose a disconcerting division between theory and practice, it also largely excludes materials and activities that promote connections between Aboriginal students' backgrounds, their communities, and the school. According to the RCAP report (1996, p. 456) curriculum relevance is seen by Aboriginal peoples as one of three fundamental issues in the education of Aboriginal children and youth (the others are Aboriginal language education and Aboriginal control and parental involvement). The relevance of curriculum to success in school learning is particularly important for minority students such as those of Aboriginal ancestry for two reasons. First, educationalists (e.g., Maxine Greene, 1993) have observed that in spite of all the exposure to difference in the world today and the increasing interest in pluralism and the existence of multiple realities, Eurocentric and patriarchal views are still prevalent where curriculum and learning are concerned. Racist ideology and a knowledge hierarchy that privileges Western knowledge still conspire to exclude minority knowledge from the school curriculum. Second, minority students continue to be treated largely as invisible when they are made to experience textbooks and linguistic conventions considered to be neutral but that actually assume a subject from the dominant white culture. Furthermore, inaccurate and negative representations of Aboriginal peoples still persist. As one of the students said during one of our conversations relating to photographs of successful Aboriginal professionals which Mrs B. had used as curriculum material for two of her Social Studies lessons, 'Aboriginal people are seen [in White society] as backward, stupid, and responsible for their own failure. When one individual fails to make it, everyone in the culture is called a failure' (Rich).

For this reason, although the students said they would appreciate exposure to non-Aboriginal curriculum content because, as Liz put it, 'the exposure will help us learn about other perspectives and other cultures,' they overwhelmingly agreed that seeing positive representations of themselves (Aboriginal people in general) more regularly in the school curriculum would validate their identity, motivate them to participate more in class, and develop pride in their own culture and people. According to one student's journal entry, such a curriculum would also nurture their aspirations for the future:

> Yeah, these pictures (of successful Aboriginal people) make you feel like you have a chance. You walk down town Winnipeg any day and all you see is Aboriginal people lying on the ground either completely drunk or asking for 'change' [money]. That feels really depressing and hopeless. But when you see Aboriginal people or pictures of Aboriginal people who have succeeded – like police officers, lawyers, and all that – you feel you have a chance and you push yourself more in school to be like them. (Ned)

The students also pointed out that in addition to positive images of Aboriginal people, curriculum should include Aboriginal perspectives, histories/traditions, and interests, which have foundations in their cultural heritage but which have been largely denied them in the formal school system:

> In my previous school, there was nothing in grade 7 or 8 social studies about us [Aboriginal people]. We learned about people during different ages – Greeks, Romans, Egyptians and their way of life but nothing really about Aboriginal people or if there was, we did not cover it in class. (Mike)

> Here in this school at least, Aboriginal students are in the majority and in social studies, some of our lessons have Aboriginal material. But in my former school, the teachers generally did not talk about us as part of the lesson … Yeah, maybe they were scared to offend us. (Liz, using her fingers to create quotation marks around the term 'offend us' to indicate the sarcasm in her use of the term)

Referring to the importance of cultural heritage in learning, William

Binz, after teaching language arts to mature-aged Aboriginal students in an Aboriginal studies program in Australia wrote:

> I began to see how they operated from and through a cultural heritage, that is, from a deeply embedded and culturally defined system of values, beliefs and meanings about the social world. More importantly, I learned that this system significantly influences and reflects what students value and why they value it and, therefore, is central, not peripheral, to creating curriculum in the classroom that is culturally relevant and personally meaningful. (quoted in Ellis, 1999, p. 177)

As Ellis elaborates, without the knowledge or the interest to begin planning curriculum from an appreciation of who students are or what they know or care about, teachers tend to diagnostically look for and remediate what they think is missing in students.

Denial of equal access to class participation was also seen by the students not only as a powerful way of excluding Aboriginal knowledge from the school curriculum but also a major cause of student disengagement from classroom learning:

> In my old school there were only three Aboriginal students in my class ... and I would raise my hand but I was hardly ever called upon to speak. It's like you are not there, so I stopped trying, there was no point (Beth).

The feeling of invisibility being conveyed here resonated very strongly with my two Aboriginal graduate research assistants in this study as they thought about their own experiences in university classrooms. One of them reflected:

> Invisibility can take many forms. With me, there was this professor, and it was frustrating that I would say something in class and this professor would barely say anything in acknowledgement or validation but then a White student would say something very similar and suddenly it became the most important point in the discussion. It made me feel like I was nothing. I could have dropped the course but I just wanted to complete my program and get out.

These data clearly highlight issues of identity and representation and the school's ability to include and engage students who are not members of the dominant culture. Analysed through the lens of 'representation' and 'positionality' in postcolonial theory of racialized other-ing (discussed in Chapter 2) this exclusion or lack of representation of Aboriginal peoples in the curriculum was curious, particularly in light of the rhetoric about Aboriginal self-determination and the numerous studies indicating increased academic performance among Aboriginal students when school curricula promote the language, knowledge, and culture of Native students. In fact, I would endorse Castagno and Brayboy's (2008) point that it is counter-intuitive to assume that students would do worse in school when the curriculum is related to their prior knowledge and everyday lives. As Joe pointed out in one of our research conversations, being ignored in this way accounts for much of the alienation Aboriginal students feel in the school system.

Theme 5: Teachers' Interpersonal Style

Students' narratives revealed three sub-themes which emerged to describe those dimensions of teacher interpersonal style that were effective in eliciting intellectual participation from the Aboriginal students in this study. In order of importance to the students, these dimensions were: Respect, firmness, and personal warmth from the teacher.

Respect: All the research participants identified 'respect' as the most important dimension of the educator's (teacher, parent, or significant others) interpersonal style. Because research on cultural difference has found that different cultures may hold very different views of behaviours that express the social value and complex norm known as respect (see for example, Wax & Thomas, cited in Kleinfeld & Nelson, 1991) participants were asked to elaborate on what they meant by 'respect' in the educator-learner interactions. For them, respect referred to the following teacher behaviours:

> Not stereotyping me as the drunken, failed Indian whose image the teacher already has in mind. (Ned)

> Treating me like I already have something the teacher respects – like my culture and my own way of doing things; not trying to control my behaviour all the time. (Beth)

> Not making me feel dumb in front of the whole class. Treat me like I know something which the teacher may not know ... everybody knows something. (Don)

It is as simple as valuing and understanding me as a person. Like, just teach the way you want to be treated ...You know, teach with respect for us as individuals and do not treat us like all Indians are the same. (Rich).

Previous research and our own observations support the students' assertions. Members of the Aboriginal community we observed frequently expressed positive opinions about each other and treated each other with gentleness, patience, and respect (e.g., some members of the community were late for a meeting we attended, but the others patiently waited for over an hour but showed no anger as the late-comers gradually arrived). Similarly, Haig-Brown and colleagues' (1997) research interviews with sixteen students of Aboriginal ancestry (Cree, Ojibway, Métis and Saultaux) from Joe Duquette High School revealed that all the students identified 'respect' as 'the number one rule' for successful interactions among the students, teachers, and staff in the school. According to these researchers, respect is integral to traditional Aboriginal values. They wrote: 'Respect encompasses the understanding that children are complete human beings given as gifts from the Great Spirit on loan to adults who share with them the responsibility for preparing them for life's journey' (p. 46). The researchers also quoted what a member of the school's Parent Council said about 'respect' during an interview: 'You are born as equal and you are born with respect ... every individual has it and you don't have to earn it' (p. 46).

Firmness: Although the practice of 'non-interference' has been documented as a prominent characteristic of parenting and social interaction in many Aboriginal cultures (see, for example, Brant, 1990) the image of the teacher as a firm disciplinarian who corrects and guides learners towards appropriate behaviours emerged as the second most important characteristic of the teacher's interpersonal style, suggesting that how Aboriginals practice the cultural value of non-interference could be changing according to what is valued in the dominant culture surrounding them. As the pressure to succeed in mainstream Canadian society has mounted, some Aboriginal parents appear to be abandoning the attitude of non-interference in favour of more direct interventions in the behaviours of their children to increase their chances of success in the society. With one exception (the Métis student in the study who was being raised by his Cree grandmother), the students seemed to expect their teachers to be firm, less tolerant of nonsense, less patronizing, and act like the authority figures they are. Otherwise the message is sent that this adult has no authority and the students react accordingly. As the following quotations show, the students strongly believed in this firm image of the teacher, especially when used to maintain classroom discipline so that learning is not disrupted, rather than as a tool for asserting power and dominance:

> I think Mrs B., I don't know what it is, but she should be tougher with us. After all she is the teacher, she has that authority. (Kem)

> I agree with Jon. She needs to be stricter to keep the class more in order. Some people call her down and treat her anyhow ... whatever, and she just stands there and the class continues to be noisy. (Mike)

> Some of the things kids do in her class, I know I can never get away with at home. I know my boundaries and how far I can take my family, especially my dad. If I go past that boundary I know I am in trouble ... probably get grounded for days or something, without any argument. I was surprised at first at what she [Mrs B.] was tolerating from students. (Andy)

Andy's surprise could have also come from the fact that in his Ojibway community, we observed that elders and parents, as respected teachers, often conveyed to the young the acceptable rules of behaviour and the values to be honoured through subtle verbal and non-verbal communication. Such a teacher is a role model whose own behaviour and attitudes are absorbed by the children.

Another possible reason that these Aboriginal students expected an authority figure to act with authority is that in Aboriginal culture, authority appears to be earned through effort and is demonstrated by personal characteristics, as opposed to authority being achieved by the acquisition of an authoritative role. According to Mike,

> In the community, like the chief – this is just an example – like the chief is chief because he has done many good things in his personal life and in the community to deserve to be chief. He has that authority. The teacher is the same ... I mean she has qualifications, and therefore, the authority. She should act with authority.

Some middle-class teachers do not perceive authority in this way and may attempt to reduce the implications of overt power in order to establish a more egalitarian and non-authoritarian classroom atmosphere.

However, if the students operate under another notion of authority, as the Aboriginal students in this study seemed to be doing, they may perceive the teacher as weak, ineffective, and insincere.

The image of the teacher as a firm individual wielding authority in the classroom did not, however, seem to hold for our Métis participant, suggesting diversity in how the cultural values and traditions of Aboriginal peoples are engaged. In response to Andy's comments about behavioural boundaries at home, this Métis student said:

> Jeez, I can never live like that. My grandmother lets me do what I want. I go and come as I like, no questions asked. Sometimes, I go for two days ... as long as I stay out of trouble. (Chris)

Chris's comment is consistent with our finding that among some Cree community members the principle of non-interference is still predominant. The child's will is respected, and adults do not interfere in the choices made by the child. The imposition of the adult's will on the child is considered inappropriate except, of course, in instances where the child may encounter harm. From our research conversations, we learned that this non-interference, non-directive approach determined a basis for a future lifestyle. According to English-Currie (1990) children matured rapidly and became adept at determining their own actions and making their own decisions, while being sensitive to the expectations of the collective and to elders.

The contrast between this laissez-faire approach and the regimentation of the classroom experience, including the authority that many teachers exert, constitute a discontinuity between the school and the home environment. This cultural conflict has been cited in several documents as a threat to the identities of some Aboriginal students in the formal education system and a major cause of school failure (for example, Elsie Wuttunee, cited in RCAP, 1996, p. 455).

Personal warmth: Nine of the ten students in the study expected their teachers to treat them with emotional warmth and have personalized relationships with them. This finding is consistent with Haig-Brown and colleagues' (1997) report that teachers at Joe Duquette High School referred to their students as 'extended families' (p. 142) and students referred to their teachers as 'friends,' 'second parents,' and 'sensitive' (p. 122). It is also consistent with Collier's (1993) position that Native students like to have personal relationships with their teachers.

Warmth as a teacher attribute emerged during our conversation about the effectiveness of the individualized instruction which we observed each student regularly receiving from the two teachers and the teacher aide during lessons. Chris's comment on this point was typical and instructive:

> When she [Mrs B.] is teaching from in front of the room, she is kind of far from you and she is usually talking to everyone, not to any of us in particular except if she is addressing a question to someone specifically. But when we are working on our own and all three of the teachers go round and help us individually, that helps a lot.

Wishing to find out more about how this personal contact/closeness, as opposed to the professional distance teachers typically maintain in the classroom, enhanced Aboriginal student learning, I asked Chris to elaborate on his comment and he said:

> Well, I mean, the close contact means personal attention. When they [teachers] come close to you, sometimes they bend down to your seat level and you tell them your specific problem and they explain and help you. When you get the point right, sometimes they pat you on the back. They are also more friendly one on one.

Individualized instruction has been found to have a positive effect on student academic achievement in general. For these Aboriginal students in particular, individualized instruction appears to carry added benefit because of its significance in communicating the warmth which they perceived as important in interactions between them and their teachers. Joe expressed this feeling best in his closing comment on this aspect of our conversation: 'When they (the teachers) are that close and personal you get the feeling they care.' The effect of teachers' personal warmth on students' academic performance needs to be explored further for its potential to increase learning, for many studies among White students have also found warmth to be a central dimension of teacher behaviour related to outcomes such as student attentiveness (see Kleinfeld & Nelson, 1991).

These data do not mean that all 'respectful,' 'firm/strict,' and 'warm' teachers are effective teachers of Aboriginal students. They do, however, suggest that there are different ideas among different cultural groups about which characteristics make for a good teacher. It is, therefore, impossible to create a model of the good teacher without taking into account issues of cultural and community contexts.

Summary

This was small-scale exploratory research, undertaken to identify aspects of Aboriginal cultural socialization which mediate and influence classroom learning for some students of Aboriginal ancestry in the Canadian formal school system. Five specific examples of such cultural socialization processes/experiences, represented in the form of themes, have been presented as cultural mediators of learning for several groups of Aboriginal students. These were: use of Aboriginal pedagogical approaches such as storytelling and scaffolds, effective communication between the teacher and Aboriginal students, communal concepts of self, relevant curriculum, and the interpersonal style of the teacher. Although the findings revealed that these cultural influences were similar for the majority of the students in this study, some differences did emerge among the students over which cultural practices facilitated or inhibited classroom learning for them. Together, however, these examples signal a vibrant counterpoint to the dominant system of education which fails to connect meaningfully to the lives of Aboriginal learners and the communities from which they come. The examples are, therefore, suggestive of a badly needed conversation about the relationship between the places we call schools and the places where students live their lives. Such a conversation would be even more powerful and meaningful if explored within: (a) today's context of educational standardization and test-driven accountability where opportunity for connecting home/community culture to classroom learning is erased or severely diminished and (b) the context of Aboriginal epistemologies, sovereignty, and self-determination. Based on this research, I offer the following list of suggestions as beginning points for such a conversation. Where suggestions are made about classroom application, these are simply intended as starting points for teachers and students. The needs of your students should help you plan more in-depth activities specific to your community and its population.

1. The use of Indigenous approaches to teaching and learning, such as story telling and learning by observation and emulation, appear to hold potential for effective classroom learning for some Abo-

riginal students and should therefore be encouraged in classrooms with Aboriginal students. Storytelling, in particular, has been found to be a most powerful teaching tool for making abstract ideas intelligibly concrete to students (Osborne, 2000) and as a hook or entry point into a curriculum topic. It should, therefore, be used more often to arouse the interest of not only Aboriginal students but all students in the classroom. General guidelines for selecting stories for classroom use include ensuring a good fit between the story and the curriculum topic/concept under discussion and ensuring that the material provides a realistic, authentic, and non-patronizing account of its subjects and does not confirm existing biases or stereotypes about Aboriginal peoples. The teacher, as the interpreter of the curriculum, must be capable of providing a context which will counteract negative portrayals. In implementing observational learning the teacher must ensure that students actively encode the information they receive from the expert (i.e., the teacher) to refine or build their cognitive representation of the domain being studied instead of passively watching the expert. Students may need extensive support and guidance in the beginning as they learn to actively engage themselves in this cognitive process but this scaffolding can be gradually removed as they acquire expertise.

2. Teaching methods characterized by fast-paced 'talk' may impede learning for some Aboriginal students by getting them lost in the details. The use of such methods in classrooms with Aboriginal students should therefore be minimized and/or complemented by other teaching methods – for example, the use of stories and observational learning.

3. Because of cultural differences in patterns of oral interactions, classroom communication by teachers should offer clarity – preferably in clear, directive language – about what is required (the product) from Aboriginal students in the classroom. For example, as Liz said in one of our interviews, if teachers require students to read Chapter 4 of a textbook for a test, they should be told so directly instead of making an inferential statement like 'You might want to read Chapter 4.' Let students know in advance what the proposed test will cover and the format it will take.

4. Learning scaffolds – in the form of clear explanations, concrete examples from the cultural and experiential backgrounds of

Aboriginal students, and explicit structures/ directions to guide performance in a given learning task – appear to offer the potential for increased classroom learning for the students in this study. These scaffolds are, therefore, worth implementing in classrooms with Aboriginal students. Particularly in regard to concrete examples from Aboriginal experiential backgrounds, the students in this study made a strong link between Aboriginal role models and motivation to learn. They also saw Aboriginal teachers, counselors, and school administrators as having an understanding and social perspective with which Aboriginal students could identify. For these reasons, and also to achieve greater cultural and educational democracy, schools should recruit more Aboriginal and other minority personnel.

5. Until conclusive research evidence emerges to disprove the claim that instruction adapted to Native groups' visual learning style will increase learning, visually based instruction should be maximized in classrooms with Aboriginal students. As seen from our research data resources like videos, posters, pictures, computer images/illustrations, or even something as simple as Power Point overheads and transparencies may enhance learning for some Aboriginal students. With the Internet and technologies like mimeos and interactive boards, the opportunities for visual-based instruction are increasing on an unprecedented scale.

6. Without minimizing the importance of independent thinking and independent work in the teaching of Aboriginal students, opportunities for cooperative and collaborative group work, where students receive peer support, should be explored for the learning potential they hold for Aboriginal students. In planning cooperative tasks, care must be taken to build in the elements of accountability, equitable distribution of work, positive interdependence where group members work toward the achievement of a common goal, and social skills (e.g., listening to everyone in the group and treating their contributions with respect). Incorporating these elements will increase the academic benefits of cooperative learning for all students, but more so for Aboriginal students, for whom this approach to learning seems to have a cultural basis. Previous researchers (e.g., Collier, 1993; Philips, 1983) endorse this recommendation when they posit that an added benefit of small group work for Native students is that it provides them with easier op-

portunities to speak and to go over the material than whole class situations.

7. Curriculum materials and classroom learning/teaching processes that include Aboriginal perspectives, histories, cultures, and successes may increase motivation for learning among Aboriginal students. Such materials may also nurture high aspirations among Aboriginal students and should be included in school curricula. Here consistent infusion, rather than occasional add-on materials and activities, should be stressed. As Banks (1994) has pointed out, culturally responsive education is a dynamic and on-going process. Occasional add-on materials often trivialize ethnic cultures and view ethnic content from the perspective of mainstream culture. In Chapter 4, I provide examples of Aboriginal perspectives that could be integrated into different school subjects as student learning outcomes – Social Studies, Mathematics, Science, Art, Music, English Language Arts, and so on.

8. Urban Aboriginal students seem to expect their teachers to be firm disciplinarians who also show personal warmth toward them. As the students in our research indicated, simple gestures such as quietly acknowledging the achievement of a challenging task or taking the time to listen to and understand their issues and experiences can make a positive difference to their learning. In addition, they expect teachers to show respect for Aboriginal students (for example, by validating their voices and their contributions) and be knowledgeable about Aboriginal culture, experiences, and the political and social issues affecting Aboriginal lives. What teacher education programs and schools can do to develop teachers' knowledge of Aboriginal cultures and issues are discussed in Chapter 8.

9. Supportive and non-threatening classroom communities/environments appear to be important for increasing verbal participation by Aboriginal students and are, therefore, required in classrooms with Aboriginal students. Again, individual accountability in small group work and respectful reception of students' classroom ideas and contributions even as teachers help them see the limitations that may be inherent in these ideas would create the confidence students need to participate in class. Whyte (1986) states that the verbal capacity of Indian/Métis students may have been underestimated, with the end result, in some cases, of these students being ignored or streamed away from academic programs.

Concluding Remark

The past two decades have seen profound changes in educational psychology that have placed psychosocial and cultural processes squarely at the centre of learning and development. We are witnessing a resolution of the antinomy traditionally heard in discussions about the primacy of individual psychogenesis[2] versus sociogenesis[3] of mind, in favour of a fusion of horizons (Gadamer, 1984) between the two positions, that is, that learning and development arise through the interweaving of individual bio-psychological processes and the appropriation of cultural heritage (Cole & Wertsch, 2001). This new view adds a political dimension to the discussion as it moves cognitive and educational study from the individual level which hides the effects of culture, race, and socioeconomic status, to a level where learning and development are understood within cultural and larger sociopolitical contexts and their effects. The new position calls for research into what different groups bring to processes of learning and how this interfaces with the culture and practices of the school. In this chapter, I have provided an example of such research, arguing that the design of any study intended to inquire into how cultural processes mediate and influence learning and development must focus on understanding individuals' or groups' histories of participation in activities in their cultural communities instead of simply attributing general traits of individuals categorically to ethnic group membership.

As the discussion of our research findings have shown, research is still inconclusive about some claims relating to specific or predominant Aboriginal cultural ways of learning, highlighting the difficulty in arriving at any final 'formula' for helping a cultural group perform better in an educational setting. Indeed, researchers still have to resolve whether in fact optimal results are achieved when the learning styles of any cultural group or individual are systematically matched to curriculum and instructional methods. Some (e.g., Agbo, 2004; Miller-Lachman & Taylor, 1995) have pointed out that accommodating culture and cultural learning styles of 'at-risk' students consistently has resulted in increased academic achievement, increased school attendance and retention, and gains in reading and mathematics (Apthorp et al., 2002). Others (e.g., Curry, 1990; Kleinfeld & Nelson, 1991), however, have noted that, although ample evidence documents that certain learning styles tend to be predominant in certain cultures (i.e., patterns exist in how members of different groups approach tasks) there is no demonstrable impact on academic achievement when teachers match specific teaching strategies to specific aspects of Native students' cultural learning style preferences.

These opposing viewpoints suggested the need for further research – designed to rigorously test key findings of our study among a larger sample of Aboriginal students in public school classrooms – in order to develop more informed recommendations to guide teaching and teacher education. A standard research grant from the Social Sciences and Humanities Research Council of Canada (SSHRCC) afforded me the opportunity to conduct such a follow-up study from 2003 to 2007. This follow-up study, in which the specific aspects of Aboriginal cultural socialization identified in this chapter were integrated into the school curriculum, is described in Chapter 4. The impact/effects of that integration on academic achievement, class attendance/participation, and school retention among Aboriginal students are discussed in Chapter 5.

QUESTIONS FOR DISCUSSION

1. Cultural deficit theorists use negative cultural stereotypes such as 'complacency,' 'indolence,' 'apathy,' and 'lack of motivation and discipline' to describe cultural minority groups and to explain their academic and economic failure relative to other ethnic groups. What is your opinion about the use of such stereotypes to explain academic and economic underperformance among some Aboriginal peoples in Canada?
2. In what ways do the research findings discussed in this chapter challenge or reinforce your identity as teacher and some of your existing views/ideas about curriculum, teaching, and learning?
3. Do you agree with Maxine Greene's observation that in spite of all the exposure to difference, pluralism, and the existence of multiple realities in the world today, Euro-centric views are still predominant in curriculum and in classrooms? Provide examples to support your answer.
4. What have you learned from the study discussed in this chapter that will inform how you teach Aboriginal students? What questions does the study raise for you?
5. Do you think culturally adapted instruction will improve learning for Aboriginal students in your classroom? What challenges does this type of instruction pose for your particular teaching context?

NOTES

1 Preliminary classroom data from the research discussed in this chapter have appeared in Kanu (2002). In their own voices: First Nations students identify some cultural mediators of their learning in the formal school system. *Alberta Journal of Educational Research, 48*(2), 98–121. In this chapter, I have combined the preliminary data in that article with new data collected from the Aboriginal community we observed to provide readers with a clearer understanding of how cultural participation mediates classroom learning.

2 Individual psychogenesis: The view that learning and development are individual mental functions that originate in the mind, unaffected and unmediated by the outside world.

3 Sociogenesis: The view that the development of mental functions are influenced and mediated by factors such as social interactions, and the contexts and environments surrounding the individual.

REFERENCES/RECOMMENDED READINGS

Agbo, S. (2004). First Nations perspectives on transforming the status of culture and language in schooling. *Journal of American-Indian Education, 43*(1), 1–31.

Apthorp, H., D'Amato, E., & Richardson, A. (2002). *Effective standards-based practices for Native American students: A review of the literature.* Aurora, CO: Mid-Continent Research for Education and Learning.

Archibald, J. (1993). Researching with mutual respect (editorial). *Canadian Journal of Native Education, 20*(3), 189–92.

Bandura, A. (1976). *Social learning theory.* Upper Saddle River, NJ: Prentice Hall.

Banks, J.A. (1994). *Multicultural education: Theory and practice,* 3rd ed. Boston: Allyn and Bacon.

Berry, J.W. (1966). Temne and Eskimo perceptual skills. *Journal of International Psychology,* 1, 207–99.

– (1969). Ecology and socialization as factors in figural assimilation and the resolution of binocular rivalry. *International Journal of Psychology,* 4, 271–80.

Brady, P. (1995). Two policy approaches to Native education. Can reform be legislated? *Canadian Journal of Education,* 20, 349–66.

Brant, C. (1990). Native ethics and rules of behaviour. *Canadian Journal of Psychiatry, 35*(6), 534.

Bogden, R.C., & Biklen, S.K. (2003). *Qualitative research for education,* 3rd ed. Boston: Allyn and Bacon.

Castagno, A.E., & Brayboy, M.K. (2008). Culturally responsive schooling for Indigenous youth: A review of the literature. *Review of Educational Research, 78*(4), 941–93.

Cole, M., & Wertsch, J.V. (2001). *Beyond individual-social antinomy in discussions about Piaget and Vygotsky.* Retrieved 8 Apr. 2010 from: http:/www.massey.ac.nz/~alock//virtual/colevyg.htm.

Collier, L. (1993). Teaching Native students at the college level. *Canadian Journal of Native Education, 20*(3), 109–17.

Corson, D.J. (1992). Minority cultural values and discourse norms in majority culture classrooms. *Canadian Modern Language Review, 48,* 472–96.

Cox, B.G., & Ramirez, M. (1981). Cognitive styles: Implications for multicultural education. In J.A. Banks (Ed.), *Education in the '80s: Multiethnic education,* pp. 122–34. Washington, DC: National Education Association.

Cruickshank, J. (with A. Sidney, K. Smith, & A. Ned) (1990). *Life lived like a story: Life stories of three Yukon Native elders.* Vancouver: University of British Columbia Press.

Curry, L. (1990, October). A critique of research on learning styles. *Educational Leadership, 48,* 50–6.

Delpit, L. (1995). *Other people's children: Cultural conflict in the classroom.* New York: The New Press.

English-Currie, V. (1990). The need for evaluation in Native education. In J. Perrault & S. Vance (Eds.), *Writing the circle: Native women of Western Canada,* pp. 47–60. Edmonton: NeWest Publishers Ltd.

Ellis, J. (1999). Children and place: Stories we have, stories we need. *Interchange, 30*(2), 171–90.

Eysink, T., de Jong, T., Berthold, K., Kollofel, B., & Opfermann, M. (2009). Learner performance in multimedia arrangements: An analysis across instructional approaches. *American Educational Research Journal, 46*(4), 1107–49.

Flemming, W.C. (2006). Myths and stereotypes about Native Americans. *Phi Beta Kappan, 88,* 213–17.

Gadamer, H.G. (1984). *Truth and Method.* New York: Crossroad Publications

Gee, J.P. (2006). What is literacy? In P. Vandenberg, S. Hum, & J. Clary-Lemon (Eds.), *Relations, locations, positions: Composition theory for writing teachers,* pp. 14–34. Urbana, IL: NCTE.

Greene, M. (1993). Diversity and inclusion: Toward a curriculum for human beings. *Teachers College Record,* 95 (2), 211–21.

Grossman, H. (1995). *Special education in a diverse society.* Boston: Allyn & Bacon.

Haig-Brown, C. (1997). *Coyote learns to make a storybasket: The place of First Nations stories in education*. Unpublished PhD dissertation, Simon Fraser University.

Haig-Brown, C., Hodgson-Smith, K. L., Regnier, R., & Archibald, J. (1997). *Making the spirit dance within: Joe Duquette High School and an Aboriginal community*. Toronto: Lorimer.

Heath, J. (1983). *Ways with words: Language, life and work in communities and classrooms*. New York: Cambridge University Press.

Jones, S. (1979). Integrating emic and etic approaches in the study of intercultural communication. In M. Asante, E. Newmark, & C. Blake (Eds.), *Handbook of intercultural communication*, pp. 57–74. Thousand Oaks: Sage.

Kanu, Y. (2006). *Curriculum as cultural practice: Postcolonial imaginations*. Toronto: University of Toronto Press.

– (2007). Tradition and educational reconstruction in Africa in postcolonial and global times: The case for Sierra Leone. *African Studies Quarterly, 9*(3) (online). Retrieved from: http://web.africa.ufl.edu/asq/v9/v9i3a3.htm.

Kirkness, V.J. (with Bowman, S.S.) (1992). *First Nations and schools: Triumphs and struggles*. Toronto: Canadian Education Association.

Kleinfeld, J.S. (1971). Visual memory in village Eskimo and urban Caucasian children. *Arctic*, 24, 132–38.

– & Nelson, P. (1991). Adapting instruction to Native Americans' learning styles: An iconoclastic view. *Journal of Cross-cultural Psychology, 22*(2), 273–82.

Miller-Lachman, L., & Taylor, L.S. (1995). *Schools for all: Educating children in a diverse society*. New York: Delmar.

Merriam, S.B. (1998). *Qualitative research and case study applications in education*. San Francisco: Jossey-Bass.

Ogbu, J., & Simons, H.D. (1998). Voluntary and involuntary minorities: A cultural-ecological theory of school performance with some implications for education. *Anthropology and Education, 29*(2), 155–88.

Osborne, K. (2000). Voices from the past: History as storytelling. *Canadian Social Studies, 35*(1) (online). Retrieved from: www. quasar.ualberta.ca/css.

Philips, S.U. (1983). *The invisible culture: Communication in classrooms and community on the Warm Springs Indian Reservation*. New York: Longman.

Rahim, L.Z. (1998). *The Singapore dilemma: The political and educational marginality of the Malay community*. Kuala Lumpur: Oxford University Press.

Royal Commission on Aboriginal Peoples (1996). *Gathering strength: Report of the Royal Commission on Aboriginal Peoples*. Ottawa: Canadian Communication Group.

Te Hennepe, S. (1993). Issues of respect: Reflections of First Nations students and experiences in post-secondary classrooms. *Canadian Journal of Native Education, 20*(3), 193–260.

Whyte, K. (1986). Strategies for teaching Indian and Metis students. *Canadian Journal of Native Education, 13*(3), 33–40.

Youngblood, J.A. (2004). Performativity identified. *Qualitative Inquiry, 10*(5), 673–90.

4 Integrating Aboriginal Perspectives into the School Curriculum: Layering at Five Levels of Classroom Practice

This chapter describes how the elements of Aboriginal cultural sociali-zation captured in the previous chapter, along with other Aboriginal perspectives from Indigenous scholarly literature, were integrated into the Manitoba Grade 9 Social Studies curriculum in two public schools with a mixture of Aboriginal and non-Aboriginal students. Beginning with a brief articulation of the challenge of defining 'Aboriginal per-spectives,' it goes on to describe the guiding principles used for the integration process, the context of the integration, and the specific pro-cedures of integration. Aboriginal perspectives were integrated at five levels of classroom practice: (a) at the level of lesson planning when learning outcomes are set; (b) at the level of curriculum content and learning resources; (c) at the level of instructional methods/strategies; (d) at the level of assessment of learning; and (e) as a philosophical underpinning of the curriculum. Each of these five levels is described, providing teachers with procedural ideas and guidelines that they may find useful for their own integration effort. Although the examples and discussions are based on Social Studies, the basic framework (i.e., the five levels at which integration can occur) is applicable to other subject areas while allowing for individual adaptations.

Defining 'Aboriginal Perspectives': The Challenge of Definition

The integration of Aboriginal perspectives into any school curriculum has to begin with some kind of agreement as to what 'Aboriginal per-spectives' are. Within the broad field of Indigenous studies diverse definitions of the term 'Aboriginal perspectives' exist, and as the lit-erature on Aboriginal formal education shows, Native parents and leaders have different perspectives on what constitutes appropriate Aboriginal content for school curricula. For example, although some parents prefer to see their children taught strictly in the old ways, others see the need for Aboriginal children to be able to function effectively in both Native and non-Native worlds and develop usable skills for today's job market (see e.g., Friesen & Friesen, 2002). Such diversity of opinion is likely to create confusion for some people, but I would argue that this is not necessarily a bad thing because the plethora of definitions and understandings of Aboriginal perspectives demonstrate a dynamic variety of voices on this topic. These voices introduce diverse interpretations by drawing on specific modes of thought, particular ideologies, and unique political and cultural experiences. Indeed, considering the radical differences among Aboriginal peoples and their cultures and experiences, one would be surprised if they spoke with only one voice.

While it is important to preserve these differences, we also have to acknowledge that some kind of agreement, at least on language form, needs to be achieved if Aboriginal perspectives are to be incorporated in a standardized school curriculum. The development of such language will have to take into account local Aboriginal communities and Ornstein and Hawkins' (2004) observation that 'Our languages and use of terms vary with regard to the scope and intent of meaning' (p. 12). For the scope and intent of our research, the term 'Aboriginal perspectives' was understood as curriculum content/materials, instructional and assessment methods/strategies, and interaction patterns that Manitoba's Aboriginal peoples see as reflecting their experiences, histories, cultures, traditional knowledges, and values. These perspectives would develop positive self-identity for Aboriginal students and help non-Aboriginal peoples develop healthy understanding of and respect for Aboriginal histories, cultures, and contemporary life styles (Manitoba Education, 2003).

Guiding Principles for Integrating Aboriginal Perspectives

Although clear about what we meant by Aboriginal perspectives, I, as a non-Aboriginal person, was acutely aware of my lack of expertise in the history and culture of Aboriginal peoples. Neither I nor my two Aboriginal graduate research assistants helping me with the integration effort had prior experience in incorporating Aboriginal perspectives into a mainstream, regular curriculum. We looked around for examples of such integration but found nothing more than a few lesson plans, at the time, that were being developed under British Columbia's initiative *Shared Learnings: Integrating BC Aboriginal Content K-10*, on the website of the B.C. Ministry of Education, materials that were very specific to the First Nations communities living in British Columbia.

Ultimately, the guiding principles for our integration effort were informed by postcolonial frameworks, in particular the work of Homi Bhabha (1990; 1994) to suggest that in order to produce significant change in perspective and understanding implied in the call for the integration of Aboriginal perspectives, integration itself would have to be viewed as existing in a 'third space' (Bhabha (1990). Bhabha describes the third space as a space of negotiation and hybridity. He writes: 'All forms of culture are constantly in a process of hybridity – this third space between two originary moments displaces the histories that con-stitute it, and sets up new structures of authority, new political initia-tives, which are inadequately understood through received wisdom' (p. 210). The third space, far from being a site for the re-inscription of essentialist narratives of culture, is a liminal space for interaction, con-flict, and mutual assimilation that every encounter between cultures involves. As Richardson (2008) explains, it is a location characterized not by liberal notions of compromise and consensus but by cultural dis-location and displacement, and the 'enunciation of cultural difference' (p. 129). Bhabha himself notes the challenge comprising the disruptive nature of this process, describing it as 'very difficult, even impossible and counterproductive, to try to fit together different forms of culture (and civic life) and to pretend that they can easily co-exist' (Bhabha, 1990, p. 210). In the third space, then, there are moments of encounter, dislocation, and negotiation as 'pre-given ethnic or cultural traits set in the fixed tablet of tradition' (Bhabha, 1994, p. 2) are disrupted. In a curricular sense, disruption can lead students and teachers to question their taken-for-granted world views and to begin to open themselves to diverse perspectives and conceptions of what it means to live with the 'other' in an increasingly pluralistic school environment.

Inspired by Bhabha's postcolonial framework of the third space, our guiding principles for integration were drawn from scholars like Friesen and Friesen (2002) who view integration as a mixing of ideas, a coming together of minds with an appreciation for alternative ways of thinking. Native Australian scholar, Martin Nakata, describes this meeting site as the 'cultural interface' which is:

'The intersection of Western and Indigenous domains…the place where we live and learn, the place that conditions our lives, the place that shapes our futures and, more to the point, the place where we are active agents in our own lives – where we make decisions – our lived world' (Nakata, 2002, p. 285).

Like Bhabha, Nakata suggests that this meeting place implies recognition of the complexities and tensions at the cross-cultural interfaces and the need for negotiation between Indigenous knowledge /perspectives and Western knowledge systems so that meanings are reframed and reinterpreted. Attending to these cross-cultural negotiations and the pedagogical practices they imply are profoundly challenging for Indigenous and non-Indigenous educators alike. It also implies that genuine transformation would only occur if Aboriginal perspectives were designed and developed in collaboration with local Aboriginal communities and infused throughout teachers' curricula and pedagogies. We therefore expanded our circle to include Aboriginal educators from the Manitoba Aboriginal Education Directorate who provided valuable advice and support, and Aboriginal resource persons at the First Nations Education Resource Centre in Winnipeg, who provided culturally appropriate curriculum materials like videos and storybooks on loan to us. We found additional resources such as print materials on current Aboriginal topics from reputable Aboriginal websites, books and articles by Aboriginal scholars, and more videos from other Aboriginal education resource centres around Winnipeg. Most importantly, we used research data such as those presented in Chapter 3 on the nine aspects and sub-aspects of Aboriginal cultural socialization which Aboriginal students had reported as influencing their learning in the public school system. By integrating Aboriginal content/themes/perspectives into the curriculum, we hoped to 'complicate' the curriculum by helping students to view textbook events, themes, and issues from diverse perspectives and develop the transformed consciousness needed to bring change in perspectives.

The Context of Integration

The context of our integration effort was a two-year study (2003–2005) – the second of the three research studies reported in this book – in which we collaborated with classroom teachers to integrate Aboriginal perspectives into their Social Studies curricula and document the impact of this integration on school success for the Aboriginal students in their classrooms. Our three research questions for this particular study were:

1. What are the most effective ways of integrating Aboriginal perspectives into the curriculum of urban public high schools?
2. How does such integration impact on academic achievement, class attendance/participation, and school retention among urban Aboriginal students in the public high school system?
3. What are the critical elements of instruction that appear to affect academic achievement, class attendance/participation, and school retention among urban Aboriginal students?

The study was carried out in two inner city high schools (we will call them School X and School Y), selected for their mix of non-Aboriginal and Aboriginal students and predominantly dominant culture teachers (mainly Anglo-Canadian). Close to 33 per cent of the 1100 students in School X and 52 per cent of the 810 students in School Y were of Aboriginal descent. Data collection occurred in the four Grade 9 Social Studies classrooms in the schools over two academic years. In the 2003/2004 academic year in School X, one Grade 9 Social Studies class was enriched by the integration of curriculum content, resources, instructional and assessment methods, and interaction patterns identified as successful with Aboriginal students (hereafter referred to as the 'enriched' classroom) and one was not (the 'regular' classroom). Enrichment materials were provided by us, the researchers, and the class teacher. Similar procedures were implemented in School Y over the 2004/2005 academic year. The intent was to document, analyse, and describe educational outcomes (in terms of academic performance, class attendance/participation, and school retention) among Aboriginal students in classrooms where Aboriginal perspectives were consistently integrated into the prescribed curriculum, and classrooms where no such integration occurred.

Research participants in the two schools consisted of 64 Aboriginal students (34 from the enriched classrooms and 30 from the regular classrooms), 20 non-Aboriginal students and the four dominant culture (Anglo-Canadian) Social Studies teachers teaching these students. Like the majority of the students in these schools, the students in the study were all from similar low socio-economic backgrounds. 75 per cent of the Aboriginal students taking part in the study reported having access to help and support at home with schoolwork if needed, suggesting that a low-income background does not necessarily preclude involvement by Aboriginal families in the education of their children. Prior to beginning the study, the teachers reported that students were assigned randomly to their Social Studies classes with respect to overall academic ability, and did not know beforehand about the differences in the content and approach to teaching in the Social Studies classrooms.

The four teachers had similar qualifications (a bachelor's degree with a major in history or geography) and each had over 10 years Social Studies teaching experience in the Grade 9 classroom. The teachers reported similar goals in their teaching of Social Studies, namely, the development of students' conceptual understanding of topics/ideas/concepts and higher-order thinking, and the ability of students to apply learning beyond the lesson. All four teachers used the same textbook and taught the same unit topics twice per week in their respective classrooms.

What set the teachers and their classrooms apart was their under-standing of, and approaches to, the integration of Aboriginal per-spectives into the curriculum. While they all expressed the belief that Aboriginal perspectives should be integrated into school curricula, the two teachers in the enriched classrooms placed such integration at the centre of their teaching, believing it to be a philosophical underpinning of the curriculum. When the integration of Aboriginal perspectives is believed to be a philosophical underpinning of the curriculum, it ceases to be an occasional add-on activity in the classroom and becomes an integral part of daily curriculum implementation. We had welcomed these two teachers' classrooms for enrichment for our study because of their strong belief that it is the teacher's responsibility to do what he or she can to motivate students to learn. To be able to live this belief for his Aboriginal students, one of these two teachers willingly attended workshops to enhance his knowledge and understanding of Aborigi-nal issues and histories and routinely used resources and pedagogical approaches found to be effective with Aboriginal students. The other teacher admitted to not integrating Aboriginal materials as much but was willing to participate in our study so that she could learn where to look for Aboriginal materials to integrate and also learn new teaching methods.

On the other hand, the teachers who taught Social Studies in the regular classrooms understood integration as occasionally adding Aboriginal content to 'the real curriculum,' which remained funda-mentally Eurocentric. One of them pointed out during an interview that although he believed that inclusion 'was the way to go' he still felt uncomfortable singling out Aboriginal perspectives for consistent integration into the curriculum because 'doing so would be unfair to the other ethnic minority students in the class' (interview, 21 Aug. 2004). The other teacher revealed that the lack of easily available student level Aboriginal material for use with his class or time to adapt materials for students meant that he could not include Aboriginal materials beyond what was given in the textbook.

The drawback, however, to including only what is given in the school textbook/curriculum is that such material typically represents what King (2001) calls 'marginalizing knowledge,' a form of curriculum information that can include 'selected 'multicultural' content that simultaneously distorts both the historical and social reality people actually experienced' (p. 274). As Swartz (1992) suggests, such a curriculum is a 'master script' from which all other accounts and perspectives are omitted unless they can be disempowered through misrepresentation. Critical race theorists see this kind of official knowledge of the school curriculum as 'a culturally specific artifact designed to maintain the current social order' (Ladson-Billings, 2004, p. 59). Except where a teacher is trained in double reading the code, distorted information is passed on to students inadvertently.

The contrast between how these two 'regular' teachers and the 'enrichment' teachers perceived integration and how these perceptions were enacted in their pedagogies and interactions with students are described in more detail in Chapter 5. Suffice it to state at this point that there were sufficient differences between the two sets of classrooms to yield a rich and complex database and to warrant our use of the regular classrooms as a frame of reference in our discussion of students' outcomes in the enriched classroom, especially how different pedagogical styles and teacher personalities may produce different outcomes.

Integrating Aboriginal Perspectives: Layering at Five Levels of Classroom Practice

The following sections describe five levels or layers of classroom practice at which we integrated Aboriginal perspectives in the enriched classrooms. Prior to the commencement of the academic year in each school, during the months of July and August (Phase 1 of the research in each school), we (the researcher, her two Aboriginal graduate research assistants, and the teachers whose classrooms were selected for enrichment) worked collaboratively to integrate the nine aspects of Aboriginal culture and other Aboriginal perspectives into the instructional planning of the Grade 9 Social Studies curriculum units (the teachers were given stipends for this summer work). Drawing partly on suggestions from the Manitoba Ministry of Education document *Integrating Aboriginal perspectives into curricula (2003)*, we integrated Aboriginal perspectives at five levels: (a) as student learning outcomes for each unit and lesson; (b) as instructional methods/strategies; (c) as curriculum content and learning resources/materials; (d) as assessment of student learning; and (e) as a philosophical underpinning of the curriculum.

What follows are some specific examples of how Aboriginal perspectives were integrated at each of these five levels, once the teaching units for the academic year had been identified by each teacher.

Integration at the Level of Student Learning Outcomes

A key feature of any rational curriculum or lesson planning is some idea of what is to be accomplished. Educators characteristically describe these intended accomplishments as their goals, objectives, or intended learning outcomes. Although there are several limitations to stating intended educational accomplishments/learning outcomes (for example, critics have argued that we can only know what we wanted to accomplish after the completion of our act of instruction. See Eisner, 2009, for more limitations), prior identification of learning outcomes provides the goals toward which the lesson or the curriculum is aimed and facilitates the selection and organization of content and learning activities. We figured that, especially for teachers learning how to integrate Aboriginal perspectives into their curriculum units and lessons, educational objectives or intended learning outcomes with an Aboriginal focus would perform a useful function. At best they could serve as heuristic devices that provide initiating consequences which can be modified or even altered as instructional activities unfold in the classroom. We, therefore, decided to identify Aboriginal perspectives for integration as student learning outcomes at the lesson planning stage. The crucial consideration here was that the teachers' planning processes came to include the ongoing question about how their curricular content, resources, and pedagogies related to and included Aboriginal peoples in positive and empowering ways.

Selection of the learning outcomes we integrated was guided by the curriculum topic, suggestions/advice from our Aboriginal consultants, and research of existing literature – for example, literature such as the RCAP Final Report, the Manitoba Ministry of Education document *Integrating Aboriginal perspectives into school curricula* and similar documents emerging in other Canadian provinces (for example, British Columbia's *Shared Learning: Integrating BC Aboriginal Content K-10*), the CAAS Proposed Learning Expectations (see reference list for their current website/URL), and our own research among Aboriginal students (presented in Chapter 3). Inspired by these sources, we targeted certain values, beliefs, practices, issues, and historical events reported as common and important among many Aboriginal communities and integrated them as learning outcomes for all students. Students were expected to demonstrate understanding/awareness of the following Aboriginal perspectives, among others:

The importance of respect for humans and non-humans in Aboriginal culture; holism – meaning the inter-relationships and connections between and among all things as fundamental to sense-making, and the holistic nature of knowledge and learning as comprising the physical, mental, emotional, and spiritual dimensions; the vital role of elders in the education of Aboriginal youth; the importance of experiential learning (i.e., the belief that knowledge is found in life itself and cannot be received as a codified canon); the importance of family and community to Aboriginal identity; the importance of oral tradition and its role in transforming and preserving Aboriginal history and cultural values; the effects of racism and stereotypes on Aboriginal peoples; the various effects of European contact and settlement on Aboriginal peoples; the inter-generational effects of the residential school system; the ten major treaties between the Canadian government and Aboriginal peoples; the ramifications of the 1763 Royal Proclamation; the 1969 White Paper and the Aboriginal response to its proposals; economic development opportunities; Aboriginal self-government; contributions of Aboriginal peoples to Canadian society; and spirituality – an integral part of life for many Aboriginal peoples which has been excluded from the education of Aboriginal students in the Canadian public school system. Because of its vital role in the learning, development, and identity formation of Aboriginal students, the concept of spirituality – as explored in our research – needs some elaboration.

Spirituality, its healing effect, and the crucial role it plays in human experience, including the experience of learning, have been well documented in the literature on Aboriginal education (see, for example, Cajete, 1994; Couture, 1991; Curwen-Doige, 2003; Forbes, 1979). For Aboriginal peoples spirituality is about meaning making, the belief in a higher power or purpose, a sense of wholeness, healing, the interconnected of all things, the ongoing development of one's identity including cultural identity, and how people construct knowledge through cultural symbols, images, music, and so on. Latino writer, David Abalos (cited in Tisdell, 2007), writing about some of the ravages of colonization, describes spirituality as playing a powerful role in healing from internalized oppression. He refers to spirituality as the 'sacred face' in the attempt by those experiencing internalized oppression to create and sustain positive social change that is grounded in their own cultural community and practices. From this description, we could see why spirituality is important to many Aboriginal peoples, as exemplified in Aboriginal cultural practices such as the sweat lodge, and the pipe and drumming ceremonies.

For Aboriginal scholars concerned with culturally appropriate education there is an intricate connection between spirituality and learning that teachers need to understand in order to provide empowering education for all students through appropriate attitudes toward students. As these scholars point out, this understanding is indispensable to an understanding of the missing link between traditional Aboriginal education and the Western system of education which is secular and appears to be oblivious to the spirituality that infuses Aboriginal epistemology and hence culturally appropriate education for Aboriginal students. To understand the necessity of spirituality in learning and education for Aboriginal students we need to explore, briefly, Aboriginal epistemology to discover the foundation of spirituality in learning. For this, I turn to Aboriginal scholars/educators for what they know that teachers need to know in order to work well with Aboriginal students.

Ermine (1995) describes spirituality as 'the inner space, that universe of being within each person that is synonymous with the soul, the spirit, the self, or the being. The priceless core within each of us' (p.103). One's spirituality, as Curwen-Doige (2003) elaborates, is the inner resource that enables one to know oneself and to find meaning for oneself in connection to one's surroundings. Connections are made through the cognitive and affective perceptions and actions of the human mind, body, and spirit. According to Couture (1991) living in the relationship between these connections is 'the manifest spiritual ground of Native being' (p.59). The Native mind, according to Couture, is therefore a 'mind-in-community' (p.59) and relationships are foundational to Native being and becoming. Comparing Western knowing prevalent in the school system and traditional Indian knowing Couture writes that traditional Indian knowing consists of experiencing matter and spirit as inseparable realities 'non-dualistically apprehended' (p. 57). He explains: 'The mode of indigenous knowing is a non-dualistic process – it transcends the usual opposition between rational knowledge and intuition, spiritual insight and physical behavior. It is inclusive of all reality. As a process of thinking and perceiving, it is irreducible. Its scope and focus are on what goes together' (p. 57). For Aboriginal peoples, therefore, the process of knowing consists of looking for holism or connections among parts in order to make meaning. It's an 'expression of an individual's spirituality in relationship, not an expression of an objectified system of beliefs or a religion' (Curwen-Doige, 2003, p. 147). It is a way of knowing that is intra-personal, subjective, holistic, spiritual, and transformative compared to Western/mainstream approaches to learning that are secular, fragmented, neutral or objective. Therefore, an Aboriginal student's spirituality must be respected and encouraged in his/her education if learning is to occur. With regard to curriculum and pedagogy, this suggests three principles: that teachers (a) accept and validate Aboriginal epistemology as a basis for learning; (b) endeavour to create a relational and safe learning environment that students value and trust; and (c) promote authentic dialogue (see Curwen-Doige, 2003 for elaborations on these principles). Authentic dialogue, according to Cajete (1994), is about the social, economic, and political situations directly affecting people's lives; it is dialogue that is readily seen as relevant because what is learned is connected to the cultural orientations as perceived by the people themselves.

Native-American educator Forbes (1979) places spirituality at the centre of education, arguing that 'knowledge without the spiritual core is a very dangerous thing' (p. 11) because learning remains at the superficial level where ideas can be formed without the influence of morals and values. Meaningful education, for Forbes, is 'learning ... how to live a life of the utmost spiritual quality' (p. 11). Hence, as Curwen-Doige deduces, the connection between learning and moral values is fundamental to Aboriginal identity. For Mi'kmaq educator, Marie Battiste, spiritual connection is a vital Aboriginal value that must be incorporated into the education of Aboriginal students. However, as she informs us, too often the presentation of Aboriginal social and cultural frames of reference in classrooms are done without an underlying understanding of the 'philosophical foundations of spiritual interconnected realities' (Battiste, 1998, p. 27), making the education of Aboriginal students 'a secular experience with fragmented knowledge imported from other societies and cultures' (p. 21).

Because it has been excluded from the education of Aboriginal students in the Canadian public school system, spirituality became an integral part of our integration effort, especially at the critical stage of formulating student learning outcomes.

In particular, two important voices in our research considered it efficacious to identify Aboriginal student learning outcomes for each unit of study and integrate those outcomes at the lesson planning stage: the Aboriginal research assistants and the enrichment teachers in whose classrooms the integration occurred. Although the Aboriginal research assistants strongly believed that Aboriginal ways of knowing are personal and experiential and, therefore, difficult if not impossible to capture beforehand in the form of prescribed learning outcomes, they also recognized that getting Aboriginal perspectives into mainstream curricula meant co-existing in the third space where traditional culture is disrupted and recreated in order to remain relevant in the modern world. From their point of view, therefore, prior identification and integration of Aboriginal perspectives as learning outcomes not only highlights those perspectives that are fundamental to sense making and hence worthy of teaching and learning in the classroom, it also provides direction and focus for teachers, particularly outlining what students are expected to know and be able to accomplish from an Aboriginal perspective. They saw this as true not only for Social Studies but also for the other school subjects.

From the perspective of the enrichment teachers, targeting any cultural group's perspectives as learning outcomes at the outset was simply sound pedagogical practice because it places students at the centre of the teaching processes – who they are, their values and aspirations and how these can be achieved. One of the teachers (who admitted to being 'wedged to Ralph Tyler's Objective Model of curriculum development') commented, 'I always keep my students in mind when I set learning goals and when I select content, resource materials and plan learning activities ... and these goals feature prominently in my assessments. I never forget the links.' This claim was certainly authenticated by what we observed in this teacher's classroom. Intended learning outcomes were shared and discussed with students at the beginning of each lesson because 'I believe that discussing learning objectives informs the students about what I am trying to accomplish in the lesson and how they can help me get there. It's one way of getting them involved in their learning … It also shows all students that Aboriginal outcomes are an important part of the learning objectives in our class' (interview excerpt). Students were required to fill out exit slips listing the learning outcomes that had been achieved and any additional learning that they had experienced during the lesson. In addition we (the researchers) were frequently invited to provide feedback on the extent to which intended learning outcomes had been addressed and to discuss other elements and unplanned outcomes of the lesson. By taking unplanned learning outcomes into account, this teacher was able to make allowance for the emergence of the newness embedded in the lived experience of each lesson rather than making learning objectives purely controllable calculations. Hence an important effect of integrating at the level of learning outcomes is that it is student-focused and it helps the students and the teacher to keep their minds firmly on the 'ball' while remaining alert to the potential of the present.

Teachers intending to integrate Aboriginal perspectives at the level of student learning outcomes must, therefore, examine the learning outcomes listed in the curriculum guides/documents pertaining to the subject areas they teach and, where missing, specify and integrate Aboriginal learning outcomes into their units and lessons. While the sample Aboriginal learning outcomes listed above pertain largely to the subject area of Social Studies and the specific Grade 9 Social Studies topics taught during our study, the values and beliefs exemplified in some of the topics – for example, the importance of respect in Aboriginal cultures, the role of elders in the education of Aboriginal youth, the importance of experiential learning, and spirituality can be applied to any subject area.

Other learning outcomes viable for integration into specific subject areas can also be explored. A few examples from Manitoba for high school classrooms are:[1]

English Language Arts. *Students will:*
- demonstrate an understanding of the importance of oral tradition in Aboriginal cultures
- demonstrate an understanding of the protocols associated with Aboriginal oral tradition (e.g., listening, showing respect when someone is speaking, appropriate times of year to tell particular stories, etc.)
- analyse selected books/readings so as to demonstrate an understanding of the social, cultural, or political issues affecting Abo-

riginal peoples portrayed in the books/readings (e.g., racism, stereotyping, land claims, health and life styles)
• evaluate the appropriateness of the portrayal of Aboriginal peoples in various media

Mathematics. *Students will:*
• describe the use of geometry in traditional Aboriginal structures
• demonstrate awareness of Aboriginal peoples' traditional techniques for measurement and estimation
• identify examples of the concepts of parallels, balance, and symmetry in Aboriginal artwork and architecture

Music. *Students will:*
• describe the role of traditional music in Aboriginal societies
• identify traditional Aboriginal music
• demonstrate awareness of the protocols associated with the performance of traditional Aboriginal songs
• demonstrate awareness of Aboriginal peoples' involvement in the contemporary music industry

Physical education. *Students will:*
• demonstrate awareness of and willingness to participate in traditional Aboriginal games and dances
• identify Aboriginal role models in different sports
• demonstrate awareness of the health benefits of physical activity
• evaluate the use of Aboriginal images in sports

Science. *Students will:*
• demonstrate awareness of Aboriginal contributions to science and technology
• demonstrate understanding of the physics principles associated with various traditional Aboriginal technologies
• understand and appreciate traditional Aboriginal knowledge of the land, plants, and cycles of the ecosystem
• identify examples of traditional medicine used by local Aboriginal peoples

Art. *Students will:*
• demonstrate an understanding of various types of Aboriginal art and their origins

- describe various aspects of the work of an Aboriginal artist (e.g., theme, style, traditional design elements)
- analyse similarities and differences in the work of contemporary Aboriginal artists

An important thing to remember is that these learning outcomes and other Aboriginal perspectives should not be treated as an add-on or as supplementary to the 'core curriculum.' They must be legitimized by placing them at the centre of the curriculum, alongside the conventionally prescribed curriculum topics.

Integration at the Level of Curriculum Content and Learning Resources

In their study of in-school determinants of educational success for Aboriginal students, Bernard Schissel and Terry Wotherspoon (2003) observed that, despite improvements, two recurrent problems are still prominent in the effort to improve the educational status and attainment of Aboriginal peoples: (a) the absence of content material that incorporates Aboriginal peoples and their histories, values, cultures, and practices in many school curricula; and (b) the frequently reiterated concern among Aboriginal peoples that an anti-Aboriginal bias remains in many school materials and pedagogical practices. Both problems have been described as not only producing the personal and social isolation, marginalization, and boredom that Aboriginal students experience, they also deny Aboriginal students the opportunity to validate their identities and heritage, thereby contributing to school failure and dropout among Aboriginal students (Kanu, 2002; Schissel & Wotherspoon, 2003; Tanner et al, 1995).

In the light of these observations, Aboriginal content materials and learning resources were copiously and consistently integrated into the Social Studies curriculum of the enriched classrooms. We visited libraries and Aboriginal education resource centres in Winnipeg in search of Aboriginal resources and found and integrated materials such as the following: Native literature including stories written by First Nations authors (e.g., Culleton, 1995; Johnson, 1990; Moses & Goldie, 1992; Olsen et al., 2001; Roman, 1998) were used to complement Social Studies units and to validate Aboriginal spirituality and other cultural beliefs. For example, First Nations origin/creation stories (often dismissed in the school curriculum as mere myths), stories describing Native ceremonies, and stories depicting the holistic and interconnected nature of

Aboriginal identity were integrated into the Grade 9 unit on Canadian identity. Through skillful use of teacher questions these materials were reinterpreted so that students could get a different perspective from an Aboriginal viewpoint. Videos and print material on Native history/issues/perspectives that enhanced certain Social Studies unit were incorporated. Some examples are, videos on the various ways in which European contact had an impact on Aboriginal lives (e.g., diseases, participation in wars, residential schools, new culture and religion, and adaptation and change); print materials on major federal Indian policies and their effects on Aboriginal peoples; materials on treaties/treaty honourings/treaty violations; materials on the Indian Act regulations and how they impacted the lives of Aboriginal peoples (e.g., human rights violations, destruction of Aboriginal cultural practices, racism); and materials on Aboriginal accomplishments, contributions, agency, and the struggle for Aboriginal self-determination today. Other Aboriginal content materials, particularly materials and perspectives that were absent from the curriculum or that were told from the viewpoints of Aboriginal peoples were integrated. These materials provided *counterstories* to what was presented in the textbook. For example, Aboriginal governing structures prior to European contact (e.g., the Iroquois Confederacy and the Great Law of Peace and its influence on democracy) were incorporated into the unit on Government and Federalism, to counter the myth that Aboriginal peoples had no organized form of government before the arrival of Europeans. Counter story-telling 'aims to cast doubt on the validity of accepted premises or myths, especially ones held by the majority' (Delgado & Stephancic, 2001, p. 144). Based on the premise that society constructs social reality in ways that promote its own self-interests or those of the elites, counter story-telling is a means of exposing, challenging, and critiquing normalized privileged discourses, the discourses of the majority. Counter story-telling therefore serves as a means of giving voice to marginalized groups (DeCuir & Dixon, 2004).

Our aggressive integration of Aboriginal materials into every unit was intended to add breadth and depth to students' understanding of the content of those units, to facilitate contrapuntal readings (Said, 1993) of the curriculum content (that is, to read and understand the content material from the perspective of the 'other,' usually the colonized and the subjugated) and to promote the development of higher order cognitive skills such as reasoning and drawing conclusions based on multiple sources of evidence and multiple interpretations of reality. It was also intended to raise students' critical consciousness by helping them to challenge and redefine the knowledge presented in their textbook.

Integration at the Level of Instructional Methods/Strategies:

Mere addition or exposure to Aboriginal content material and resources without learning experiences that incorporate Aboriginal pedagogical methods would be ineffective for achieving targeted learning outcomes and building genuine cultural understanding among students. Learning experience refers to the interaction between the learner and the external conditions in the environment (e.g., content material and resources) through which the desired outcomes are attained. Compatibility between the targeted outcomes and the teaching methods and strategies utilized to achieve these outcomes is of critical importance. In our study, therefore, lesson activities in the enriched classrooms were planned in ways that allowed the integration of instructional methods and interaction patterns which have been documented as effective in the teaching/learning of Aboriginal students. For example, where appropriate, stories were used as a teaching method to enhance students' understanding of curriculum content; sharing/talking circles were utilized to facilitate classroom discussion on an equal, respectful and non-threatening basis; learning scaffolds that helped students process and understand social studies concepts were provided in the form of concept frames, graphic organizers, information processing maps, and illustrations and examples from Native culture/experience; field trips to a Pow-wow, an Aboriginal art gallery, and a sweat-lodge were arranged through an Aboriginal elder; community support through small group work and classroom visits by knowledgeable guest speakers from Native communities were features of the Social Studies lessons; and opportunities for kinesthetic, visual, and auditory learning were provided. Also present were individual work and collaborative group projects that provided plenty of opportunity for independent decision-making and problem solving, both of which are listed as valued pedagogical goals in Aboriginal child rearing (see Manitoba Education & Youth, 2003). 'Silencing,' in which students are denied the opportunity to discuss and examine their concerns and interests, has been a powerful form of school control that often leads to marginalization and disengagement (see Wotherspoon, 1998). Therefore, students in the enriched classroom were given ample opportunity to voice their opinions, discuss issues of interest to them, and examine their experiences.

Language issues are fundamental to effective learning in the content areas; yet the most recent review of the literature on this topic (Janzen, 2008) suggests that very few teachers explicitly teach the language/discourse of their subject areas to students, thereby seriously compromising students' understanding of content/concepts in these areas. Linguistic analysis by Schleppegrell and colleagues (2004) demonstrates that reading and writing make unique demands on students in general and that the language of history textbooks can be particularly difficult for students, requiring Social Studies teachers to explicitly teach their students the grammatical features of history language to develop learner proficiency in reading and writing. Therefore, in teaching the Social Studies content/concepts and in setting tests/examinations during our research, care was taken both to teach the grammatical features of Social Studies language in the text materials we used and to eliminate or minimize any unnecessary complexity in the use of the English language that might interfere with students' understanding of the concepts or test items (for example, simpler words and shorter sentences were often used).

Integration at the Level of Assessment Methods/Strategies

Assessment practices do far more than provide information; they also shape people's understanding about what is important to learn, what learning is, and who learners are. Emerging conceptions of learning, especially those based in socio-cultural and cognitive studies, have substantial implications for educational assessment. Socio-cultural studies of learning construe learning in the interaction between learners and their environments, including all the conceptual tools (e.g., language of instruction), physical tools (e.g., computers, books, etc.), and other people – all of which serve as resources for or constraints on learning (see Moss, 2007).

Whereas the emphasis in cognitive studies of learning is on the way knowledge is represented, organized, and processed in the mind, the emphasis in socio-cultural studies of learning is on participation and performance assessment where the acquired knowledge is deemed as meaningful and useful. Learning in this latter sense entails becoming a person and a member of a community for whom such knowledge is meaningful and useful. Thus, as Lave and Wenge (1991, p. 53) put it, 'learning involves the construction of identities.' Along these lines Indigenous educators (e.g., Demmert, 2001) have argued that school assessment standards have the potential to be a powerful tool for Indigenous communities if these communities become involved in the development of culturally responsive assessment procedures. For example, Indigenous youth from reservation communities have a number of cultural predispositions that may impede their success on standardized assessment tests (see Rhodes, 1994). These predispositions include norms such as taking time to reflect so that decisions and choices are made slowly and accurately (which may result in Native students not completing tests in the given amount of time), and helping others in need (which may distract Native students where individual work is required). More recently Nelson-Barber and Trumbull (2007) have added a 'cultural validity' dimension to this argument, explaining why cultural validity is so important:

Because socio-cultural groups create meaning from experience in culturally determined ways, individuals have predisposed notions of how to respond to questions, solve problems, and so forth. It follows that these predispositions influence the ways in which they respond to test items (p. 134).

In highlighting the implications of socio-cultural theories of learning for assessment, Gipps (2002, p. 76) writes: 'The requirement is to assess process as well as product; the conception must be dynamic rather than static; and attention must be paid to the social and cultural context of both learning and assessment.'

Clearly, a socio-cultural approach to assessment challenges our conception of assessment as a distinct component of learning. As Delandsheere (in Moss, 2007) explains: 'we are moving from an educational practice of assessment where we have defined a priori what we are looking for, to an educational practice where we are participating in activities in which we formulate representations to better understand and transform the world around us.' To understand assessment for this transformation in the context of Aboriginal education is to *not* allow test-driven accountability to blind us to authentic indicators of learning for Aboriginal peoples. This means using practices that are consistent with norms in Aboriginal communities, that provide space for students to assess their own progress, and that allow students alternative ways of demonstrating knowledge and skill.

Taking into account these socio-cultural and cognitive discourses of assessment and the Manitoba standards of student assessment, we applied the following assessment strategies in the enriched classrooms. Strategies such as the use of journals and portfolio artifacts, which allowed students to reflect on classroom activities and their own progress, were included as tools for assessing student learning. Also included were students' written assignments and class work, and class presentations of collaborative inquiry projects. Many of these projects were on Aboriginal peoples and issues (e.g., the early economic activities of Aboriginal peoples in Canada's six physical regions, the position of the major political parties on Aboriginal issues, and how the legal system relates to Aboriginal peoples). Other assessment tools included story/drama performances, and traditional paper and pencil tests testing students' academic skills and higher order thinking. To enhance the chances for student success on the tests and exams, the enrichment teachers carried out extensive reviews of previously taught content material and skills just before each test/exam and students in both the enriched and the regular classrooms were given ample time for reading and writing the tests/exams.

Integration as a Philosophical Underpinning of the Curriculum

As stated earlier, when the integration of Aboriginal perspectives is approached as a philosophical underpinning of the curriculum, it is no longer seen an occasional add-on activity in the classroom; instead, it becomes an integral part of daily curriculum implementation. Perhaps one reason for the commitment of one of the enrichment teachers in particular was his belief in the transformative power of integration 'to enhance students' understanding of Aboriginal culture and issues, increase the self-esteem and pride of Aboriginal students, and alleviate ignorance and racism among dominant cultural groups' (interview, 24 Aug. 2004). For this reason, he integrated Aboriginal perspectives into not only the Social Studies course but also his other teaching courses and his extra-curricular activities with students. For instance, because of the increase in diabetes among Aboriginal youth, this teacher reported encouraging more Aboriginal students to participate in gym and other physical activities: 'The students love lacrosse, so I stay after school to play it with them' (interview, 24 Aug. 2004).

Everywhere on the walls of his classroom were pictures, illustrations and pithy sayings reflecting Aboriginal spiritual values such as the Seven Sacred Teachings (Wisdom, Respect, Love, Courage, Humility, Truth, and Honesty). There was an enlightening poem explaining the Aboriginal practice of 'smudging' (e.g., 'We smudge our eyes so that we'll only see the truth in others; We smudge our whole being so that we may portray the good parts of ourselves through actions'). Dis-

played in the other enrichment teacher's classroom was a poster enti-
tled 'Great Peoples of the Past' with portraits and accomplishments of
Inca, Aztec and other Indians among other prominent explorers, inven-
tors, artists, and architects, and there was a huge wall map showing the
names of North America's First Peoples and where they are located.
Prominently displayed on what the teacher called a 'Consciousness
Cupboard' were George Ancona's vividly illustrated book on the pow-
wow, Diane Hoyt-Goldsmith's 'Potlatch: Tsimshiam Celebration,' and
Basil Johnson's 'Ojibway Ceremonies.' Students were often asked to do
research projects that required them to utilize these resources.

The foregoing five approaches to the integration of Aboriginal perspectives continued throughout the academic year in each school as the
Social Studies units were being taught. No such integration was carried
out in the regular classrooms. The next chapter discusses the effects of
these integration efforts on academic achievement, class attendance/
participation, and school retention among the Aboriginal students in
the enriched classes compared to those in the regular classes.

Summary

This chapter has described five levels or layers of classroom practice at
which the integration of Aboriginal perspectives could occur. These are:
integration as (a) student learning outcomes for curriculum units and
lessons; (b) instructional methods/strategies; (c) curriculum content
and learning resources/materials; (d) assessment of student learning;
and (e) as a philosophical underpinning of the curriculum. It is evident
from these integration approaches that teachers are not being asked to
create a program or a new curriculum. Rather, integration of Aboriginal
perspectives might best be understood as consistently adding layers to
what teachers are currently doing in their classrooms. Integration will
be implemented in classrooms most richly if teachers understand it as
existing in Bhabha's third space of negotiation and hybridity and as
a way of thinking or 'habit of mind' – that is, that their planning and
instructional and assessment processes come to include ongoing questions about how the curriculum content they are teaching can be made
to include Aboriginal peoples in positive and empowering ways. The
teacher in the enriched classroom in School Y expressed this spirit during an interview with a member of our research team:

At first, I did not see how I was going to be able to incorporate Aboriginal cultural knowledge and perspectives into every unit of the Social Studies curriculum I was teaching. Then I reminded myself again that the integration of Aboriginal perspectives was for the benefit of all of us – after all Aboriginal culture and history is Canadian culture and history. There are Aboriginal accomplishments, values, histories, and struggles that are not in the Social Studies curriculum and that I can include. When I began to warm up to this thought, for the first time, ideas about available resources started flowing in my mind and through my participation in this study, I have come to realize that it's difficult but not as difficult as I had feared … No one is asking me to re-write my entire curriculum. Instead, I need to develop a new habit of mind so that the integration of Aboriginal perspectives becomes part of my planning, my resource collection, and my teaching – I shall do this, not only to enrich everyone's understanding but also to finally welcome my Aboriginal students in the classroom.'

QUESTIONS FOR DISCUSSION

1. Do you agree with the author's guiding principle that integration is a mixing of ideas, a coming together of minds, and negotiations at cross-cultural interfaces? Provide reasons for your answer.
2. What do you think of the five levels/approaches to the integration of Aboriginal perspectives described in this chapter? List the strengths of integrating at each level and the areas needing improvement.
3. Do you know of other approaches that have been used to integrate Aboriginal perspectives into school curricula? If so, what are those approaches and how effective are they for increasing learning and school retention among Aboriginal students?
4. Reflect on the five levels of integration presented in this chapter in connection with your subject area(s). At which of these levels do you foresee the most difficulty with integrating Aboriginal perspectives into your subject areas?
5. What is your position on the integration of spirituality into the school curriculum?

NOTES

1 This list is adapted from the Manitoba Ministry of Education's (2003) document *Integrating Aboriginal perspectives into curricula*. See it for learn-

ing outcomes for more subject areas and the CAAS document *Learning about Walking in Beauty* (2003) for more Aboriginal learning outcomes that you may find useful for incorporation in your unit or lesson topics.

REFERENCES/RECOMMENDED READINGS

Battiste, M. (1998). Enabling the autumn seed: Toward a decolonized approach to Aboriginal knowledge, language, and education. *Canadian Journal of Native Education, 12*, 16–27.

Bhabha, H.K. (1990). The Third Space: An interview with Homi Bhabha. In J. Rutherford (Ed.), *Identity, community, culture and difference*, pp. 207–21. London: Routledge.

– (1994). *The location of culture*. London: Routledge.

Cajete, G. (1994). *Look to the mountain: An ecology of Indian education*. Durango, CO: Kivaki Press

Couture, J. (1991). Exploration in Native knowing. In J. Friesen (Ed.), *The cultural maze: Complex questions on Native destiny in western Canada*, pp. 53–73. Calgary: Detselig.

Culleton, B. (1995). *In search of April Raintree*. Winnipeg: Peguis Publishers.

Curwen Doige, L.A. (2003). A missing link: Between traditional Aboriginal education and the Western system of education. *Canadian Journal of Native Education, 27*(2), 144–160.

DeCuir, J.T., & Dixson, A.D. (2004). 'So when it comes out, they aren't that surprised that it is there': Using critical race theory as a tool of analysis of race and racism in education. *Educational Researcher, 33*(5), 26–31.

Delgado, R., & Stephancic, J. (2001). *Critical race theory: An introduction*. New York: New York University Press.

Demmert, W. (2001). *Improving schools' academic performance among Native-American students: A review of the literature*. Charleston, WV: ERIC Clearinghouse on Rural Education and Small Schools.

Eisner, E. (2009). Educational objectives: Help or hindrance? In D.J. Flinders & S.J. Thornton (Eds.), *The curriculum studies reader*, pp. 107–13. New York: Routledge.

Ermine, W. (1995). Aboriginal epistemology. In J. Barman, Y. Hebert, & D. McCaskill (Eds.), *Indian education in Canada*, Vol. 1: *The legacy*, pp. 101–12. Vancouver: University of British Columbia Press.

Forbes, J. (1979). Traditional Native American philosophy and multicultural education. In *Multicultural education and the American Indian*, pp. 3–13. Los Angeles: American Indian Studies Center, University of California.

Friessen, J.W., & Friessen, V.L. (2002). *Aboriginal education in Canada: A plea for integration.* Calgary: Detselig Enterprises Ltd.

Gipps, C.V. (2002). Socio-cultural perspectives on assessment. In G. Wells & G. Claxton (Eds.), *Learning for life in the 21st century,* pp. 73–83. Malden, MA: Blackwell.

Haig-Brown, C., Hodgson-Smith, K.L., Regnier, R., & Archibald, J. (1997). *Making the spirit dance within: Joe Duquette high school and an Aboriginal community.* Toronto: Lorimer.

Janzen, J. (2008). Teaching English language learners in the content areas. *Review of Educational Research, 78*(4), 1010–38.

Kanu, Y. (2002). In their own voices: First Nations students identify some cultural mediators of their learning in the formal school system. *Alberta Journal of Educational Research, 48*(2), 98–121.

King, J.E. (2001). Culture-centered knowledge: Black studies, curriculum transformation, and social action. In J.A. Banks & C.A.M. Banks (Eds.), *Handbook of research on multicultural education,* pp. 265–90. San Francisco: Jossey-Bass.

Ladson-Billings, G. (2004). New directions in multicultural education: Complexities, boundaries, and critical race theory. In J.A. Banks & C.A.M. Banks (Eds.), *Handbook of research on multicultural education,* pp. 50–65. New York and Toronto: Wiley.

Lave, J., & Wenge, E. (1991). *Situated learning: Legitimate peripheral participation.* Cambridge: Cambridge University Press.

Manitoba Education and Youth (2003). *Integrating Aboriginal perspectives into curricula. A resource for curriculum developers, teachers, and administrators.* Winnipeg: Author.

Moses, D., & Goldie, T. (Eds.). (1992). *An anthology of Canadian Native literature.* Oxford: Oxford University Press.

Moss, P.A. (2007). Reconstructing validity. *Educational Researcher, 36*(8), 370–476.

Nakata, M. (2002). Indigenous knowledge and the cultural interface: Underlying issues at the intersection of knowledge and information systems. *IFLA Journal, 28*: 281–91.

Nelson-Barber, S., & Trumbull, E. (2007). Making assessment practices valid for Indigenous American students. *Journal of American-Indian Education, 46*(3), 132–47.

Olsen, S., with Morris, R., & Sam, A. (2001). *No time to say goodbye.* Victoria, BC: Sono Nis Press.

Ornstein, A.C., & Hawkins, F.P. (2004). *Curriculum: Foundations, principles, and issues* (4th ed.). New York: Pearson.

Rhodes, R. (1994). *Nurturing learning in Native American students*. Hotevilla, AZ: Sanwei Books.

Richardson, G. (2008). Within the luminal space: Repositioning global citizenship education as politics of encounter. In A. Abdi & G. Richardson (Eds.), *Decolonizing democratic education*, pp. 127–38. Rotterdam: Sense Publishers.

Roman, T. (Ed.). (1998). *Voices under one sky: Contemporary Native literature*. Scarborough, ON: Nelson Canada.

Said, E. (1993). *Culture and imperialism*. London: Chatto and Windus.

Shepard, L.A. (2006). Classroom assessment. In R.L. Brennan (Ed.), *Educational measurement*, 4th ed., pp. 623–46. Westport, CT: American Council on Education/Praeger.

Schleppegrell, M.J., Achugar, M., & Orteiza, T. (2004). The grammar of history: Enhancing content-based instruction through a functional focus on language. *TESOL Quarterly, 38*(1), 67–93.

Schissel, B., & Wotherspoon, T. (2003). *The legacy of school for Aboriginal people: Education, oppression, and emancipation*. Don Mills, ON: Oxford University Press.

Swartz, E. (1992). Emancipating narratives: Rewriting the master script in the school curriculum. *Journal of Negro Education, 61*, 341–55.

Tanner, J., Krahn, H., & Hartnagel, T.E. (1995). *Fractured transitions from school to work: Revising the dropout problem*. Toronto: Oxford University Press.

Tisdell, E. (2007). Without using the 'S' word: The role of spirituality in culturally responsive teachingand educational psychology. In J.L. Kincheloe & R.A. Horn (Eds.), *The Praeger handbook of education and psychology*, vol. 2, pp. 418–27. Westport, CT: Praeger Publishers.

Wotherspoon, T. (1998). *The sociology of education in Canada: Critical perspectives*. Toronto: Oxford University Press.

5 Aboriginal School Success through Integration? Learning Opportunities and Challenges

This chapter discusses the effects of the integration processes on academic achievement, class attendance/participation, and school retention among the Aboriginal students in the study described in Chapter 4. Although it was not a direct focus of the research, the views of some non-Aboriginal students on how the integration of Aboriginal perspectives had an impact on their learning are also presented. Some learning opportunities and challenges involved with the integration of Aboriginal perspectives are discussed. The chapter opens with a brief description of how the data presented were collected and analyzed.

Documenting the Effects of Integration: Methods and Procedures

Documentation of data on the integration processes began during Phase 2 of the study in each school, when the integrated curriculum was being implemented/taught in the enriched classrooms and the regular (non-integrated) curriculum was being taught in the regular classrooms. The following methods of data collection were used: (1) Data from both classroom types (enriched and regular) were collected on teaching processes and classroom interactions through field notes, audio-tapes, and sometimes video-recording to permit more intensive analysis of interactions, episodes, and processes. These data later provided the material for semi-structured interviews with the students. (2) In each school, texts such as classroom-based scores on three tests, two end-of-term exams, and two class assignments/projects, samples of Aboriginal students' written work, exit slips where students summarized what they had learned in each lesson, and records of student attendance, class participation, and school retention were collected. The tests/exams and assignments/projects were similar for both types of classrooms and care was taken to target conceptual understanding and higher level thinking in setting the tests/exams and assignments. (3) The enrichment teachers and the students kept journals where they reflected on classroom activities, assignments, and the integration processes. (4) Focus groups, semi-structured and open-ended interviews were conducted among the 64 Aboriginal students from the two participating schools to gain insights about their reactions to the teaching processes, episodes and interactions. Although not a target of the study, twenty non-Aboriginal students (five from each classroom type in the two schools) were also interviewed for their insights. Using stimulated recall techniques (Calderhead, 1987), interviewees were asked to view/read/listen to and then interpret and comment on classroom episodes, interactions and processes in order to identify the critical elements of instruction that appeared to affect academic achievement, class attendance/participation, and school retention. To assist this process, interviewees were provided with guiding questions such as 'Does this origin/creation story by the Haida/Cree/Ojibway help you better understand how myths work to help people understand their past?' Overall, however, they were left free to express any views and comments they had that were relevant to the research investigation. Interviews were audio-recorded, transcribed verbatim and shared with the participants for verification before analyzing them as data.

Data analysis: Collected data on teaching processes and interactions in both classroom types were examined by the research team and the student interviewees through a successive iterative process to discern critical elements of instruction that appeared to affect academic achievement, attendance and retention. Identified elements were analyzed through an extensive ongoing process of constant comparative analysis (Bogdan & Biklen, 2003). Scores on class tests/exams and assignments, as well as data on class attendance and school retention among Aboriginal students in both classroom types were compared and charts were used to display the findings clearly and concisely. Exit slips and collected samples of students' written work were examined for evidence of conceptual understanding and higher-level thinking versus simple recall of information, and these were also compared.

Results: Impact of Integration

Impact on Academic Achievement

Results of the study revealed that, in both the participating schools, students in the enriched classrooms significantly outperformed their counterparts in the regular classrooms on Social Studies test/exam scores. They also demonstrated a better understanding of Social Studies content/concepts, higher level thinking, and improved self-confidence as the academic year progressed. Consistently on the Social Studies tests/exams and assignments in School X there was a pass rate of 88.2 per cent among the Aboriginal students who were regular attendees in the enriched classroom (overall scores ranged between 61% and 83%), compared to a 44 per cent pass rate among regular attendees in the regular or non-integrated class (where overall scores ranged between 40% and 60%). In School Y, the pass rate among regular attendees in the enriched class was 84%, although scores were lower (ranging between 51% and 72%) compared to the regular classroom where the pass rate among Aboriginal students was only 50.3 per cent (and scores ranged between 50% and 67%). Although students in the enriched class in School Y did not demonstrate as much conceptual understanding, higher level thinking, or self-confidence as those in the enriched class in School X, they performed better on these items than the Aboriginal students in the regular classroom in that school. Variations in the classroom contexts (for example, variation in teacher capacity, defined as the teacher's knowledge of subject matter including knowledge of Aboriginal perspectives, and instructional and interactional style), in individual student abilities, and in class attendance/absenteeism among the Aboriginal students in the two schools may have accounted for the differences in the performance of the students in the enriched classrooms in the two schools.

In both schools, the students in the enriched classes attributed their superior performance to factors such as: better conceptual understanding due to the use of learning scaffolds such as examples and illustrations from Native culture during the teaching of Social Studies topics (for this, the Ojibway and Cree research assistants were very helpful); the inclusion of Aboriginal content/perspectives, especially the counter-stories which added depth and breadth of understanding for all students; the inclusion of pedagogical methods such as using stories to motivate students and to teach and reinforce content directly or indirectly and talking/discussion circles where students shared views and ideas; small group work where students felt supported; group projects which provided opportunities for ownership, decision-making, and demonstrating learning in diverse ways; one-on-one interactions with the teacher; the use of clear language on tests and in the teaching of content material; the extensive test preparation students received (e.g., extensive review of previously taught content and previous exam questions, and getting longer time to read and write tests); and (in School X) the teacher's superior knowledge of the unit topics and of Native issues, culture and history, his ability to explain concepts clearly, and his extraordinary faith in the students which translated into student motivation and respect and warmth towards the students. Neither the teacher attributes nor the Aboriginal-focused activities listed above were present or actively promoted in the regular classrooms, a situation that could have contributed to the poor performance of most of the Native students in those classes.

Empirically, our findings on these positive effects of integration are supported by previous studies which had reported gains in academic achievement when Native content/perspectives were added to the curriculum (e.g., Simard, 1994; Ezeife, 2001; Lipka, 2002; SAEE Report, 2009). The findings also appear to support the cultural discontinuity theory that when school curriculum and teaching/learning processes are compatible with students' cultures and cultural socialization patterns, the chances of academic success are increased and conversely, cultural discontinuity increases the chances of school failure (Vogt, Jordan & Tharp, 1987; Giles, 1985).

Although, as indicated above, a variety of teaching/learning methods were used in the enriched classrooms, five of these methods were found to be particularly appealing to the Aboriginal students and effective for promoting learning for all the students in the enriched classes. These methods were: the use of stories, the use of Aboriginal elders/ guest speakers as a learning resource, field-trips to Aboriginal communities, the use of learning scaffolds, and talking/discussion circles. These methods are discussed in more detail in the next chapter which specifically describes some critical elements of instruction that positively influenced the academic achievement of the Aboriginal students.

Impact on School Retention

In both the enriched and the regular classrooms, no correlation was found between Aboriginal student attrition and the integration of Aboriginal perspectives. When the academic year began in September 2003 in School X, there were a total of thirty-nine Aboriginal students in both classroom types in that school. By mid October eight of them (three from the enriched class and five from the regular class) had left, either because their parents relocated elsewhere in the city, province, or country or because these students were transferred into the school's transition program, an alternative program for students designated as not yet being able to cope with high school academic work. In School Y we lost seven of the forty Aboriginal students in the two classroom types for similar reasons but also one case of pregnancy. These findings contradict previous research establishing correlations between the integration of Aboriginal perspectives and school retention among Native students (for examples of such correlations, see Coladarci, 1983 and Silver et al. 2002).

Of significance, however, is the fact that the study revealed factors, other than the integration of Aboriginal perspectives, that accounted for attrition among Aboriginal students, in particular those from unstable and low-income family situations – for example, factors such as frequent mobility due to lack of affordable good quality housing. Consistent with this finding, a profile of Native students interviewed by Silver and colleagues (2002) during their study on Aboriginal education in Winnipeg's inner city high schools suggested a high degree of mobility among Native students both within Winnipeg and between Winnipeg and rural areas. Our finding was also consistent with the findings of a federal/provincial study (Statistics Canada, 2002) which reported annual moving rates in some inner city districts as exceeding 70 per cent, and an earlier Manitoba Health study (1995) in which the lowest and highest migrancy rates in inner city schools (where most Aboriginal students attend school) were reported as 40.6 per cent and 84.7 per cent, respectively. Other factors which previous studies have found to account for school dropout among Native students have included the lack of relevance of the curriculum in terms of future employment, peer pressure to leave school, pregnancy, problems at home (Coladarci, 1983), perceived insensitivity of teachers (Silver et al., 2002), and low test scores and GPA (Eberhard, cited in Ledlow, 1992).

Impact on Class Attendance/Regularity

No remarkable differences were found among the enriched and regular classrooms in terms of physical class attendance/regularity. In both the enriched and the regular classrooms in School X, there was a steady group of Aboriginal students who regularly attended Social Studies classes – ten students with an average attendance rate of 87% in the enriched class, and seven students with 83.2 per cent attendance rate in the regular class. The enriched classroom in School Y had seven regular attendees with an average attendance rate of 82.4 per cent and the regular classroom had eight regular Aboriginal students with 80.2 per cent attendance rate. Attendance among the rest of the Native students in both classroom types remained sporadic and this was reflected in the lower test scores of these students.

However, a clear difference emerged when regular attendees in both classroom types were asked to provide *reasons* for their regularity in Social Studies classes. In the enriched classrooms, the cultural discontinuity theory appeared to have been supported again when a correlation became apparent between class attendance and the integration of Aboriginal perspectives. During our interviews, frequent reasons given by Aboriginal students for their regular attendance in these classes included the following:

'Mr B. (the Social Studies teacher from School X) is an awesome teacher, he is very knowledgeable about Aboriginal issues'; 'We are learning a lot about Native issues in this class – for example, from the books *April Raintree* and *No Time to Say Goodbye* we learned issues about Aboriginal women and about residential schools, and we are also learning about other Native cultures outside Canada. For example, I enjoyed the video *Whale Rider,* which was about Maori culture in New Zealand. Their culture has some similarities with Cree culture'; 'The video we saw on Soweto Township in South Africa during Apartheid had similarities to life on some Native reserves here'; 'In this class, we get to express our views and ideas in the discussion circles and we work together a lot and I like that'; 'I look forward to this class every week (referring to the enriched class in School Y). We learn something new about Native issues, like successful Native professionals, politicians, and businesses, and this whole idea of urban reserves in Winnipeg ... suddenly I don't feel that bad about the future any more'; 'She [Mrs J, the enrichment teacher in School Y] is trying hard to include us [Aboriginal peoples] and our perspectives; I am learning to speak up in class and I now understand more clearly the legal categories between Inuit, First Nations, and Métis.' A non-Aboriginal student in School X reported 'learning a lot in the enriched class' but thought 'there was way too much focus on Aboriginal content and perspectives.'

By contrast, several of the Aboriginal students in the regular classrooms reported that the only reason they attended Social Studies classes regularly was because they were 'required/forced' to do so. One of them elaborated: 'If I don't get my attendance slip signed by Mr H.

[the Social Studies teacher in the regular class in School X] I will lose the government financial assistance I am getting for attending classes.' Another said, 'My parents wake me up every morning and make sure I leave home for school. Once in school, we are not allowed to hang around in the hallways during class periods. The teachers on duty are always patrolling the hallways.'

When asked what they thought about their Social Studies classes and about the integration of Aboriginal perspectives, their comments included the following: 'Mr H. hardly talks about Aboriginal issues except on one or two occasions when he talked about the people who lived in Canada before the White people came and the role of the Aboriginal people in the fur trade'; ' We do not have discussions or express our opinions in this class ... we copy notes from the overhead or from the board'; 'He has no respect for us ... like he kicks us out of class for coming late without even asking us any questions'; 'He gets easily angry and yells all the time'; 'I wouldn't be here if I didn't have to ...'; 'Yes, Mr J. [the Social Studies teacher in the regular class in School Y] talks about Aboriginal topics but only what is in the textbook, which is not a lot, really.' One Native regular attendee, however, reported enjoying Mr H's class because 'I have learned quite a bit about the geography and government of Canada, and other topics. Yes, maybe I would have liked the class even more if he had included Aboriginal perspectives.'

In both schools, frequent or prolonged absenteeism among Aboriginal students was attributed to reasons other than the integration of Aboriginal cultural knowledge/perspectives into the Social Studies curriculum. These reasons included: having to take care of younger siblings at home; poverty, so students have to work; problems at home with parents/ foster parents/ guardians; incarceration at juvenile centers; attendance at juvenile court; and returning to the reserve for funerals, weddings, or just to be with family.

This complex array of reasons/issues suggests the need to look beyond the cultural discontinuity theory in accounting for irregular school attendance among Aboriginal students, and take into account Ogbu's macro-structural explanations of school failure – for instance, the culture of poverty perpetuated by the low participation of Aboriginal peoples in the labour market. According to a 2009 report released by *Campaign 2000* (a coalition of anti-poverty groups) the highest poverty rate in Canada is found among Aboriginal children and the children of new immigrants – 40 per cent of Aboriginal children and 49 per cent of new immigrant children were reported as living below the

Canadian poverty line. Using Statistics Canada information for the year 2008, the Coalition stated that one in ten Canadian children live in poverty, that one-quarter of Aboriginal children and nearly half of those living on reserves are poor, and that Canada's child poverty rate ranked thirteenth among seventeen similarly well-off countries. In Manitoba, which has the second highest population of Aboriginal peoples in Canada, the Social Planning Council of Winnipeg (2009) reports that 18.8 per cent of all children – nearly one in five – live in poverty and Manitoba was referred to in that report as the Child Poverty Capital of Canada. Thirteen years earlier, in 1996, the unemployment rate in the Winnipeg inner city was 15.4 per cent and for Aboriginal youth it was 35.1 per cent (Silver et al., 2002). Silver and colleagues' (2002) study, which looked at a wide range of variables affecting Aboriginal education in inner city Winnipeg, reported that conditions are so harsh for many Aboriginal families in the inner city that these families are just basically surviving and that these home conditions may cause students to be pulled out of school to look after younger siblings as parents (many of them single mothers) are simply 'swamped' at home. Some Aboriginal students have had to find part-time work in order to help themselves and, sometimes, their families. Overall, however, Silver et al. reported that the majority of Aboriginal students in school are hardly able to find and hold paying jobs, for reasons such as racial discrimination and the perception among them that they do not have the skills necessary to get a job or that few employers hire Aboriginal people. Within such a culture of poverty Aboriginal adults in some households have sometimes turned to drugs and alcohol for comfort, leaving the older children to fend for themselves and care for their younger siblings (Silver et al., 2002). These grim findings were confirmed by a 2007 report of the Urban Aboriginal Task Force (UATF) in Ontario, which stated that, despite anti-racism initiatives related to education and employment and despite improved rates of employment of Aboriginal peoples in recent years, blatant racism against Aboriginal peoples still persists and the Aboriginal community remains overwhelmingly poor and disadvantaged.

The absence of secondary schools on some Aboriginal reserves has also meant that Aboriginal students who aspire to an education beyond the elementary or middle school level have to leave their home communities and live in dormitories or with guardians and extended family members in the city. Unsatisfactory living conditions in the city and missing their own families have often caused these students to either drop out of school and return home for good or be absent from school for extended periods of time visiting their families for one reason or another. Prolonged absences may lead to low grades, school failure, and dropout, which, in turn, perpetuate the culture of poverty by severely reducing the opportunity for Aboriginal peoples to participate in the labour market. These macro-structural explanations (Ogbu, 1987) suggest that the effort to increase school achievement for Aboriginal students by integrating their culture into the school curriculum cannot be pursued in isolation from other factors, a suggestion already put forward by other studies. For example, a SAEE (2009) report has suggested that strategies need to be developed to reduce the negative effects of transition on Aboriginal students (that is, moving away from families and communities to attend high school in urban areas), and Binda (2001) has referred to the dire need to improve the socio-economic conditions of urban Aboriginal students and their families.

Challenges

Despite the documented positive effects of integration among diverse Aboriginal students across two school settings, the integration of Aboriginal perspectives into the school curriculum revealed challenges that must be highlighted. The first of these is the resource challenge. Although much has been written about Aboriginal peoples in Canada, relatively little is still available from the perspectives of Aboriginal peoples themselves. Much of the history of Aboriginal peoples and information about Aboriginal issues such as economic development, Aboriginal self-government, and Aboriginal relations with successive federal governments are written from Eurocentric perspectives that almost always exclude or diminish Aboriginal experiences and interpretations of these issues. Materials that could be used to counter or challenge these Eurocentric perspectives are difficult to find and we therefore spent countless hours in libraries, Aboriginal education resource centres, and on the Internet locating credible materials to supplement unit topics or challenge the Eurocentric perspectives in the textbook. In addition, although there are now more resources available, particularly on Aboriginal websites, than when we first embarked on our research, it is still not easy to get materials that are ready for classroom use by teachers and students. Where we were able to locate materials, countless more hours were spent by us (the researchers) and the enrichment teachers re-writing them to meet the needs of Grade 9 level students. Integration at the resource level was therefore found to be the most difficult to accomplish. All four teachers in our study identified this problem as a serious challenge to the integration of Aboriginal perspectives in the classroom. For example, the enrichment teacher in School X wrote in his research journal: 'The biggest single issue has been the lack of appropriate resources for students. Most of the resources I have found are at a reading level too difficult for the students ... I believe that appropriate (grade level) resources are the key to integration.' In a similar vein, the teacher from the regular classroom in the same school cited the lack of student level resources as one of his two main reasons for not integrating Aboriginal perspectives on a regular basis (the other reason was his perception that Aboriginal issues are too controversial). During our interview with him, he said: 'Apart from the controversial nature of Aboriginal topics that I mentioned earlier, there is also the problem of resources. Adapting the available materials to classroom level takes an incredible amount of time.' The enrichment teacher from School Y made similar comments when interviewed, for example: 'If they want teachers to take this work seriously, they have to focus on developing the resources we need. I mean, I am grateful for the materials you have brought to my Social Studies class during this research because, on my own, I would not have been able to find them, there is no time.' This finding suggests the need for greater attention to resource development to facilitate successful integration and it supports my earlier study (see Chapter 7) in which teachers perceived similar lack of resources as a major impediment to the integration of Aboriginal perspectives. Similar findings were also reported by SAEE (2004) in their study of ten schools across Western Canada where the integration of Aboriginal perspectives into the school curricula was being undertaken. The SAEE study recommended that funding should be provided for the resource support and infrastructure needed if the intent of the government is to ensure that Aboriginal students receive a level of education equivalent to their non-Aboriginal peers from the mainstream culture. To this effect, the federal government should ensure that a substantial part of the over 1 billion dollar annual budget on Aboriginal education is spent on resource development.

Another challenge involves presenting information in a way that honours the unique culture, history, and perspectives of each Aboriginal group. There is no single 'Aboriginal way' of knowing that is shared by all Aboriginal peoples and cultures. Although Aboriginal peoples share certain beliefs, values, practices, and historical experiences, in general

Aboriginal groups are quite distinct from each other in their cultural practices and experiences, suggesting the need for historically accurate and culturally appropriate materials about the different groups. Developing curriculum materials from each of these distinct perspectives is no easy feat and yet it is important to pay attention to this requirement, especially in the production and dissemination of curriculum materials as 'official' Aboriginal histories, knowledge, experiences, and values to be taught in schools. As with the definition of Aboriginal perspectives, we wrestled with this challenge in our research and, in consultation with our Aboriginal collaborators, settled on materials which reflected patterns of thought held in common by a broad spectrum of the Aboriginal communities from which our students came. Even at this, we were not always sure, highlighting the need for Aboriginal resources that are locally developed and agreed-upon for use in local school jurisdictions.

Compounding the challenge of honouring the unique cultures of diverse Aboriginal groups is the challenge of infusing distinctively Aboriginal epistemologies and pedagogies into a distinctively Eurocentric education system with longstanding privilege and dominance, without marginalizing, compromising, and even disrespecting the former. The power differential between these two distinctive systems is so heavily weighted in favour of Eurocentrism in the public school system that it becomes a real challenge to teach for genuine cultural understanding, mutual respect, and social justice. Despite racially and culturally diverse school demographics, many public schools in Canada still welcome multiculturalism only to the extent that it fits into, rather than challenges or disrupts, Eurocentric epistemologies and pedagogies. Although we provided alternative perspectives that challenged or 'complicated' the content of the Grade 9 Social Studies textbook, by fitting our integration materials and activities into a Western Eurocentric system (a hybrid approach integral to Bhabha's third space) authentic Aboriginal ways of knowing and being were unintentionally compromised and even endangered. A case in point was the assessment of student learning where we adjusted/negotiated our assessment strategies to fit Eurocentric ways of understanding and demonstrating knowledge. One of the enrichment teachers (from School X) pointed out how such adaptation distorts and misrepresents Aboriginal knowledge, thereby stymieing educators' abilities to help students gain a genuine understanding of Aboriginal culture. He said:

So what are we doing to knowledge or to a concept when we subject it to

an exam? We are breaking it into its component parts to facilitate exami-
nation. This totally contravenes Aboriginal conception of knowledge as
holistic. Even the way we divide Social Studies, and school subjects in
general, into units would be un-Aboriginal because for Aboriginal people,
everything is interconnected, a big whole, which stands in total contradiction to the Western tradition of compartmentalizing knowledge and
understanding. (interview, 18 June 2004)

Similarly, the restricted opportunity for experiential learning (which
accounts for the personal nature of Aboriginal epistemologies) in favour
of content-centred pedagogies in the school system completely distorts
and marginalizes a way of teaching valued by Aboriginal peoples and
interferes with genuine cultural understanding among both Aboriginal
and non-Aboriginal students. It may even distance Aboriginal students
away from their own culture rather than connecting to it and drawing
on it to make sense of curriculum materials and classroom learning.
Equally important is that something gets lost in the process of fitting in
or aligning distinctively Aboriginal epistemology with a Western system of education. For Aboriginal communities what gets lost is authentic and unique Aboriginal knowledge and culture. Maori scholar Linda
Tuhiwai Smith (2007), illuminating how the global market place works
to put local communities and local knowledge at risk, writes: 'In biological terms the 'something lost' is our diversity; in socio-linguistics terms
it is the diversity of minority languages; culturally it is our uniqueness
of stories and experiences and how they are expressed. These are the
"endangered authenticities" of which Ray Chow (1994) speaks, ones
that are being erased through the homogenization of culture' (p. 95).

With the challenge of distorting or marginalizing Aboriginal epistemologies comes the challenge of legitimation. Currently there are no
structures within our measurement-driven public education system to
measure a way of knowing that is holistic, experiential, and personal.
The contrast between Aboriginal and Eurocentric ways of understanding and evaluating knowledge is so profound that it creates dilemmas
for public school teachers over what knowledge should be prioritized
in the learning process. Here is how the enrichment teacher in School Y
expressed this dilemma:

You know within yourself as an educator that experiential learning is
good for their personal development but then that takes quite a chunk of
the scheduled class time and you have all these prescribed outcomes and

topics which you have to cover to meet the exam requirements. Is it really possible to remain faithful to Aboriginal cultural perspectives within the present system?

It is obvious that the colonial system of control and suppression of Aboriginal knowledge is still alive and well and will continue to be that way until an epistemic shift occurs that challenges our understanding of what constitutes legitimate knowledge, its purpose, and how it can be assessed.

Resistance from students, both non-Aboriginal and Aboriginal, was also a challenge we had to grapple with. Like all young people of their age, the Aboriginal students did not particularly like being singled out for the kind of attention entailed in our study and a number of them were initially reluctant to disclose their Aboriginal identity, particularly in the light of the negative stigma associated with being Aboriginal in mainstream Canadian culture. Some even refused to participate in the interviews to which we invited them after their experiences in the enriched and regular classes in their school. Others simply failed to write anything in their journals about how they were experiencing the integration processes. One student said to me in a conversation, 'I don't really care one way or the other, I don't see the benefit.' He was probably thinking of the job market discrimination he might experience even with educational credentials.

Resistance to the integration of Aboriginal perspectives into the Social Studies curriculum was also evident among some non-Aboriginal students in the enriched classrooms. For example, during focus groups, two of these students commented that there was too much focus on Aboriginal peoples and issues in their Social Studies classes. As one of them put it, 'I have nothing against the inclusion of topics about Aboriginal people, it's just that it's been too much!!' Another said, 'I am Polish and there is nothing in our Social Studies book about my culture, and yet we have spent almost this whole year focusing on Aboriginal perspectives. I am getting fed-up.' These concerns echo those raised earlier by one of the teachers in the regular classrooms who resisted consistent integration of Aboriginal perspectives because 'doing so would be unfair to the other ethnic minority students in my class' (interview, 21 Aug. 2004). The question/challenge arising from these legitimate concerns is this: How do we acknowledge Aboriginal perspectives in the school curriculum without continuing to create hierarchies that privilege some of our students while excluding others?

Put more directly, can focusing too much on Aboriginal perspectives recreate asymmetrical power relationships between different ethnocultural groups and confine some to the margins of the curricular map? In a general sense, this concern can be seen as a cautionary tale that illustrates the tensions and complexities of attempting an act of cultural redemption for any group through curriculum reform.

Chronic absenteeism among many of the Aboriginal students, mainly for some of the reasons discussed earlier in this chapter, was a challenge we had not anticipated. We had assumed, perhaps naively, that consistent integration of Aboriginal perspectives into the Social Studies curriculum content and learning resources, classroom activities, and assessment practices would translate into motivation for learning, regular class attendance, and school retention among the Aboriginal students in the enriched classrooms. Researchers and even members of Aboriginal communities have concluded that the academic achievement gap prevalent among Aboriginal students is the result of failing school policies and practices such as culturally incompatible curriculum and pedagogy, teachers' low expectations of these students, the absence of Aboriginal teachers in schools or a combination of these factors. The common belief is that if schools and teachers do their jobs well, family economic circumstances and race should not influence how well a child learns. Elsewhere, I have written that to view achievement solely through the lens of 'failing schools' is to ignore how, in a stratified society like Canada, factors such as social class and in particular two of its characteristics – race and income – influence school learning (Kanu, 2008, p. 137). Foster (1997) describes such a narrow view of the problem as being lodged within a fundamentally liberal position which assumes that differences of race, socio-economic location, and gender do not preclude equal participation in society, or that differential treatments which result from being a member of these marginalized groups can be overcome by an inclusive approach that helps these individuals achieve to the same level as their mainstream counterparts.

The macro-structural barriers to Aboriginal academic achievement which were revealed in this study are a clear indication that the collection of conditions and characteristics which define social class differences inevitably influence school success. According to Rothstein (2004), socio-economic class differences which have implications for learning include poor health, poor housing, frequent mobility, and absenteeism. It is hard to imagine how school reform, including improved teacher capacity to integrate Aboriginal perspectives into school curricula, could be effective for students who move in and out of their classrooms as they can be for students whose attendance is regular. This is not to suggest that improved school practices will not contribute to narrowing the achievement gap; rather, it is to argue that an inordinate focus on in-school reforms as the only vehicle for reversing achievement trends is dangerous and misleading because it draws attention away from the effects which social and economic reforms may have on closing the achievement gap (Kanu, 2008). As the enrichment teacher in School X put it, 'We cannot get them (Aboriginal students) to come to school when they are plagued by all these other problems.'

Political, economic, and power issues always come into play when those who have historically been marginalized or suppressed are now to be included. As I argue in Chapter 7, these issues are particularly poignant among members of the dominant culture who include the vast majority of teachers in the Canadian public school system and who have historically benefitted from the powers and privileges of White society. Although these teachers might acknowledge that some students do poorly in school and drop out, they attribute these conditions to other factors such as unstable family situations or lack of motivation to succeed. Their vantage point does not always equip them with a clear understanding of how systemic barriers like racism, cultural and social marginalization/exclusion, personal and structural poverty, and powerlessness can hinder the progress of those who are less privileged based on their ethnic and racial identity. Convincing such teachers to integrate Aboriginal perspectives could be a real challenge, for they are too blinded by their privilege and their unexamined institutionalized educational practices to believe that integration would necessarily make a difference in terms of teaching quality and student engagement. This was certainly the case for the White teacher in the regular classroom in School Y, who said in our interview, 'I completely agree that Aboriginal students should learn about their own culture and we should hire qualified Aboriginal teachers to help make this happen. But if you mean by this that Aboriginal students are not currently being served academically, I disagree with that' (interview, 10 June 2005).

Two schools which we had initially approached as potential participants in our integration study turned us down because, as they put it, there were less than ten Aboriginal students in their schools and racism was not a problem in these schools. As one of the principals said during my first visit to his school, 'Here we do not see skin colour. We treat and teach our students the same. You might want to try School so and so which has more Aboriginal students.' The implication was that the integration of Aboriginal perspectives was only a valid issue in schools with large numbers of Aboriginal students and that other students did not need to learn Aboriginal perspectives. Not only does this point of view render the education of these other students fragmented and incomplete, their school's colour-blind approach to their education also leaves them ignorant about societal inequities that empower and privilege some while subordinating others (like Aboriginal peoples) on the bases of race and class, and how to work to correct such injustices. As Dei and colleagues (1997) noted in their study of school dropout among African-Canadian students in Toronto, schools have the potential either to reproduce the social relations existing in society or function as a site for social change. Working towards issues of equitable representation within schools clearly transcends the boundaries of the schools and have broader implications for power relations in the society.

Finally, there is the challenge of dealing with the backlash that often emerges from the settler communities whenever disenfranchised groups have fought for equal rights – for example, equal access to education and other resources. In the case of Canada's Aboriginal peoples the backlash has focused most of its recent energy on fighting against recognition of the legal rights granted to Aboriginal peoples under the 'protective' provisions of the Royal Proclamation of 1763, in negotiation of the surrender of vast Aboriginal territories, and affirmed by Section 35 of the Constitution Act of 1982. An example of such backlash is the Nisga'a Treaty in the province of British Columbia. This treaty provides the Nisga'a with 2,000 square kilometers of land (a modest 5% of Nisga'a traditional land), about $253 million in cash, and self-government powers that are similar to those of municipal government. Modest as the provisions of this treaty were, they provoked an unprecedented backlash in British Columbia. A leading newspaper in that city, *The Vancouver Sun*, wrote: 'as Native peoples get more land, timber, fish, and as they reap and allegedly abuse fantastic amounts in tax-payers' compensation, the potential for backlash grows and grows.'[1]

Similar backlash, more violent in nature, emerged in the province of New Brunswick after the Marshall decision. In that decision the Supreme Court of Canada found that a 1760 treaty gives the Mi'kmaq the right to earn a 'modest livelihood' by fishing, hunting and gathering, When Mi'kmaq fishers took to the water to exercise this right, non-Aboriginal fishers, in clear defiance of the law, destroyed Mi'kmaq fishing traps. The backlash movement engaged in extensive bashing of the Supreme Court and inflaming of non-Aboriginal Canadians against the Marshall decision. After the outbreak of the violence, the *National Post* wrote in an editorial: 'Rioters of any race must be brought to justice, but the original cause of the riots, "racially awarded economic spoils," must be excised too.' In a commentary titled 'Special rights for Natives threaten our otherwise civilized society,' Barbara Yaffe of *The Vancouver Sun* said: 'The total registered Indian population is less than 3% of the population [of Canada]. It's doubtful the other 97% will standby peacefully as this select group proceeds to live by different rules.'[2]

Most recently significant media coverage of allegations of corruption in certain First Nations communities has been used by the backlash movement to bolster their argument that Aboriginal peoples are not ready for self-government. Obviously, any allegation of mismanagement must be investigated thoroughly. However, there has been similar media coverage of corruption scandals in some non-Aboriginal communities in which politicians, civil servants, and other workers have been convicted for fraud and breach of trust. The degree of corruption and theft of tax-payers' money has been enormous in such cases but no one ever concluded that people in those communities/provinces should not be able to govern themselves so one wonders why this argument is used whenever a financial scandal erupts in a First Nations community.

These examples of backlash against Aboriginal rights suggest the likelihood that the integration of Aboriginal perspectives into school curricula will be seen as another preferential treatment for Aboriginal peoples, provoking another firestorm of racist backlash. This is a challenge that must be met squarely – for example, by educating the public about the legal treaty rights of Aboriginal peoples and the self-evident moral issue that the quality of life for Aboriginal peoples is well below that of other Canadians and that this is directly related to the conditions which have evolved in Aboriginal communities largely as a result of unresolved land and title issues, for example, an increasing reliance on federal government support programs. In addition, federal and provincial governments must develop contingency plans for dealing with any ramifications resulting from implementing the decision to integrate Aboriginal perspectives in schools.

Concluding Remark

The research results discussed in this chapter suggest cautious optimism about increasing school success for Aboriginal students by integrating Aboriginal cultural knowledge/perspectives into the school curriculum. It appears that integration at the levels of student learning outcomes, instructional methods and resources, assessment of student learning, and as a philosophical underpinning of the curriculum results in higher test scores, better conceptual understanding/higher level thinking, improved self-confidence, and, among Aboriginal students from stable home environments, increased motivation to attend classes regularly. Teacher knowledge, teacher caring, positive teacher attitude, and high teacher expectations appear to be the most important factors affecting academic achievement, class attendance and participation. Aboriginal resources, community involvement, and respectful and nurturing learning environments were also identified as contributing factors to high academic achievement.

Caution, however, needs to be applied in interpreting these results as unproblematic endorsements of socio-cultural and cultural discontinuity theorists of learning. For one thing, during the study, an Aboriginal student from the enriched class in School X commented that it did not really matter whether or not Aboriginal perspectives were integrated into the curriculum because: 'I get that sufficiently at home and in my community.' This comment is significant because it appears to support research evidence (e.g., Deyhle, 1995; Ledlow, 1992; Smith, 2001) that students with a strong sense of traditional cultural identity (for example, speaking the Native language fluently and consistently engaging in traditional spiritual and social activities in their homes and communities) have an advantage in that they already have strongly developed identities, and do not need to resist White culture to have an identity. Since this particular student belonged to the top five in her class in terms of academic achievement, class attendance, and participation this would seem to contradict the argument that the more differences there are between the school and the home culture, the more problems students will experience in school. It appears, therefore, that Native students from homes with little participation in their Native culture and language may fit more closely into Ogbu's category of castelike minorities whose resistance to school poses a far more significant factor.

In addition, as indicated by the data I presented on absenteeism and school retention, culturally responsive curriculum and pedagogy *alone* cannot provide a fully functional and effective agenda in reversing achievement trends among Aboriginal students or dismantling the persistent dynamics by which educational opportunities for Canada's

Aboriginal peoples are constrained. It is one thing to integrate Aboriginal perspectives into the school curriculum on a regular basis (as we did) but quite another to ensure that all Aboriginal students, particularly those who are socio-economically disadvantaged, are actually in the classroom to benefit from such integration. As McConaghy (2000) has pointed out in the case of this kind of curriculum reform in Australia, the inclusion of Aboriginal perspectives can be achieved without any substantive transformation of the basic structures from which the mainstream curriculum derives its authority. In other words, 'the voyage in' is only possible if those important structural and institutional forces which thwart the capacity of some social groups are disrupted. As Schissel and Wotherspoon (2003, p. 5) have argued in relation to human agency and social structures, 'Individuals bear considerable responsibility for their own choices and destinies, but none of these is independent of powerful circumstances that often lie beyond the capacity of the individual to manage or control.'

In combating school underperformance among Aboriginal students, therefore, macro-structural variables which perpetuate material injustices that contribute to phenomena such as chronic absenteeism and dropout among Aboriginal students – for example, the poor socio-economic conditions of many Aboriginal families and inadequate resources and poor educational financing for certain segments of the society (e.g., some schools serving Aboriginal populations) – may in fact be significant factors to consider. In fact, according to Ogbu (1978), these conditions are a far more significant factor in the educational underachievement of North American Natives than their cultures and languages. Ogbu explains: 'This does not mean that cultural and language differences are not relevant; what it does mean is that (the conditions of) castelike status makes it more difficult for them to overcome any problems created by cultural and language differences than it is for voluntary immigrant minorities' (p. 237). This suggests the need to explore the relationships between microlevel and macrolevel variables affecting schooling and the realization that meaningful and lasting intervention requires a systematic, holistic, and comprehensive approach. As Nancy Fraser (1997) asserts in her book *Justice Interruptus*, in the fight for social justice the growing stress on cultural politics undermines the efforts to redistribute wealth to improve the lives of marginalized citizens in the current political economy dominated by Western capitalism's pervasive materialistic individualism. Describing what she calls the 'postsocial condition' Fraser writes:

Many actors appear to be moving away from a socialist political imaginary, in which the central problem of justice is redistribution, to a post-
socialist political imaginary, in which the central problem of justice is
recognition. With this shift, the most salient social movements are no
longer economically defined 'classes' who are struggling to defend their
'interests,' end 'exploitation,' and win 'redistribution.' Instead, they are
culturally defined 'groups' or 'communities of values' who are struggling
to defend their 'identities,' end 'cultural domination,' and win 'recognition.' The result is a decoupling of cultural politics from social politics,
and the relative eclipse of the latter by the former ... This, then, is the postsocial condition: an absence of any credible overarching emancipatory
project despite the proliferation of fronts of struggle; a general decoupling
of the cultural politics of recognition from the social politics of redistribution; and a decentering of claims for equality in the face of aggressive
marketization and sharply rising material inequality. (pp. 2–3)

What Fraser proposes are remedies that combine a politics of recognition with a politics of redistribution for, on the one hand, an inordinate
focus on cultural recognition can distract from the economic marginalization and powerlessness of impoverished people; on the other hand,
an emphasis on the redistribution of social goods does not necessarily challenge the social structures that sustain and perpetuate unequal
power relations. In Fraser's analysis, recognition and redistribution are
mutually irreducible dimensions of justice. For far too long, culturalism has been the dominant factor influencing Aboriginal education and
social policies. While it has successfully pushed forward issues of identity, representation, and the politics of recognition, the time is ripe to
heed critics like McConaghy (2000) who have suggested that we now
move beyond culturalism towards an alternative, *postculturalism*, which
'contends that culture is significant, but not always the most significant
factor in issues of ... social policy, and can never be dissociated from
issues of race, class, gender, and other forms of social analysis' (p. 44).
The strategies and technologies that produce and reproduce Aboriginal
school failure are numerous and complex, and the expectation that the
inclusion of Aboriginal cultural perspectives in the school curriculum,
on its own, will fully effect social change is another colonial desire that
unfairly places an onerous responsibility on Aboriginal peoples.
Because equality of opportunity is the fundamental promise of a liberal democratic society such as Canada, and because Canada has so
far failed to deliver on this promise in the case of Aboriginal students

who now comprise a significant proportion of our urban school population, we must put the required structures in place for the realization of Aboriginal students' aspirations. The challenges that became evident during the course of our research do not reflect insurmountable obstacles; rather, they are tensions that are an inevitable part of the attempt to implement dissonant knowledge and pedagogies within a system that has historically functioned to subjugate them. These tensions provide a unique opportunity for a better understanding of the workings of the mainstream education system, its mechanisms of excluding, and how to make it work in more socially just ways. Most crucially, the tensions present an opportunity for educators to critically examine and transcend their taken-for-granted understandings of what it means to teach, particularly when their own identities and epistemic values and traditions are substantially different from those they teach. As Haig-Brown (1995) has noted, observing, naming, and analyzing tensions can lead to knowledge which, in turn, can lead to transformation.

Summary

This chapter has discussed the effects of the integration of Aboriginal perspectives on academic achievement, class attendance/participation, and school retention among the Aboriginal students in a research study conducted in two Canadian inner-city high schools. Although not a direct focus of the research, the views of some non-Aboriginal students on how the integration of Aboriginal perspectives impacted their learning are also presented. The learning opportunities and the challenges entailing integration were discussed. A major finding discussed in this chapter is that while the integration of Aboriginal cultural knowledge and perspectives results in positive outcomes such as higher test scores, better conceptual understanding/higher level thinking, improved self-confidence, and, among Aboriginal students from socio-economically stable homes, increased motivation to attend class, culturally responsive curriculum and pedagogy *alone* are insufficient for reversing achievement trends among Aboriginal students. A multi-pronged approach that takes into account macro-structural variables affecting Aboriginal schooling – for example, the poor socio-economic conditions of many Aboriginal families, structural racism, and insufficient educational financing and/or poor financial management of schools serving some Aboriginal communities – is also called for. Following Fraser (1997) in *Justice Interruptus*, I argued that what we need are remedies that combine a politics of (cultural) recognition with a politics of wealth redistribution. In other words, recognition and redistribution are mutually irreducible dimensions of justice in Aboriginal education.

QUESTIONS FOR DISCUSSION

1 In groups of three, choose one of the challenges of integrating Aboriginal perspectives described in this chapter and discuss how it can be addressed to facilitate integration. Present your views to the class.
2 What would you do in your school and in your classroom to promote genuine understanding of and respect for Aboriginal cultural knowledge/perspectives? Make a list and discuss the items on your list with your classmates.
3 To what extent has this chapter helped you acquire a better understanding of educational underperformance among some Aboriginal students?
4 Do you think the integration of Aboriginal perspectives should only occur in schools with Aboriginal students? Why or why not? Provide reasons to support your answer.

NOTES

1 See the Dr Abdul Lodhi Memorial Lecture (27 March 2000) titled 'Who is flaming the fires against anti-racism initiatives in Canada?' delivered by Moy Tam (Executive Director and CEO of the Canadian Race Relations Foundation) at the Canadian Race Relations website: http://www.crr.ca/content/view/106/401/lang.English, accessed 15 January 2010.
2 Ibid.

REFERENCES/RECOMMENDED READINGS

Binda, P.K. (2001). Native diaspora and urban education: Intractable problems. In P.K. Binda with S. Caillou (Eds.), *Aboriginal education in Canada: A study in de-colonization*, pp. 179–94. Mississauga: Canadian Educators' Press.
Bogdan, R.C., & Biklen, S.K. (2003). *Qualitative research for education* (4th ed.) Boston: Allyn and Bacon.

Calderhead, J. (1987). *Exploring teachers' thinking*. London: Cassell Educational.

Campaign 2000 (2009). *Report card on child and family poverty in Canada: 1989–2009*. Retrieved 24 Nov. 2009 from www.campaign2000.ca

Coladarci, T. (1983). High school dropout among Native Americans. *Journal of American Indian Education, 23*(1), 15–22.

Dei, G.S., Mazzuca, J., McIsaac, E., & Zine, J. (1997). *Reconstructing dropout*. Toronto: University of Toronto Press.

Deyhle, D. (1995). Navajo youth and Anglo-racism: Cultural integrity and resistance. *Harvard Educational Review, 65*(3), 403–44.

Ezeife, A.N. (2001). Integrating the learner's schema, culture and environment into the science classroom: Some cases involving traditional and Aboriginal societies. *Canadian and International Education, 30*(1), 17–44.

Foster, V. (1997). Feminist theory and the construction of citizenship education. In K. Kennedy (Ed.), *Citizenship education and the modern state*, pp. 54–64. London: The Falmer Press.

Fraser, N. (1997). *Justice interruptus: Critical reflections on post-socialist conditions*. New York: Routledge.

Giles, K.N. (1985). *Indian high school dropout: A perspective*. Milwaukee: Midwest National Origin Desegregation Assistance Center.

Haig-Brown, C. (1995). Taking control: First Nations adult education. In M. Battiste & J. Barman (Eds.), *First Nations education in Canada: The circle unfolds*, pp. 262–86. Vancouver: University of British Columbia Press.

Kanu, Y. (2008). Closing the Aboriginal academic achievement gap: Why school reforms alone are not enough. In A.A. Abdi & G. Richardson (Eds.), *Decolonizing democratic education*, pp. 137–47. Rotterdam: Sense Publishers.

Ledlow, S. (1992). Is cultural discontinuity an adequate explanation for dropping out? *Journal of American Indian Education, 31*(3), 21–36.

Lipka, J. (2002). Schooling for self-determination: Research on the effects of including Native language and culture in the schools. ERIC Document Reproduction Service No. ED459989. Retrieved 14 May 2007 from www.IndianEduResearch.net.

McConaghy, C. (2000). *Rethinking Indigenous education: Culturalism, colonialism, and the politics of knowing*. Flaxton, Queensland: Post Pressed.

Ogbu, J.U. (1978). *Minority education and caste: The American system in cross-cultural perspective*. New York: Academic Press.

– (1987). Variability in minority school performance: A problem in search of an explanation. *Anthropology and Education Quarterly, 18*, 312–34.

Rothstein, R. (2004). A wider lens on the black-white achievement gap. *Phi Beta Kappan, 86*(2), 105–10.

Schissel, B., & Wotherspoon, T. (2003). *The legacy of school for Aboriginal people:*

Education, oppression, and emancipation. Don Mills, ON: Oxford University Press.

Silver, J., Mallet, K., with J. Greene & F. Simard (2002). *Aboriginal education in Winnipeg inner city high schools.* Winnipeg: Canadian Center for Policy Alternatives.

Simard, L. (1994). Curriculum adaptation: Just do it. In P. K. Binda (Ed.), *Critical issues in First Nations education,* 78–86. Brandon, MB: BUNTEP, Brandon University.

Smith, L.T. (2007). On tricky ground: Researching the Native in the age of uncertainty. In N. Denzin & Y. Lincoln (Eds.), *Handbook of qualitative research,* pp. 85–107. Thousand Oaks: Sage.

Smith, M. (2001). Relevant curricula and school knowledge: New horizons. In K.P. Binda with S. Caillou (Eds.), *Aboriginal education in Canada: A study in decolonization,* pp. 77–88. Mississauga ON: Canadian Educators Press.

Social Planning Council of Winnipeg (2009). *Manitoba child and family poverty report card for 2009.* Retrieved 24 November 2009 from www.Campaign2000.ca/reportcards/provincial/Manitoba/2009.

Society for the Advancement of Excellence in Education (SAEE)(2004). *Sharing our success: Ten case studies in Aboriginal schooling.* Retrieved 4 December 2007 from www.saee.ca/publications/A_021_HHH_MID.php

– (2009). *Synthesis of Aboriginal education: Cross Canada policy directions.* Retrieved 20 June 2009 from www.saee.ca/index.php?option=com_content&

Statistics Canada (2002). *Census of population questionnaire.* Ottawa: Author.

Urban Aboriginal Task Force (UATF) (2007). *Urban Aboriginal Task Force: Final report.* Ontario Federation of Indian Friendship Centres, Ontario Metis Aboriginal Association, and Ontario Native Women's Association.

Vogt, L.A., Jordan, C., & Tharp, R.G. (1987). Explaining school failure; producing school success: Two cases. *Anthropology and Education Quarterly, 18,* 276–86.

6 Critical Elements of Instruction Influencing Aboriginal School Success

Chapter 5 discussed the effects of the integration of Aboriginal perspectives on academic achievement, class attendance/participation, and school retention among Aboriginal students, suggesting cautious optimism about increased academic achievement when Aboriginal cultural knowledge and perspectives are integrated into the curriculum, instructional methods, and assessment practices. This chapter identifies and discusses some of the critical elements of the integration processes that accounted for the gains described in chapter 5. Documentation of the critical elements of instruction influencing the school success of Aboriginal students in dominant culture school contexts is particularly important because, as school personnel ponder equitable ways of delivering education and preparing all students along the K–12 pipeline to post-secondary institutions, teachers could draw on these elements to enhance and support classroom learning for Aboriginal students. Teacher educators could also incorporate these elements into teacher preparation programs for cross-cultural instruction in classrooms with Aboriginal students.

From analyses of the teaching/learning tasks and the environments in the enriched classrooms (discussed in Chapter 5) several elements of the integration processes emerged as critical for increasing academic achievement, class attendance and participation among the Aboriginal students in our study. These elements are: teachers' sense of efficacy (teachers' belief that they are able to engage in courses of action that will improve educational outcomes for their students); teacher capacity; integration of Aboriginal content and resources; use of teaching and assessment methods compatible with Aboriginal cultural knowledge/ perspectives; and a nurturing learning environment. Each of these elements is discussed next, along with suggestions/questions about how teachers could develop them in their own practice.

Teachers' Sense of Efficacy

Albert Bandura's (1986) social cognitive theory posits that the beliefs which people hold about their capabilities and about the outcomes of their actions powerfully influence the ways in which they behave. These self-efficacy beliefs determine the choices people make, the effort they put forth, and the persistence and perseverance they display in the face of difficulties. Research in many arenas has demonstrated the power of efficacy judgments in human learning, performance, and motivation. For example, efficacy beliefs are related to smoking cessation, diet and exercise programs, political participation, and academic achievement (Bandura, 1997). The last arena, academic achievement, is of particular importance to educators, for research over the past two decades has found links between student achievement and the self-efficacy beliefs of teachers.

A teacher's sense of efficacy or a teacher's efficacy beliefs connotes judgments about the teacher's own perceptions of his or her capability to accomplish a task. Compared to teachers with low self- efficacy beliefs, teachers with strong perceptions of their own capability tend to employ classroom strategies that produce the courses of action required to have positive effects on students. Teachers' sense of efficacy is related to their classroom behaviours. It affects the efforts they put into teaching, the goals they set, and their level of aspiration. Teachers with a strong sense of efficacy are open to new ideas and are more willing to experiment with new methods to meet the learning needs of students. According to Ashton and Webb (1986) efficacy influences teachers' persistence when things do not go smoothly and their resilience in the face of setback – an invaluable attribute when implementing change such as the integration of Aboriginal perspectives into school curricula.

In our study, the strong self-efficacy beliefs of the enrichment teachers in regard to the integration of Aboriginal perspectives led them to take measures that low-efficacy teachers may have found time-consuming or extraordinarily difficult. For instance, the enrichment teacher from School X reported attending efficacy seminars like informational workshops, reading materials on Aboriginal education, and mingling with Aboriginal peoples to enhance his knowledge and understanding of Native cultures and Native issues. He sometimes used his own resources to acquire the instructional materials he needed and routinely spent time adapting material for student use in his lessons. From his interview comments such as 'where there is a will, there is a way ...' and 'I believe we can learn a lot from Native cultures' (interview, 12 Aug. 2004) we deduced that this teacher's strong sense of self-efficacy was the reason he perceived and approached the integration of Aboriginal perspectives as a philosophical underpinning of the curricula he taught. Similarly, the enrichment teacher in School Y reported experiencing 'a dip in my belief that I could do this' when we first began the integration process in her classroom. However, as she received instructional materials from us and support and encouragement from her school principal (a Métis man), she became more confident 'as I repeatedly tested out my newly acquired knowledge and skills and noticed positive changes in my students' participation in the circle discussions' (interview, 10 June 2005). Change is difficult and stressful. Initially the implementation of change may produce a negative effect on teachers' self-efficacy. However, as they develop new strategies to cope with the change and gain evidence of improved student learning, teachers' personal teaching efficacy returns, as we saw in the case of this teacher.

This finding and previous others (e.g., Anderson, Greene, & Loewen, 1988; Ross, 1994) suggest positive links between teachers' beliefs about their efficacy and student outcomes such as increased motivation to learn, increased efficacy beliefs about completing learning tasks, and higher academic achievement. In the light of these promising findings, schools should explore effective ways of developing or strengthening teachers' beliefs about not only their personal but also their collective capability to execute required courses of action to increase school success for their Aboriginal students. From a theoretical perspective, the link between collective efficacy beliefs and student achievement occurs because 'a robust sense of group capability establishes expectations (cultural norms) for success that encourages organizational members to work resiliently toward desired ends' (Goddard, Hoy, & Hoy, 2004, p. 8). Groups or organizations also create and strengthen members' sense of collective efficacy for goal attainment through what Bandura (1997) calls *social persuasion*. Social persuasion may entail encouragement from a colleague, a supervisor, the community or the media about the ability of teachers to influence student outcomes. Although social persuasion alone may be limited in its power to create enduring changes in efficacy beliefs, it may act as a counter-force against occasional setbacks that might have instilled enough self-doubt to interrupt persistence. Persuasion can encourage group members to innovate in order to overcome difficult challenges. Chapter 8 will describe school-level variables that can be addressed to enhance teachers' collective efficacy beliefs – for example, providing teachers with professional development opportunities, opportunities for teachers to influence instructionally-relevant school decisions, and helping teachers feel a greater sense of control over their professional lives in schools.

At the pre-service level, faculties of education across Canada, particularly in provinces with high Aboriginal populations, have introduced measures aimed at the development of the efficacy of individual teacher candidates. These measures include the introduction of courses in Native studies and courses in the integration of Native perspectives as a graduation requirement, and an increased hiring of qualified Aboriginal faculty to teach these courses. The intent is to strengthen teacher candidates' efficacy beliefs by enhancing their knowledge of Aboriginal perspectives, how to integrate such knowledge into school curricula, and where to find resources that facilitate such integration. Graduates from these programs are expected to continue to build on this knowledge to increase their personal capacity as well as collaborate with other teachers to form supportive coaching networks that lead to higher efficacy among teachers. It would be interesting and useful to follow these graduates as they enter the workforce to investigate the extent of the effectiveness of these measures for the preparation of teachers to integrate Aboriginal perspectives.

Teacher Capacity

Directly related to the teacher's sense of efficacy as having a positive effect on students' outcomes is *teacher capacity*, defined here as the teacher's knowledge (of the subject matter and of Aboriginal perspectives), attitude, personal interactions and instructional style, expectations for students, and commitment. Analysis of our research data suggested that for *all* the students interviewed, teacher capacity appeared to be the most critical factor affecting academic achievement. In the enriched classroom in School X, Aboriginal and non-Aboriginal student interviewees mentioned the following teacher capacities as critical factors in their superior academic performance: the 'awesome ability of Mr B (their Social Studies teacher) to explain concepts in clear and simple language,' his 'use of a variety of teaching methods and strategies' which appealed to different learning needs, 'his knowledge of Native culture' and his consistent 'effort to integrate Native culture and content into Social Studies,' his ability to 'encourage and motivate all students,' 'his positive attitude and high expectations for students,' and 'his respectful interactions with all students, especially Native students' (excerpts from student interviews, 15 June 2004). In a somewhat similar vein students in the enriched classroom in School Y remarked on Mrs J's (their Social Studies teacher) effort to include Aboriginal perspectives: 'This year she is really trying hard to include us. Like when we watched and discussed the movie *To Kill a Mockingbird*, many of her examples of racism in that movie were compared to what is happening to Aboriginal people right here in Canada'; 'She brought in John Underwood [pseudonym for a respected Aboriginal athlete], that was awesome'; 'She took us to the Manitoba Museum to see the displays on Aboriginal hunting and residential schools, that was good too'; 'Mrs J. lets us discuss in class and I really like the talking circle' (excerpts from student interviews, 10 June 2005).

By contrast, interviewees from the regular classes frequently expressed the need for a teacher 'who cares,' 'who is interested in us,' 'who understands Aboriginal issues,' and 'who can use teaching methods and resources other than transparency notes or the textbook and its end-of-chapter questions most of the time.' (excerpts from student interviews, 18 June 2004 and 10 June 2005).

Teacher capacity may account for the observed differences in student academic performance in the enriched and the regular classrooms in our study, suggesting that successful integration requires sensitive caring teachers who are knowledgeable about Aboriginal issues/cultures and value them sufficiently to integrate them into the school curriculum on a consistent basis. This finding is supported by Bishop, Berryman, and Richardson's (2002) study which identified similar teacher personal attributes and pedagogical style as the crucial factors that promoted literacy learning skills among Native Maori students in years 1 to 5 in New Zealand. It is also supported by Kanu's (2002) study in which Aboriginal students in Canada identified positive teacher attitude and teacher warmth and respect toward Aboriginal students as important factors that enhance their learning in the public school system. Couture (1988) also supports this finding by his reference to the responsibility of the classroom teacher in accepting and accommodating Aboriginal students in the class, stating that the challenge (for the teacher) is to acquire an understanding of fundamental Native cultural values and to create the conditions for maintenance and reproduction of these values.

Curwen Doige (2003) too has argued – based on a Canadian study of Native and non-Native students in a university course she taught – that accepting and accommodating Native students must go beyond whether they are visual learners, towards an understanding and acceptance of the knowledge paradigms from which they maket meaning. For example, through skillful classroom discussions of beliefs and values held in common by Aboriginal peoples (e.g., the role of Aboriginal myths, rituals, and ceremonies in identity formation) the enrichment teacher in School X was able to infuse Native spirituality (an important source of meaning-making for many Aboriginal peoples) into the Grade 9 Social Studies curriculum, thereby enabling the students to develop a stronger sense of who they are. These discussions turned out to be a mutually beneficial process which provided learning opportunities not only for the students but also the teacher whose enhanced knowledge and understanding of Aboriginal culture liberated him from the position of the outside authority (Cajete, in Curwen Doige, 2003). Together, these findings suggest the need for the government and policy makers to provide sustainable funding and encouragement for programs that improve the capacity of teachers for integrating Aboriginal perspectives effectively.

Culturally Compatible Teaching and Assessment Methods

As indicated in Chapter 4, a variety of teaching/learning methods were used in the enriched classrooms. The Aboriginal students in those classrooms identified several of these methods as particularly appealing and effective in promoting learning for them, including: the use of stories, Aboriginal elders and guest speakers as learning resources, field trips to Aboriginal communities, learning scaffolds, and discussion/talking circles. According to some of the students, stories were effective for building interest and motivation and hence readiness for learning, for example: 'The story grabs your attention and builds your appetite to listen and want more ...' (Aboriginal student interview, 10 June 2005). Stories were also seen as effective for teaching content material and for developing higher-level thinking skills such as making inferences and drawing similarities and differences: 'First we listen to the story as Mr B [the teacher] reads it aloud and then we are asked to explain the events in the story and how they are different or similar to our lives or to what we are discussing that day. And then we pull out the lessons [values, ideals, and knowledge] in the story and discuss them' (Aboriginal student interview, 12 June 2004). As the lessons of a story are not always implicit, each student would have to find his or her own lesson from the information in the story. And hearing the story repeatedly allows the listener to sharpen and refine the lessons learned. According to Fitznor (2002) children are also able to develop their ability to retrieve information from their short and long-term memories as well as refine their higher-order thinking skills.

Learning scaffolds were most useful as information processing strategies. Concept frames and information maps were used to organize information, outline main and supporting ideas in an article or a video, and review and apply information. When reinforced by examples from their own cultural experiences, these forms of scaffolding were described by the students as 'helping us to understand the topic more'; 'helps me organize my thinking on paper'; and 'it just makes you understand better when you first list down the main ideas and then draw arrows pointing to the supporting ideas or the evidence' (student interview excerpts). Students do more analysis, synthesis, and evaluation when they complete a problem-solving frame or a concept analysis frame, and the information mapping can lead to a descriptive or expository writing assignment. Students use these frames as learning scaffolds until they are able to internalize the structures the frames provide and organize the processes on their own.

The fieldtrips to a sweat lodge, a Pow-wow, an Aboriginal art gallery and the ensuing circle discussions were described by the students as particularly valuable for two reasons. First, prior to the trips students had researched and reported their findings on the Pow-wow (the drums, songs, the dances, the outfits, and traditional Pow-wow etiquette) and the sweat lodge. The actual trips provided them the opportunity for experiential learning, which in turn helped them to develop personal knowledge of and pride in their cultural ceremonies and what these ceremonies represent in terms of Aboriginal spirituality and identity. For example, an Aboriginal student commented: 'My grandmother always says that real learning is about going out there and experiencing something. I felt something inside me, a connection, when we saw the Pow-wow and the sweat-lodge. I will never get that from a textbook or a video or the interviews we conducted for our research.' Another reported increased interest and motivation for learning: 'In the art gallery we visited, I was very interested to know more about the beadwork, the patterns and the colours. I would like to design my own beadwork' (interview, 10 June 2005). Second, the circle discussion

accorded them voice, respect, and confidence in discussing their learning and their opinions. As their confidence grew over the academic
year, especially in School X where the teacher was adept at the use of
higher-level thinking questions to probe, extend, and scaffold students'
responses to elicit critical thinking, Aboriginal students were observed
openly challenging views they considered as racist, stereotypical, or
discriminatory in their classroom. A vivid example of this was when
an Aboriginal student challenged a non-Aboriginal Catholic student to
'explain why the burning of incense and other materials in your church
is not considered to be superstitious but the burning of sweet grass in
an Aboriginal smudging ceremony is seen as superstitious.'

Classroom visits by Aboriginal elders, experts, and role models from
the Aboriginal community were also found to motivate all the students,
enhance the pride of Aboriginal students in Aboriginal knowledge, culture and achievements, inform Aboriginal and non-Aboriginal students
about Aboriginal issues, and create connections between curriculum
topics and the real world of Aboriginal students. During the research
in each school, through the help of an Aboriginal education resource
centre, we arranged for three separate visits by respected Aboriginal
elders, experts, and role models to the enriched classrooms. The experts
we brought in were identified by the Aboriginal Education Resource
Centre as authorized knowledge-keepers. These are elders of their Aboriginal communities who have gained humble authority by displaying
wisdom in life. As we found out, not all seniors become elders and not
all elders are seniors although the latter is common as wisdom is gained
through experience. Elders, as keepers of knowledge and tradition,
have been recognized by their communities and by the Creator because
they hold in their hearts many important lessons that they are willing
to share with others to make their community a better place. According to the Royal Commission on Aboriginal Peoples (1996) elders do
not hoard their knowledge. Their most important task is to pass on
their knowledge so that the culture of their people can stay vital and
responsive to changing times and contexts. Their credibility and the
continuity of their Nations depend on such responsiveness. They are
today's connection to the past, a living link to the customs and beliefs
of the ancestors. They help to renew and perpetuate traditions which
are rooted in a shared past and are crucial to the identity of Aboriginal
peoples today. They do this by passing on their cultural knowledge, traditional languages, beliefs and sacred spiritual practices to the younger
generations. Often this is done during ceremonies such as the Sweat

Lodge, which the elders help conduct. Elders also lead by example, living their beliefs to bring the world closer to harmony. Elders are teachers, philosophers, linguists, historians, healers, judges, counselors, and more. They come from many communities, are of many ages, and have unique experiences that have shaped their views of the world. The one thing they have in common is the desire to help their people live the right way.

Aboriginal and non-Aboriginal students alike described the visits of these elders/experts and role models as beneficial for enhancing cultural understanding and the self-efficacy judgments of Aboriginal students. For instance, after a classroom visit and follow-up circle discussion with Joe (all names are pseudonyms), a First Nations athlete and teacher who reported struggling in his early life but later finding fulfillment through sports, an Aboriginal student in one of the enriched classes had this to say: 'Joe's story was awesome. I can see myself going in that direction too.' According to Bandura's social cognitive theory, students build their efficacy beliefs through the vicarious experience of observing others. Social models play a powerful role in the development of self-efficacy, especially when students are uncertain about their own abilities. Students compare themselves to individuals as they make judgments about their own capabilities. For example individuals, like Joe, who struggle through problems until they reach a successful end are more likely to boost the confidence of observers than those who do not persevere in the face of difficulty. Bandura (1997) also contends that students are most likely to alter their beliefs following a social model's success or failure to the degree that they feel similar (e.g., in age, gender, or ethnicity) to the model in the arena in question. The vicarious information gained from Joe became a powerful source of self-efficacy for the Aboriginal students as they convinced themselves that they too can conquer challenges and do well in life. Research (e.g., Eccles et al., 1984) suggests that social models may be particularly influential during transition periods such as adolescence when youngsters become more attuned to social comparison information.

A non-Aboriginal student, reflecting on a classroom visit by an Aboriginal elder, wrote: 'I have often heard that the sweet-grass ceremony is superstition. Last week, I learned from Les [the Aboriginal elder] that the sweat-lodge, the drumming ceremony, and the sweet-grass are part of Aboriginal spirituality. We all have ways of expressing our spirituality.' Clearly, the opportunity to experience the presence and teachings of an Aboriginal elder may have played a significant role in the development of the kind of cultural understanding expressed by this student and we regretted that the school's schedule and resources could not accommodate more of this experiential approach to learning.

Student narratives in regard to the assessment of learning, suggested that some of the strategies we integrated were more effective than others. For example, like the students in our first study (discussed in Chapter 3) the majority of the sixty-four Aboriginal students interviewed throughout this second study expressed low self-efficacy beliefs in reference to doing individual oral presentations in front of a class. They reported a high level of discomfort with this approach to their learning and assessment for the following reasons, among others: 'I always feel nervous and anxious when I have to present'; 'In front of the class, I tend to freeze and forget what I want to say; like my mind kind of goes blank'; 'Sometimes, it's the way I express myself in English that is difficult. I fear that I am being judged by everyone'; 'I just can't do it, I hate it' (excerpts from Aboriginal student interviews, 18 June 2004 and 10 June 2005).

Self-efficacy beliefs are informed by emotional and physiological states such as anxiety, stress, and mood (Bandura, 1997). Students learn to interpret their physiological arousal as an indicator of personal incompetence by evaluating their performance under various conditions. High anxiety and stress, such as those expressed by these Aboriginal students, can undermine self-efficacy and students who experience a feeling of dread toward a particular school-related task interpret their apprehension as evidence of lack of skill in that area. It bears noting that the self-efficacy beliefs which students hold when they approach a task serve as a filter through which they interpret that task. Those who are overly anxious over a task performance may falsely interpret their anxiety as a sign of incompetence and inability and such an interpretation can lead to the very failure that students dread. Conversely, a good mood increases self-efficacy beliefs, motivation, and subsequently achievement (Usher and Pajares, 2008). It appears, therefore, that increasing students' physiological and emotional well-being – for example, by decreasing stress and anxiety – strengthens self-efficacy. Strategies such as letting the students present with others as a small group where students feel supported and building an atmosphere of trust and respect in the classroom have also been described as effective in decreasing anxiety (Kanu, 2002; Usher & Pajares, 2008).

In sharp contrast to the students' expressed aversion to presenting in front of a class, journal writing as a form of assessment seemed acceptable to everyone. We were surprised by this finding, for we thought that journal writing would be incompatible with the ways of thinking predominant in cultures, such as Aboriginal culture, which have a strong oral tradition. The finding supports Ogbu and Simon's (1998) assertion that there are both individual and sub-group variations in school attitudes and behaviours. It also suggests that, as pointed out in Chapter 2, learning style is not a genetically fixed trait but is constructed by the social and physical environment and the demands of the learning task. More important for our investigation of culture and Aboriginal student learning, we gathered from the interviews that journal writing was preferred because of the opportunity it provided for the students to explore their inner selves as they reflect on how they felt, thought, and experienced the curriculum material and the classroom activities. Such reflective processing of information requires a relaxed atmosphere and ample time, both of which are accorded by journal writing. According to Curwen Doige (2003) strategies such as journal writing add an element of spirituality to Aboriginal student learning as the students actually get the chance to spiritually work curriculum content and classroom experiences from the inside out for transcendence, that is, transforming the given (the external and imposed curriculum) into new meanings and new forms of life. The informed teacher helps Aboriginal students make this spiritual connection so that they are able to interpret meaning. However, as Curwen Doige points out, the Aboriginal students can only do this well if their spirituality is respected and accepted in classroom discussions and activities.

Student also described the small group projects as effective both as a teaching/learning method and as an alternative way of demonstrating their knowledge to the teacher for assessment. Interviewees' comments on this point included the following: 'First of all, we got to choose and research topics that were of interest to us ... [*intrinsic motivation*] and then we worked together in our small groups and shared ideas that we brought [*community support*] and then we got to present our report in any way we felt comfortable with' [*independent decision-making*]. 'My group presented on Aboriginal lobster fishing through interactive drama, a play. Everyone enjoyed it and we were learning at the same time'; 'I am not very good at writing an essay so I was happy that we were allowed to present our project through role play and stories'; 'We really enjoyed making the video we presented for our project. People from our community were eager to be interviewed about what they think of Aboriginal people and the criminal justice system. It was awesome.' (Interview excerpts, 18 June 2004 and 10 June 2004, italics mine).

In summary, then, the projects provided the students with intrinsic motivation and opportunities for hands-on experiential learning, goal setting and independent decision-making, working together in groups where they felt supported, and opportunities for appreciation of their unique talents. As well, the projects gave them opportunities for kinesthetic, visual, and auditory learning and learning outside the four walls of the classroom. In addition they were able to demonstrate their learning (for the teacher's assessment) in ways that were compatible with their cultural socialization.

Students also appreciated the extra preparation they received for their exams and the longer time they were given to read and write the exams, as the following comments show: 'Yes, I like it when they [teachers] revise all the topics just before the exams. If you were absent, you get another chance to hear the topic from the teacher'; 'Sometimes you understand the topic more clearly during the review time'; 'Oh, we ask a lot of questions during revision time'; 'The longer time for the exam gives me time to think about what I am going to write'; 'Some students don't use up all the time we are given but for me, I use it to read over my answers and change what I want to change. Also I write slowly so more time is good' (interview excerpts, 18 June 2004 and 10 June 2005).

Targeting Aboriginal Content and Resources

Among other benefits, the integration of Aboriginal content and resources appeared to increase breadth and depth of understanding of curriculum content and promote higher cognitive skills such as reasoning and drawing conclusions. In both respects, students reported that among the materials used to supplement and/or complement the content of their Social Studies units, the counter-stories we brought in, or which they found on their own through structured library research, were particularly useful for understanding and challenging what was presented as unproblematized factual content in the textbook. For example, after a unit on Human Rights during which several supplemental content materials were added to the textbook information, an Aboriginal student remarked: 'Our discussion of the Aboriginal interpretation of the 1876 Indian Act provided a different perspective and that really opened my eyes ... I cannot believe that Aboriginal people were not allowed to leave their reserves without a Pass permitting them to leave, in their own country, that's shocking!' Another said: 'I now see the banning of Aboriginal ceremonies in the past as an attempt at cultural genocide, and I can defend my position on that if asked...' (informal conversations, 24 March 2004).

The use of Aboriginal elders and guest speakers as learning resources was praised for the way it validated and accorded respect and recognition to Aboriginal knowledge in the classroom. We interpreted the inclusion of Aboriginal content and resources as having a liberating effect in that these elements released Aboriginal students from the constraints of dominant cultural canons of knowledge and ways of knowing.

These positive effects of integrating Aboriginal content and resources were, however, undermined by the challenge of accessing these resources, as pointed out in Chapter 5. I have appended a list of available resources (Appendix A), some of which we found useful during our research – resources that readers may also find useful for generating ideas for their own integration efforts.

A Nurturing Learning Environment

Students in the enriched classes identified what can be described as 'a nurturing learning environment' as a critical element of instruction that promoted learning for them. By this they meant a learning environment 'that is open' (freedom to speak when you feel ready), 'creates opportunity for our voices to be heard,' 'somewhere I feel I really belong, like a community,' and 'a place where I don't feel anxious or unsafe' (interview excerpts). Asked how such an environment had contributed to her learning, an Aboriginal student from the enriched class in School X responded, 'I feel respected in this class. During the talking circles, Mr B. (the teacher) always insists that we listen to each other with an open mind and respect what each of us has to say. And, we are not forced to speak, if we do not feel like it. That's also respecting our silence.' Several non-Aboriginal students attested to the positive effect of this sort of classroom environment as indicated by the following comments: 'I have learned more by listening to what they [Native students] feel when they are stereotyped' (non-Aboriginal student interview, 18 June 2004). This student revealed that the counter-stories and the respectful circle discussions in class, where views were openly expressed and challenged under the guidance of the teacher, had helped him to better understand certain Aboriginal issues and to change some negative stereotypical views he had held about Aboriginal peoples. This revelation, which was echoed by other non-Aboriginal students, was an important breakthrough in the effort to increase academic achievement for Aboriginal students because research on *stereotype threat* suggests that when a student's social identity is tagged with a negative stereotype, the student tends to underperform in a manner that is consistent with the stereotype (see, e.g., Aronson & Steele, 2005). Steele (1999) suggests that students whose social identities are attached to the negative stereotypes which others hold about their academic abilities tend to 'disidentify' with or shift their self-perceptions away from academic tasks. For these students, avoiding school work is a safeguard against being seen as inferior. However, as Steele notes, 'disidentification is a high price to pay for psychic comfort' (1999, p. 46). Aboriginal students in Canadian classrooms have had to pay this price for far too long. The level of trust and psychological safety felt in the learning environment plays a critical role in Aboriginal students' academic achievement. Creating such an environment requires a better understanding, by teachers, of how Aboriginal students attend to the sources underlying their academic confidence.

Curwen Doige (2003) highlighted the crucial importance of an appropriate learning environment in fostering the spirituality of Native students in the learning process. Based on a self-study of her own teaching in a class of Native and non-Native students enrolled in an Aboriginal Children's Literature course (ED4688) in an eastern Canadian university, Curwen Doige discerned that an appropriate learning environment helps students gain insights into their own values and beliefs, connect learning to their prior knowledge systems, and value persons for who they are. She wrote, 'Holding the spirit of each student in genuine respect is crucial to the learning that occurs in ED4688. I believe it is also foundational to cross-cultural understanding in any classroom with any age group' (p. 157). I would add that building such an environment in the classroom is also grounded in sound theories of learning and development (see, for example, Rogers, 1969; Bruner, 1971; Battiste, 1998; Cajete, 2000) which engender pedagogical practices that enable students to develop mentally, physically, socio-emotionally, and spiritually – a balance that is integral to the lives of many Aboriginal peoples.

Summary and Caveat

This chapter has discussed some critical elements of instruction that appeared to enhance classroom learning for Aboriginal students when Native cultural knowledge/perspectives were integrated into the Social Studies curriculum. Although previous studies had reported gains when Native perspectives were included in school curricula, there is still a dearth of knowledge about the specific aspects/elements of such inclusion on which teachers and teacher educators could draw to enhance their understanding of how best to teach Native students. Our study suggests that teacher capacity, motivated by strong teacher efficacy beliefs, is a most crucial factor affecting academic achievement, class attendance and participation among the Aboriginal students in this study. The use of Aboriginal content material and resources from Aboriginal communities, teaching and assessment methods that are compatible with Aboriginal cultural socialization, and respectful and nurturing learning environments were also identified as critical elements of instruction that enhance classroom learning for Aboriginal students.

One caveat, however, is that, as elaborated in Chapter 5, it would be naive to conclude that the integration of these critical elements *alone* will close the academic achievement gap between Aboriginal students and their White middle-class counterparts without addressing macro-structural variables such as poverty and high rates of migrancy which contribute to the achievement gap. But, at a time when schools are increasingly being held accountable for student achievement in the K–12 system, the pipeline to higher education, processes which contribute to equitable and effective delivery of education for particular groups of students are invaluable. In this regard, the critical elements of instruction identified in this chapter are important for teachers to implement in classrooms with Aboriginal students. Ongoing evaluation of such implementation will enrich our understanding of the factors influencing the efficacy and sustainability of these elements.

QUESTIONS FOR DISCUSSION

1. Why are efficacy beliefs important for the success of school reforms such as the integration of Aboriginal perspectives into the school curriculum?
2. In your opinion, what can schools and faculties of education do to

enhance teachers' sense of efficacy for integrating Aboriginal perspectives?

3. What would you do personally to enhance your sense of efficacy and your capacity as teacher to be able to integrate Aboriginal perspectives into your curriculum?

4. Briefly examine each of the critical elements of instruction described in this chapter as increasing learning for Aboriginal students. List those that you consider the easiest to implement and those that you consider the hardest to implement in your classroom. What measures would you take to help you implement those elements that you listed as difficult to implement?

REFERENCES/RECOMMENDED READINGS

Anderson, R., Greene, M., & Loewen, P. (1988). Relationships among teachers' and students' thinking skills, sense of efficacy and student achievement. *Alberta Journal of Educational Research, 32*, 148–65.

Aronson, J., & Steele, C.M. (2005). Stereotypes and the fragility of academic competence, motivation, and self-confidence. In A.J. Elliot & C.S. Dweck (Eds.), *Handbook of confidence and motivation*, pp. 436–56. New York: Guilford Press.

Ashton, P.T., & Webb, R.B. (1986). *Making a difference: Teachers' sense of efficacy and student achievement*. New York: Longman.

Bandura, A. (1997). *Self-efficacy: The exercise of control*. New York: W.H. Freeman and Company.

Bandura, A. (1986). *Social foundations of thought and action: A social cognitive theory*. Englewood Cliffs, NJ: Prentice Hall.

Battiste, M. (1998). Enabling the autumn seed: Toward a de-colonized approach to Aboriginal knowledge, language and education. *Canadian Journal of Native Education, 22*(1), 16–27.

Bishop, R., Berryman, M., & Richardson, C. (2002). Te toi huarewa: Teaching and learning in total immersion Maori language educational settings. *Canadian Journal of Native Education, 26*(1), 44–61.

Bruner, J. (1971). *The relevance of education*. New York: Norton.

Cajete, G.A. (2000). *Native science: Natural laws of interdependence*. Santa Fe, NM: Clear Light Publishers.

Couture, J. (1988). Native culture in the classroom: A possible end run. Unpublished manuscript, Athabasca University.

Curwen Doige, L.A. (2003). The missing link: Between traditional Aboriginal education and the Western system of education. *Canadian Journal of Native Education, 27*, 144–60.

Eccles, J.S., Migley, C., & Adler, T. (1984). Grade-related changes in the school environment: Effects on achievement motivation. In J. Nicholls (Ed.), *Advances in motivation and achievement: The development of achievement motivation*, Vol. 3, pp. 283–331. Greenwich, CT: JAI Press.

Fitznor, L. (2002). *Aboriginal educators' stories: Rekindling Aboriginal worldviews.* Toronto: University of Toronto Press.

Goddard, R.D., Hoy, W.K., & Hoy, A.W. (2004). Collective efficacy beliefs: Theoretical developments, empirical evidence, and future directions. *Educational Researcher, 33*(3), 3–13.

Kanu, Y. (2002). In their own voices: First Nations students identify some cultural mediators of their learning in the formal school system. *Alberta Journal of Educational Research, 48*(2), 98–121.

Kleinfeld, J. (1995). Effective teachers of Eskimo and Indian students. In L. Roberts & R.A. Clifton (Eds.), *Cross-currents: Contemporary Canadian Educational Issues.* Toronto: Nelson Canada.

Ogbu, J., & Simons, H.D. (1998). Voluntary and involuntary minorities: A cultural-ecological theory of school performance with some implications for education. *Anthropology and Education, 29*(2), 155–88.

Rogers, C. (1969). *Freedom to learn: A view of what education might become.* Columbus, OH: Merrill.

Ross, J.A. (1994). The impact of an inservice to promote cooperative learning on the stability of teacher efficacy. *Teaching and Higher Education, 10*, 318–94.

Steele, C.M. (1999). Thin ice: Stereotype threat and Black college students. *Atlantic Monthly, 284*(2), 44–54.

Usher, E.L., & Pajares, F. (2008). Sources of self-efficacy in school: Critical review of the literature and future directions. *Review of Educational Research, 78*(4), 751–96.

FURTHER RESOURCES

This list is intended to provide educators and curriculum developers with learning resources that will assist with the integration of Aboriginal perspectives into the content areas, especially at the high school level. It is not exhaustive; therefore users are expected to do further research to enrich their understanding of integrating Aboriginal perspectives into their curricula. Please note that some website content may have changed since retrieval of the information provided below.

PRINT RESOURCES

Battiste, M. (2002). *Indigenous knowledge and pedagogies in First Nations educa-tion: A literature review with recommendations.* Ottawa: Indian and Northern Affairs Canada.

Coaltion for the Advancement of Aboriginal Studies (CAAS) (2003). *Learning about walking in beauty: Placing Aboriginal perspectives in Canadian classrooms.* Printable from CAAS website: www.edu.yorku.ca/caas.

Caduto, M.J., & Bruchac, J. (1992). *Native stories from keepers of the animals (told by Joseph Bruchac).* Saskatoon: Fifth House Publishers.

Dickason, O. (1992). *Canada's First Nations.* Toronto: McClelland and Stewart.

Diversity in the Classroom Series (1996). *Aboriginal cultures and perspectives: Making a difference in the classroom.* Regina: Saskatchewan Book Bureau.

Hall, M. (1996). Full circle: Native educational approaches show the way. *Journal of Experiential Education, 19*(3), 141–44.

Keller, E. (2005). *Strategies for teaching science to Native Americans.* Retrieved 18 January 2007 from www.as.wvu.edu/~equity/native.html.

Lipka, J., & Adams, R. (2003). *Building a fish rack: Investigations into proofs, prop-erties, perimeter and area.* Calgary and Bellingham, WA: Detselig.

Lipka, J., Hogan, M.P., et al. (2005). Math in a cultural context: Two case stud-ies of a successful culturally-based math project. *Anthropology and Education Quarterly, 36*(4), 367–85.

Lipka, J., Shary, N., et al. (2007). Creating a third space of authentic bicultural-ism: Examples from math in a cultural context. *Journal of American Indian Education, 46*(3), 94–115.

Manitoba Education, Citizenship and Youth (2003). *Integrating Aboriginal perspectives into curricula: A resource for curriculum developers, teachers, and administrators.* Winnipeg: Author.

Manitoba Education, Citizenship and Youth (2007). *Kindergarten to Grade 12 Aboriginal languages and cultures: Manitoba curriculum framework of outcomes.* Winnipeg: MECY, School Program Division.

Native Education Directorate and Instructional Resources Unit (2000). *Abo-riginal peoples: Resources pertaining to First nations, Inuit, and Metis.* Winni-peg: Manitoba Education and Training. Consists of 235 pages of annotated bibliography.

Nelson-Barber, S., & Estrin, E. (1995). *Culturally responsive mathematics and sci-ence education for Native students.* Washington, DC: Native Education Initia-tives of the Regional Educational Labs.

Reynolds, G. (2000). Teaching First Nations history as Canadian history. *Cana-dian Social Studies, 34,* 44–7.

Royal Commission on Aboriginal Peoples (1996). *Final Report,* Vols. 1–5. Ottawa: Communication Group.

Saskatchewan Education (2001). *Aboriginal elders and community workers in schools: A guide for school divisions and their partners.* Regina: Community Education, Saskatchewan Education.

Tippeconnie, J., & Faircloth, S. (2006). School reform, student success for educators working with Native K–12 students. *Tribal College Journal of American-Indian Higher Education, 17*(4), 1–6.

Slapin, B., Seale, D., & Gonzales, R. (1989). *How to tell the difference: A checklist for evaluating Native American children's books.* Berkeley, CA: Oyate.

Western Canadian Protocol (2000). *The Common Curriculum Framework for Aboriginal Language and Culture Programs: Kindergarten to Grade 12.* Western Canadian Protocol for Collaboration in Basic Education.

Growth of the First Metis Nations/Grades 8–10 (Teacher Resource). First Nations Education Division, 923 Topaz Avenue, Box 700, Victoria, BC V8T 2R1. Phone: (250) 360-4350. This resource focuses on the development of Western Canada told from Métis and Aboriginal perspectives.

Indian Education in Canada (Teacher Resource). University of British Columbia Press, Vancouver. Phone: (604) 822-5959. Provides a range of articles on Aboriginal education in the traditional, contact, and post-contact contexts. Written mainly from Aboriginal perspectives.

Our Bits of Truth: An Anthology of Canadian Native Literature. Pemmican Publications Inc., Winnipeg, MB. Phone: (204) 589-6346. An anthology of traditional and contemporary poems, myths, legends, short stories, and memoirs from various Aboriginal peoples from across Canada.

Raven Steals the Light (grades 9–10). Douglas & McIntyre Ltd., 1615 Venables Street, Vancouver, BC. Phone: 1-800-667-6902. This resource is an anthology of ten episodes of Raven and other characters that explore the values and beliefs of the Haida people told through stories.

Through Indian Eyes (K–12 Teacher Resource). New Society Publishers. Phone: (250) 247-9737. Useful for beginning teachers not familiar with assessing Aboriginal images. Practical examples and guidelines are provided.

INTERNET RESOURCES/LINKS

CAAS report/document on the integration of Aboriginal perspectives into curriculum: www.edu.yorku.ca/caas

Aboriginal Super Information Highway: www.abinfohwy.ca/

Aboriginal Web Links: http.cyberspc.mb.ca/~fullmoon/aborig.html

Aboriginal Youth Network (Canada): http://ayn-0.ayn.ca/
Assembly of First Nations: www.afn.ca
Canadian First Nations: http://indy4.fdl.cc.mn.us/~isk/canada
Bill's Aboriginal Links: www.bloorStreet.com/300block/aborl.html
Indian and Northern Affairs Canada: www.inac.gc.ca/index_e.html
British Columbia Ministry of Education: Shared Learning: Integrating BC
    Aboriginal Content K–10: www.bced.gov.bc.ca/abed/shared.pdf
Cradleboard Teaching Project: www.cradleboard.org
Manitoba Education, Citizenship and Youth: Instructional Resources Unit,
    Library: www.edu.gov.mb.ca/ks4/iru/index.html
Métis Nations Home Page: www.vcn.bc.ca/michif/
Rekindling Traditions: Cross-cultural Science and Technology Units: www.
    capes.usask.ca/ccstu/
School Net: http.school2.carlton.ca/English/ext/aboriginal/index2.html
Village of First Nations: http://firstnations.com/welcome.html
National Aboriginal Achievement Foundation: www.naaf.ca/cnaf.html
Statistics Canada website (latest Aboriginal population profiles, e.g., demo-
    graphic data): www.statcan.gc.ca/pub/89-638-x/89-638-x2009001-eng.htm
Common Curriculum Framework for Aboriginal language and Culture Pro-
    grams: Kindergarten to Grade 12: www.wcp.ca
Aboriginal Peoples' Television Network (APTN), for daily information on
    Aboriginal issues and concerns, Aboriginal leaders, and Aboriginal stories.
Marcuse, G., & Svend, E. (Producers) (1993). *First Nations: The circle unbroken*.
    Vancouver: Face to Face Media and National Film Board of Canada. Thir-
    teen videos and teacher's guide.
National Film Board of Canada (Montreal). *Keepers of the Fire* (a 55-minute
    video profiling diverse Aboriginal 'warrior women' who have defended the
    traditions of their ancestors).

RESOURCE CENTRES

Manitoba First Nations Education Resource Centre
1151 Sherwin Road
Winnipeg, MB R3H 0V1
Phone (204) 940-7020

Manitoba Indian Cultural Education Centre
119 Sutherland Avenue
Winnipeg, MB R2W 3C9
Phone: (204) 942-0228

Aboriginal Education Directorate
Murdo Scribe Centre
510 Selkirk Avenue
Winnipeg, MB R2W 2M7
Phone: (204) 945-7886

Prince Charles Education Resource Centre
1075 Wellington Avenue
Winnipeg, MB R3E 0J7
Phone: (204) 788-0203

Users are advised to locate and contact Aboriginal educational resource centres in their own areas.

7 Teachers' Perceptions of the Integration of Aboriginal Perspectives

An important dimension of the integration of Aboriginal perspectives that has rarely been addressed in previous research is the voices of teachers on this issue. This chapter reports on the third of our research studies, which investigated Manitoba teachers' perceptions of the integration of Aboriginal perspectives into the school curriculum. Results of the study suggest that while, in principle, teachers accepted the integration of Aboriginal perspectives and perceived it as timely and important, their lack of knowledge of Aboriginal cultures and issues, the exclusion of teachers from deliberations about integration, lack of classroom-ready Aboriginal learning resources, lack of sustained support from school administrators, incompatibility between school structures and some Aboriginal cultural values, and teachers' own socio-political investments in the educational status quo posed significant challenges to the integration of Aboriginal perspectives in schools. The result is an incoherent approach to integration that is disconnected from true understanding of Aboriginal perspectives and replete with tensions on several levels. Insights from the study are used to provide recommendations/suggestions for helping teachers and schools to integrate Aboriginal perspectives into school curricula.

Centrality of the Teacher to Curriculum Change

Thus far, a crucial omission from the discussions surrounding the integration of Aboriginal perspectives into the school curriculum is the voices of teachers, the very people who are mandated to implement this reform in classrooms. In studies of curricular reforms/innovations involving change in experienced teachers' practices (e.g., an innovation such as the integration of Aboriginal materials, perspectives and pedagogical practices into the teaching of existing curricula) teachers' attitudes, beliefs, and perceptions about the change have been identified as the crucial factor that can make or break the innovation (Day, Calderhead & Denicolo, 1993; Kanu, 1995). Part of the past history of failure of educational and curricular reform has been due to the marginalization of teachers in curriculum implementation and the instrumental view that teachers are merely a 'conduit' for carrying out predetermined changes over which they have no influence. In his works on educational change, Michael Fullan informs us that we have learned from this mistake, and that almost without exception, reformers now agree that the teacher must hold a central place in any educational reform (Fullan, 1993; 2001).

Particularly underlying the central role of the teacher in curriculum reform is the issue of teacher identity and its mediating influence on curriculum change. In socially transformative reform such as that involving the integration of Aboriginal culture into the school curriculum, it is the identity of the teacher that is being negotiated. As Terrance Carson expressed it in a paper on teacher identity and curriculum change, 'The teacher is the change that is being sought' (Carson, 2003, p. 7). This is because the integration of Aboriginal perspectives is being introduced within contexts of already existing identities, histories, and socialities. The public school educators being enlisted to carry out this reform have histories and identities that have been constructed within social norms and school structures that have historically functioned to protect their linguistic and cultural rights and interests. Change not only threatens comfortable identities, but also unsettles the integrity of those whom it affects (Carson, 2003). New and difficult knowledge, new relationships with curriculum and with students, especially students who are different, constitute a threat to the existing identities and the integrity of the teachers being enlisted to change public education by integrating Aboriginal cultural knowledge into school curricula. Especially in the existing conditions of unequal power, this threat can trigger resistance to, and regression from, the change being sought. Attention, therefore, needs to be paid to teacher identity and subjectivity in the context of these new demands for change, especially how teachers perceive the change. Identity is linked to perception in the sense that we perceive from our particular locations in the social order.

So far, however, little research has been done focusing on teachers' perceptions of curricular innovations, as most researchers have continued to focus on students' responses to innovations. This chapter addresses this knowledge gap by presenting Manitoba's teachers' perceptions of the integration of Aboriginal cultural perspectives into the school curriculum.

Investigating Teachers' Perceptions: Methods and Procedures

The primary question investigated in our study of teachers' perceptions was: How do teachers perceive the integration of Aboriginal cultural knowledge/perspectives into the teaching of the Manitoba high school curricula? Several subsidiary questions guided the exploration of this major question: What are teachers' beliefs/views about the integration of Aboriginal cultural knowledge/perspectives into the school curriculum? What are the reasons for these beliefs/views? Do teachers currently integrate Aboriginal cultural knowledge/perspectives into the teaching of their school subjects? If so, what do they integrate and how do they integrate? What do teachers perceive as facilitators of, and challenges/impediments, to the integration of Aboriginal cultural knowledge/perspectives? What support structures and resource requirements do teachers perceive as needed to be able to integrate Aboriginal cultural knowledge? What concerns do teachers have and how, in their view, could their concerns and challenges be addressed? Are there important differences among teachers in their perceptions of the integration of Aboriginal perspectives?

Research participants were ten teachers from three Winnipeg inner city high schools with a mix of Aboriginal and non-Aboriginal students and predominantly mainstream/dominant culture teachers. Nine of the teachers belonged to one of Canada's two dominant cultures (English) and each had taught Social Studies and English Language Arts (ELA) for over ten years. One teacher was Aboriginal (Ojibway) and had taught ELA for five years and Native Awareness for two years. All ten teachers had been identified by their colleagues and their school principals as integrating Aboriginal perspectives into their classrooms. Also participating in the study from the margin (because he was not a certified or recognized classroom teacher) was an Aboriginal community liaison worker hired by the school division to serve as 'the bridge' connecting schools with the Aboriginal community, provide cultural teachings/resources/information, and generally support 'at risk' Aboriginal students in the school division.

A disproportionately high number of dominant culture teachers participated in this study because, as mentioned earlier in the book, they constitute the vast majority of public school teachers and their perceptions and views about the integration initiative have not been previously investigated. However, Aboriginal voices are important to the integration process; therefore, Aboriginal participants were purposely included in order to have their perspectives on the research questions under investigation.

Classroom observations and open-ended interviews served as data collection methods.

Classroom observations: Throughout the one-year duration of the study a total of fifty-four classroom observations were carried out by the research team in Social Studies, ELA, and Native Awareness classrooms ranging from Grade 9 through Grade 12. Our observations focused on teaching processes and interactions, particularly as they pertained to the integration of Aboriginal perspectives going on in these classrooms. Separately, the research team wrote down field notes on classroom observations and these were compared later for inter-researcher reliability.

Interviews: The interviews probed salient issues observed in the classrooms, how the teachers approached/engaged integration, and what they perceived as resource/support needs and facilitators/challenges/ impediments to integration, their fears, concerns, and feelings about the integration of Aboriginal perspectives.

Data analysis was ongoing during the research. Data were examined to discern what was being said in regard to the research questions and the teachers' overall perceptions of the integration of Aboriginal perspectives. Once identified, key dimensions of these data were coded, using a coding system developed collaboratively by the research team, and then organized into themes. Interpretive comments on each theme, supported by quotes from the interviews, were written and returned to the teachers for comments, changes and/or confirmation before writing them up as research reports (Lincoln & Guba, 1985). Where teachers are quoted in the following discussions of the research findings, pseudonyms have been used to protect their identity. Hence the teachers are referred to as Dan, Tim, James, Ann (the

Aboriginal teacher), Nick, Mike, Neil, Ted, Sam, Doug, and Arnie (the Aboriginal liaison worker).

Teachers' Perceptions

Teachers' Beliefs about Integration and Reasons for These Beliefs

All ten teachers in the study expressed the strong belief that the integration of Aboriginal knowledge/perspectives into the school curriculum was absolutely crucial and gave the following reasons for this belief:

The need to learn from Aboriginal peoples: The teachers acknowledged the existence of a rich body of Aboriginal cultural knowledge, values, and contributions that needed to be learned and understood by all Canadians. Cited examples of such knowledge and values included: Aboriginal stories/classics/legends and the teachings they convey; Aboriginal spirituality; caring for the extended family; respect for humans, nature and the environment; sharing/cooperation/harmony; traditional knowledge of the land; and belief in the circle of life (that everything is connected). Aboriginal contributions to science, art, and the development of Canada were also cited as important for Canadians to know.

Learning has to be culturally relevant: To be meaningful, curriculum and learning have to be culturally relevant for all students, not simply students from the dominant cultures. Teachers felt that the integration of Aboriginal perspectives would support and enhance classroom learning for Aboriginal students. For example, during our interview Ann (the Aboriginal teacher) said: 'My experience of teaching literature to kids from diverse cultural backgrounds is that they are more attached and interested in the material if it is relevant to them and their own history, culture, and experiences.'

Improvement of self-image and identity of Aboriginal students: Eight of the teachers mentioned that the integration of Aboriginal perspectives would greatly improve the images and perceptions Aboriginal students have about themselves and their backgrounds. For example, Doug observed in an interview: 'Aboriginal students are the only cultural group in my classes who hide their identity...'

Economic implications of school dropout: The economic implications of school failure or dropout were mentioned as a strong reason for supporting the integration of Aboriginal perspectives. Teachers felt that integration may lead to school success and school retention among Aboriginal students. Ted, for instance, rationalized the economic link in this way: 'I mean, Aboriginals are a fast growing population, so we need to pre-figure how to make a connection with Aboriginal nations because school dropout is becoming an economic burden on the whole country ...'

The need for inclusion: Four teachers expressed the view that Canada is a multicultural democracy where everyone should be fully included and represented. However, as Tim put it, 'Too often, Aboriginal peoples are left out or not treated as equals ... The curriculum should carry their views and perspectives.'

Need to inform Aboriginal and other students: It was agreed by all the teachers that Aboriginal students needed to learn about their cultural heritage, history, and the issues affecting their lives (e.g., issues such as Aboriginal economy, self- government, land claims, and health), and that non-Aboriginal students would benefit from this education. Teachers reported that a good number of students did not have adequate knowledge of these issues and felt that the school would provide the opportunity for complex analyses of the issues, compared to the inaccurate representations of Aboriginal peoples and issues that students typically heard at home or on the media.

Because of these beliefs the teachers reported that they have made the effort to get to the stage where they felt comfortable integrating Aboriginal perspectives, although not always fully knowledgeably as they themselves had been taught poorly about Aboriginal peoples. On their own, the teachers have collected Aboriginal curriculum materials, paid honorariums to Aboriginal guest speakers, and attended workshops on Aboriginal education to increase their understanding of this population. Undoubtedly, not all teachers are able to make this move. According to the Coalition for the Advancement of Aboriginal Studies (CAAS, 2003) teachers who embark on the journey of integration often credit some sort of transformational experience for helping them acquire the interest and desire to improve their teaching. It may begin elsewhere and then expand to an interest to improve teaching about Aboriginal peoples, or this focus may be the initial goal. Transformational experiences are 'those by which the individual operates, evaluate, and makes decisions' (CAAS, 2003, p. 22).

For the non-Aboriginal teachers in this study, the move to integrate Aboriginal perspectives into their curricula and classroom practices was clearly the result of transformational experiences. For example, James said in an interview:

> It hit me a few years ago ... We had Judge Murray Sinclair (an Aboriginal) in our school a couple of years ago, and he told us that in the not very far future, one out of every five people living in Winnipeg is going to be Native in one way or another. So I mean, if that's true and that's coming, it's kind of amazing that it doesn't get more attention in the school system.

For Social Studies teachers Tim and Dan the transformation came about as a result of years of teaching the Canadian Charter of Rights and Freedoms, according to which:

> Everyone is supposed to be included and everyone is supposed to be equal, and that's still not true ... it certainly isn't necessarily true in the case of the Aboriginal community ... either real or perceived in the way others or themselves perceive the issues. I think their culture does have a place in the curriculum in order to understand and include them as part of our society and our history (Tim).

> Ethically, it's the right thing to do if we as a nation are to uphold our ideals of democracy and justice as a multicultural country (Dan).

These data suggest the need for studies that investigate catalytic ways of encouraging this process of transformation for more teachers.

It was important to explore the current beliefs/views of teachers regarding integration because these prior conceptions can serve as triggers or barriers to change as well as provide frameworks for interpreting and assessing new and potentially conflicting information and ideas. Conceptual change theory (Strike & Posner, 1985) suggests that changing teachers' beliefs depends on their recognizing discrepancies between their own views and those underlying new visions of teaching and learning. The dominant culture teachers in this study described why new practices in Aboriginal education, and their associated values, are better than conventional approaches. This provides an important insight about one of the conditions likely to influence teachers towards the integration of Aboriginal perspectives into the public school system.

How Teachers Understand and Approach Integration

Although the teachers generally supported the integration of Aboriginal perspectives into school curricula, there were clear differences among them in how they understood and approached integration. To make sense of these differences, I turned to James Banks' typology of teachers' engagement of the inclusion of multicultural perspectives in the classroom. Banks (1989) identifies four approaches to the inclusion of multicultural perspectives: (a) The contributions approach, where the focus is on teaching students about the contributions made by each cultural group; (b) the additive approach, where content, concepts/topics, and perspectives from other cultures are occasionally added to what is perceived as the 'real' (meaning Eurocentric) curriculum; (c) the transformational approach, where curriculum topics are taught from cultural perspectives, enabling students to understand issues/topics from multiple perspectives and voices; and (d) the social action approach where, based on the transformational approach, students are encouraged to take action for social change.

In this study, participants' understandings of and approaches to the integration of Aboriginal perspectives spanned Banks' first three categories; the fourth approach was not addressed either in their classrooms or in their responses to the interview questions. To varying degrees, teachers moved between the contributions, additive, and transformational approaches, depending on the topics they were teaching. By far, the most consistent use of the transformational approach was exemplified by Ann, the Aboriginal teacher, who understood integration as the infusion of Aboriginal content/perspectives into every aspect of the school curriculum. She said, 'I am Aboriginal ... I include my culture in everything I teach.' For Ann, integration also meant teaching one's subject from diverse perspectives:

> I teach kids from several different backgrounds ... My literature circles work because we study a huge amount of books from Canada, America, the Caribbean, traditional European texts, Spanish novels, Aboriginal literature(Ann).

Ann's transformational approach was further exemplified by particular behaviours, attitudes and activities we observed in her classroom, including the following:

- Prominent displays of Aboriginal cultural artifacts, posters, and flyers about Aboriginal events on her classroom walls and bulletin boards
- Discussion of books and other publications by Aboriginal and international authors
- Conduction of classes through sharing circles that encouraged diverse views
- Teaching methods that included the use of Aboriginal guest speakers, and stories, legends, and folktales about Aboriginal ceremonies and customs
- Publicly sharing her own stories about her dreams, vision quests and spiritual experiences
- Integration of Aboriginal art and symbols into ELA writing classes
- Use of culturally sensitive assessment (e.g., students were observed choosing class projects based on their cultural strengths and experiences)
- Consistent use of positive content materials about Aboriginal peoples
- Demonstration of respect and warmth towards students (e.g., Ann did not scold a female Aboriginal student who had been absent from her ELA class for almost three weeks. When the student walked in, Ann simply said: 'Welcome, I knew you would come today.')
- Going with the mood of the class: Sometimes Ann abandoned her lesson plans to go along with what she called the 'mood' of students (e.g., 'In my literature class last week, we were supposed to study a poem. Students did not appear to be in the mood for that. They wanted us to discuss Steinbeck's novel, *The Pearl*, and I went along with them on that').

By contrast, the dominant-culture teachers mainly tended to adopt Bank's additive and contributions approaches to integration. Although these teachers were unanimous in their agreement that school curricula were 'assimilating' Aboriginal students through omission or token additions of Aboriginal perspectives, they unwittingly contributed to this process of assimilation by allowing the prescribed curriculum topics, not Aboriginal issues/perspectives, to remain at the centre of their teaching. The teachers perceived integration as occasionally adding Aboriginal perspectives, where convenient, to a curriculum that remained largely Eurocentric. Some of the teachers integrated Aboriginal perspectives more often than others, but on average each of the teachers had integrated Aboriginal perspectives into their curricula only six times over the entire academic year.

Classroom observations and the interviews revealed that when teachers integrated, videos on disparate Aboriginal topics were the most common resource used. For example, we observed that in all three schools the video *Black Robe* was shown in Grade 11 Social Studies classrooms when teachers taught the unit on Europeans' first contact with Aboriginal peoples, and the video series *Daughters of the Country* was used to teach about the contributions of Aboriginal women to the fur trade. In one school, a Grade 11 Social Studies teacher, Doug, identified the news media as an occasional educational resource (e.g., 'I discuss current Aboriginal issues with my class whenever they come up on the news'), while another claimed to engage his students in content analyses of old textbooks either to point out the omission of Aboriginal perspectives or to discuss or challenge stereotypical images of Aboriginal peoples in those books. Some teachers reported drawing on Aboriginal community members as an educational resource whenever possible (e.g., as guest speakers in their classrooms) but lamented that this pool of available community members was limited. When available, the guest presentations were sometimes followed by discussions of the topics presented (e.g., James said, 'I think the discussions facilitate students' understanding of the issues'). On a number of occasions, however, we observed guest presentations that were neither linked to any curriculum topic nor discussed in order to help students develop a transformation in consciousness. For example, in one school a Grade 11 Social Studies teacher, Mike, brought in two Aboriginal guest speakers who spoke about an array of topics including the ceremonial importance of the pipe, the drum, and sweet grass in Cree and Ojibway cultures; naming ceremonies and rites of passage in these cultures; boundaries between men and women in Ojibway culture; and residential school experiences. The presentations took the form of personal stories from the guest presenters' lives, and the class, which consisted of a white majority and a few Filipino and Chilean students, reported finding the presentations 'interesting' and 'informative.'

Informal conversations with representative students from each of the Grade 11 Social Studies classrooms where these 'integrations' were being carried out revealed that these activities had little or no impact on them in terms of either how they perceived Aboriginal peoples or moving them towards the interrogation of power structures in society. Their frames of reference remained firmly fixed within their own vantage points, confirming Britzman and colleagues' (1993) point that in multicultural education, rational understandings did not always lead to sensitivity or better attitudes. In this case the teacher failed to help his Grade 11 students see Aboriginal cultural practices in terms of cultural diversity in a multicultural country like Canada or the residential school experience in terms of injustice.

Revealingly, the same professional vulnerability cited by Mr H in the regular classroom in School X (see Chapter 4) was also reported by some of the teachers in this study as a reason why they did not integrate Aboriginal perspectives on a regular basis. For instance, referring to his Social Studies class, Dan said:

> It's not a Natives Studies class, and I have students from other cultures in the class, not just Aboriginal students. I can integrate Aboriginal perspectives only so much, without getting into trouble with the other kids.

On a positive note, Dan reported that when he incorporated Aboriginal perspectives in his History units, he tried to present the European perspective in the textbook and the Aboriginal perspective (if the resource to do so was available). By presenting the two perspectives, he was exposing his students to the notion of social construction of knowledge and the understanding that all historical accounts are fundamentally politicized. For example, he reported that when he taught about the origins of Aboriginal peoples in North America, he presented the land-bridge theory in the textbook and the emerging theories supporting the claim that Aboriginal peoples have been living in North America from time immemorial. Clearly, presenting two different perspectives on this topic was a transformational approach to integration that would be effective in broadening students' understanding of the topic, and Dan regretted that he did not always have the time and the resources to teach history topics in this way.

Overall, what emerged from these data was that although there is an expressed openness to the inclusion of Aboriginal perspectives in the school curriculum, in practice little or moderate headway is being made, except for a few unique cases like Ann. Applying a critical race theory (CRT; see Chapter 2) framework to the analysis and interpretation of these data, the liberal incremental factor becomes quite evident. The dominant culture teachers' additive and contributions approaches to the integration of Aboriginal perspectives, their limited use of Aboriginal-centred resources, their use of classroom activities (e.g., guest presentations) that seemingly have no impact on how non-Aboriginal students view Aboriginal people, and their reasons for not integrating Aboriginal perspectives on a regular basis are all indicators of a token commitment to integration. They are actions which ensure that curricular reform in this area of Aboriginal education 'would not be sweeping and immediate' and which guarantee that the integration of Aboriginal perspectives, if it happens at all, would not happen quickly but 'incrementally and superficially' (DeCuir & Dixson, 2004, p. 29).

What Teachers Perceive as Challenges/Impediments to Integration

The interviews revealed several issues which the teachers perceived as challenges/impediments to the meaningful integration of Aboriginal perspectives in their schools and classrooms. These issues can be described as: teachers' own lack of knowledge about Aboriginal culture/issues and an accompanying lack of confidence to integrate Aboriginal perspectives; the exclusion of teachers from discussions pertaining to integration; the lack of classroom-ready Aboriginal resources; the racist attitudes of some non-Aboriginal staff and students; school administrators' lukewarm support for integration; and incompatibility between school structures and some cultural values of Aboriginal peoples.

Teachers' lack of knowledge: Topping the teachers' list of challenges was their own lack of the Aboriginal cultural knowledge and understanding required for effective integration. This challenge was identified by all the teachers in this study – Aboriginal and non-Aboriginal alike. The non-Aboriginal (dominant culture) teachers repeatedly mentioned their lack of knowledge about Aboriginal content/topics/issues, the cultural backgrounds and other characteristics of their Aboriginal students, and Aboriginal cultural ways of learning. Teachers' lack of familiarity with Aboriginal approaches to teaching and learning was identified as a particularly serious impediment to integration because it meant that the teachers did not have the pedagogical content knowledge (i.e., the useful forms of knowledge representation, analogies, illustrations, and examples from Aboriginal culture) to make the curriculum comprehensible to Aboriginal students. This diminished teacher capacity seriously compromised teachers' ability to act as 'cultural brokers' (Stairs, cited in Aikenhead & Huntley, 1999) negotiating and moving back and forth between the two cultures (Aboriginal culture and the Eurocentric culture of school and curricula), and helping students deal with cultural conflicts that might arise; it also undermined teachers' efficacy beliefs vis-à-vis the integration of Aboriginal perspectives.

An important question arising from these data, however, is whether the dominant culture teachers' lack of knowledge was simply a passive lack of information, or, in part, an active resistance to the difficult knowledge of cultural differences arising routinely in educational encounters between white, middle class, Euro-Canadian teachers and their ethnic minority culture students such as Aboriginal students. As McPherson (2005) has noted, encounters with difference can generate an uncomfortable sense of strangeness and estrangement between teacher and students; dissonant knowledge therefore tends to be subverted by the ideal of 'ignorance' of its existence, and the promise of cultural reproduction embedded within such an ideal.

For Ann, the Aboriginal teacher in this study, her lack of 'expertise in Aboriginal ways' posed challenges that sometimes left her vulnerable and uncertain. She reported that when she integrated certain aspects of her Ojibway culture into her teaching, or when she was called upon as 'the expert' to deal with some trauma having to do with an Aboriginal student in her school, she was not always sure if she was doing things correctly:

> When, for example, when you have me a young woman, considered a baby in the community, handling and dealing with the kind of spiritual traumas that I am dealing with in this school, and I am doing spiritual teachings in my Native Awareness class because you cannot teach Native perspectives without teaching spirituality, I don't know if I am doing it right … There's lots of rules, lots of protocols about specific times that you don't do certain things and that you do certain things … Every Aboriginal Nation does things differently, you know. Ojibways in Ontario do things differently than Ojibways in Winnipeg … So I feel I am doing a lot of things completely independent and separate from the Aboriginal communities because the non-Aboriginal community wants it, is demanding it, asking for it … but they (the non-Aboriginal community) are doing it in fragments, they are going about it in an unholistic, fragmented way … Now if there was a Native elder here to guide me and say 'this will be the right protocol,' then I'll feel more secure. You cause offence, deep offence if you don't follow protocol (Ann).

On the few occasions that participation from the Aboriginal community had been invited by her school, the knowledge of those invited had been 'treated with disrespect by the school.' Ann referred to the 'conflict' and 'struggle' over knowledge that ensued when the participation of Aboriginal elders and parents was invited by her school:

We've brought in elders before and there's conflict because the elders say it has to be done this way. The principal wants it done this way or the school division wants it done this way, or the teachers want it done this way – it's a struggle. But here is my message for them: If you're going to bring in an elder, you better be prepared to give them the respect and the authority they deserve.

Another example is we had this struggle over how we were going to host the Pow-wow. I mean, we had the (Aboriginal) parents wanting it done a certain way, we had the teachers having another idea about how it should be done … I am really excited about our Aboriginal parent council. It seems like a very empowered group but we need to keep them empowered. We need to act on their voice as if it has meaning. I have seen [White] parents come to this school and make changes happen in this school, individual parents, and I would like to see our Aboriginal parents have that power. I don't feel our Aboriginal parents are as collectively heard as other parents.

Viewed through the lens of racism/anti-racism discursive frameworks (see Chapter 2) the suppression of Aboriginal voice and agency (i.e., individuals' empowerment and abilities to affect their environment and act on their own behalf) in initiatives pertaining to the integration of Aboriginal perspectives in Ann's school constitutes what Scheurich and Young (1997) call 'epistemological racism' – the tendency by the West to marginalize the worldviews of ethnic minorities and people of color, thus excluding them from selfhood and, by definition, political self-representation. As Goldberg (1993) aptly put it, 'The universal claims of Western knowledge, then, colonial or postcolonial, turn necessarily upon the deafening suppression of its various racialized others into silence' (p. 151).

Particularly distressing for the two Aboriginal participants in this study were public school teachers' and school administrators' lack of knowledge about what they (the Aboriginal participants) perceived as the 'real issues' causing school failure and dropout among Aboriginal students who leave their communities to live and study in urban centres. These issues, some of which were captured earlier in Chapter 5, included: homesickness and missing families and cultural traditions; strict boarding home rules; absence of families in the cities; drug and alcohol abuse in families; lack of money; pregnancy or becoming a father; racism; parental worries over their kids in the big cities; death and other important events in the family; preference for life in the 'North'; and difficult school courses delivered in non-Aboriginal languages (English or French) that Aboriginal students may not clearly understand. According to Ann,

> These are some of the real issues. It is difficult, if not impossible to integrate these aspects of Aboriginal culture into the school curriculum and yet they are the important reasons why these kids fail or drop out ... How can the teachers and administrators inform themselves about these issues? It comes back to the basics of learning about Aboriginal communities and building connections and relationships that way. You've got teachers saying I can't make connections with Aboriginal kids and Aboriginal families; we've got a school system saying we can't keep them in, we can't keep them interested, they're feeling isolated.

Arnie (the Aboriginal liaison worker) added:

> The schools do not understand these issues or pretend they do not understand ... and they punish Aboriginal students by failing them and making them repeat courses over and over.

It is obvious here that for both Ann and Arnie, culture was not only the complex and changing phenomenon on which individuals and groups draw to make sense of their lives, it was also the social and economic conditions framing students' lives, conditions which require educators to pay attention to the contexts and communities within which schools operate and to use this community-based knowledge to advance the academic learning of marginalized and low-income students. Gonzalez and colleagues' (2005) 'funds of knowledge' approach provides one way in which teachers could do this. According to this approach, teachers conduct ethnographic studies of the racially, ethnically, and/or socio-economically diverse communities where students live, and develop an understanding and appreciation of the multiple cultural resources or funds of knowledge that students bring to the classroom. Ideally, teachers incorporate this community-based knowledge into the daily processes of classroom teaching and learning. This, in turn, undermines pervasive deficit theories held about people and communities that are not middle-class or do not belong to the dominant culture of the school.

Accompanying the teachers' lack of knowledge base was their lack of confidence, the result of to not having what the teachers called 'the right' to teach Aboriginal cultural knowledge. Ann (the Aboriginal teacher) felt that, because of her relative youth (early 30s), inexperience, and lack of authority pertaining to certain aspects of Aboriginal culture, she had not earned the right to teach certain Aboriginal cultural practices. The dominant culture teachers expressed a similar lack of confidence, because of both to their lack of an Aboriginal knowledge base and the fact that they were not Aboriginal. For example:

> Who am I to be teaching Aboriginal perspectives to Aboriginal kids? Will my knowledge be seen as genuine and congruent with Aboriginal perspectives? (Nick)

> I'll feel like a fraud. As an outsider largely ignorant about Aboriginal issues and cultures, I may end up teaching Aboriginal perspectives in ways that may be seen as disrespectful or denigrating. (Ted)

> Do I have the right to be teaching about Aboriginal culture and issues? Perhaps as a teacher, yes; but as a non-Aboriginal person, I'm not sure. (Doug)

The argument that the non-Aboriginal teachers are propounding here is one that has been the subject of much bitter debate about whether 'outsiders' are taking possession of the knowledge of formerly colonized peoples just as Europeans once took possession of their countries. Taken to its inevitable conclusion, such an argument indicates that the only culture one can study or teach about is one's own. Trends in cultural theory have, however, argued against such a stance and suggested that in cross-cultural situations, we need to move away completely from metaphors of 'possession' of culture towards a consideration of cultural encounters as a new scene of learning (see Dasenbrock, 1992). The evidence from this study suggests the need for teachers to make this move and come to see the integration of Aboriginal perspectives as a site of learning. At this site resides the possibility for mainstream educators to learn who they are in relationship to alternative knowledge frameworks, critically examine how their own culture and biases impact on the students they teach, and transcend taken-for-granted conceptual and organizational arrangements of curriculum, teaching, and learning. It is also the site where teachers weigh concerns about not having 'the right' to teach Aboriginal cultural knowledge against their obligation as public school teachers. As teachers in publicly fund- ed schools, their first moral obligation is to provide excellent instruc- tion by being informed properly about all of their students and using that knowledge to provide a learning environment that promotes and celebrates how students come to know and understand in their learn- ing. This responsibility – fundamental to culturally appropriate, anti- oppressive education, and social justice – should outweigh the concern they expressed that they are not Aboriginal and therefore did not have the right to teach Aboriginal cultural knowledge. In my opinion, teach- ers can always do what it takes to earn that right, as we saw in the case of Mr B in School X (see Chapters 5 and 6).

Exclusion of teachers: Another main concern expressed by the teachers was their perception that teachers were excluded from deliberations pertaining to the implementation of integration in schools and class- rooms. Integration involves not only theoretical abstractions and prin- ciples at the curriculum planning level in ministries of education but also, and most importantly, decisions about actions in the concrete situ- ation of the classroom with real students. Teachers know firsthand that the concrete case cannot be settled by mere application of principle as every concrete case will possess some cogent characteristics that defy even the best-thought-out principle. It is deliberation which operates in such cases to choose appropriate actions. The dominant culture teach- ers, in particular, felt that effective implementation of the integration of Aboriginal perspectives would require deliberation and some unusual kinds of collaborations – for example, school administrators communi- cating with Aboriginal leaders, teachers working and thinking together with Aboriginal communities, and Aboriginal and non-Aboriginal peo- ples interacting with the deepest respect on both sides. Neil felt that 'Manitoba's Ministry of Education will have to coordinate these efforts … we must all work together to implement this reform successfully.'

For these teachers, the excitement about the integration of Aboriginal perspectives resided in the fact that, unlike most new reforms, 'there is yet no established model to follow. It breaks new ground everyday and the task for those involved is to bring all the complex threads into a viable vision of what integration will become' (Sam). According to the teachers, however, this collaboration was not happening. Instead,

> We are witnessing some of the struggle involved in realizing this vision. Some people think that the whole program of reform surrounding the integration of Aboriginal perspectives should be driven solely by the Aboriginal community, forgetting that because teachers are responsible for bringing these changes to the real world of the classroom, we (teachers) should be involved in many aspects of the decision-making. (Nick)

For this same reason, James felt that it would be necessary to include teachers in decisions about how some of the money allocated to the integration initiative should be disbursed: 'We have ideas about how the funds can best be spent to meet the needs of teachers and students. After all, we all know how money assigned for meeting one need in a school system can easily be diverted towards other needs and teachers are left to pick up the pieces.'

Neil commented on what he perceived as the narrow vision (as opposed to a more inclusive vision) in the integration documents he had seen so far: 'Most of the documents focus on the benefits for Aboriginal students and how to get through to Aboriginal students, leaving teachers to figure out how to make this work for the other students in a mixed classroom. It [integration] is a laudable idea that should have been happening already but we need to sit together and figure out how to make it work for all students.' Starnes (2006) concurs that the integration of Native perspectives relies on collaboration among unusual allies if it is to succeed. As each of the parties enters this unfamiliar territory there will be disagreements and moments of frustration but 'to expect less would minimize the depth and breadth of the revolutionary vision we are seeking to bring into being' (p. 19).

Lack of resources: Integration of Aboriginal perspectives requires culturally appropriate Aboriginal resources that are ready for classroom use in schools. Like the teachers in our two-year study in Schools X and Y (see Chapters 4 and 5) the teachers in this research often cited the lack of such resources as a significant challenge to integration. Often, appropriate Aboriginal content is not part of the mandated curriculum and eight of the non-Aboriginal teachers in this study referred to the non-availability of relevant Aboriginal curriculum resources. For example, teachers pointed out that most curriculum materials available on the

Internet were relevant to Native American students in the United States, not Canadian Aboriginal students. However, while this assertion may have been true a few years ago, many of the items on the resource list I provided in Appendix A at the end of Chapter 6 show that Internet and other resources relevant to Aboriginal students in Canadian classrooms are now available. The committed teacher only needs to avail himself or herself of this learning opportunity by locating and adapting these materials for their own classroom use.

Lack of funding for the services of Aboriginal community members/ elders as an educational resource, coupled with the fact that the teachers did not personally know these community elders, was also cited as a challenge to integration. For instance:

'I don't know these people personally. I don't know who has the expertise and the authority to speak in my class ... I think that's a problem for many of us.' (Neil)

The community elders are asking to be paid for their time as guest speakers ... and who can blame them for asking? But the school has no funds set aside for that. (Dan)

I invited Arnie and Ann to speak in my class. Four weeks passed before they were able to come ... four weeks! It's frustrating. (James)

On the other hand, Tim said he could not relate to the other teachers' inability to access resources. According to him, he took personal responsibility for taking advantage of the Aboriginal resources available at Aboriginal education resource centers in the city: 'I telephone the Aboriginal education directorate for guest speakers and other resources, and I always get good responses.' However, James and Doug felt that if Aboriginal resources are available, they should be easily accessible to schools rather than have teachers calling or running around Aboriginal centers looking for them: 'I know that good teachers go searching anyway, but I am teaching two new courses this year ... so I'm doing lots and lots of searching. But it's tiring, searching for all this stuff' (James).

Professional development workshops on Aboriginal education were generally not considered a helpful educational resource because: 'The workshops are typically run on weekdays when we are in class ... and there is no funding to bring in substitute teachers for us to attend consistently' (Neil).

Furthermore, some of the teachers reported that they were turned off by 'the blame and victimization approach' to many of these educational workshops, conferences and meetings:

> It depends on how it (workshop/conference/meeting) is presented. I mentioned the blame and victimization approach a few minutes ago. If it is presented like that, it's a real turn off for people ... if it's proactive, you can see that it's got a purpose. Then it's much more effective. I have been to both kinds, believe me. (Tim)

> At this meeting we asked, 'What can we do to help?' And they told us about how the land was stolen 400 years ago and it's the white people's fault, etc. And you know what? It turned off quite a few people, a few people like me. I don't react against those stories but it's not enough. (James)

What appears to be emerging here is an ahistorical view of integration among some dominant-culture teachers. While they expressed regret about not having the resources to learn and teach about the issues affecting the lives of Aboriginal peoples today, they seemed reluctant to see the relevance of history to a fuller understanding of these issues. By describing any reference to the origins of some of today's Aboriginal issues as a 'blame and victimization approach,' and by proposing a 'proactive' approach that left the issues unexamined, the teachers were undercutting the specific historical and cultural struggle that should be part of any particular life in the present. Monture-Angus (1999, p. 26) describes why a historical perspective is necessary, given the impact of colonial legacies on Aboriginal peoples:

> To try to address the present-day manifestations of the historical oppression as singular, distinct and individualized, without a clear understanding of colonial causation and the subsequent multiplication of forms of social disorder, is to offer only a superficial opportunity for change ... Such remedies, as they are incomplete, do not offer any real change. The need for historical honesty is not a need to blame others for the present-day realities, but a plea for the opportunity to deal with all of the layers and multiplications of oppression that permeate Aboriginal lives and Aboriginal communities today.

She goes on to declare that when any process that is intended to address historical wrongs is received with guilt or anger by non-Aboriginal people, 'Aboriginal pain is appropriated and then transformed. This transformation is a recreation of colonial relationships' (p. 26).

The two Aboriginal participants in the study insisted that this history – 'this return to the past in order to move forward' – must be brought to deliberations about integrating Aboriginal perspectives.

Racism: Racist attitudes of dominant cultural groups were also identified as posing a challenge to integration. Teachers pointed out that there is a perception among some teachers and school administrators that integration is not relevant to majority culture students and is, therefore, not worth spending money or other resources on. Doug cited an example of this perception: 'There is a feeling out there that we have nothing to learn from Aboriginal people, and this is simply not true.'

For Ann, integration would be much more effective and likely to succeed if dominant culture teachers abandoned their racist attitudes and went out into the Aboriginal community 'to learn about the people, the culture, the language, and the issues.'

Overwhelmingly, the teachers identified racist, stereotypical images of Aboriginal peoples held by some of their non-Aboriginal colleagues and students as a most difficult challenge. For example:

> In my school the anger and resentment are sometimes palpable. They always feel these people [Aboriginal people] are getting something for free.' (Sam)

> I think the discussions in my class help students a bit to understand some of the issues, for instance why Natives are making land claims. But what I think a lot of them have from home is resentment over Natives getting special treatment or special consideration. (Mike)

According to the teachers, changing these images and attitudes was proving to be difficult. Textbooks and other curriculum materials may no longer carry overt racist portrayals of Aboriginal and other non-European peoples but, as the foregoing discussion suggests, negative images of Aboriginal peoples are still prevalent in the minds and attitudes of the mainstream. Unfortunately, the teachers' apparent unwillingness to locate and analyse Aboriginal issues within historical contexts may be inadvertently contributing to the difficulty they were experiencing changing these attitudes among their students.

Negative, stereotypical images of Aboriginal peoples were cited by all the teachers as the main reason why Aboriginal students tended to deny their Aboriginal ancestry/identity and disconnect themselves from Aboriginal culture, a phenomenon that poses a major challenge to integration. The Aboriginal participants in this study pointed out their frustration with this disconnect, but described it as a coping and survival mechanism for Aboriginal peoples in a racist society: 'I mean, you wouldn't want to ask my mom to identify herself because she was taught by her grandmother that you want to look and act as white as possible because it's just easier for you' (Arnie).

Aikenhead and Huntley (1999) wrote that teachers reported a similar disconnect among Aboriginal students when they (teachers) attempted to incorporate Aboriginal cultural knowledge in Science classes in Saskatchewan. Such disconnectedness has been identified as a concern for many Aboriginal educators (e.g., Battiste and Barman, 1995; Cajete, 1994). According to Ann, meaningful integration of Aboriginal perspectives could change this attitude among Aboriginal students:

> In my classroom, when it's purposeful and in the right context, then the kids will identify themselves. Like in my Native Awareness class everyone is proud to identify themselves as Aboriginal – the context makes it easier for them to do so.

The challenge for schools, it seems, is to find sensitive and meaningful ways of integrating Aboriginal traditional values and knowledge so that students will feel connected to their Aboriginal culture even as they acquire the knowledge and codes of the dominant culture through school curricula.

Schools administrators' lukewarm support for integration: Teachers perceived their schools' or school divisions' support of integration as lukewarm and inconsistent with integration defined as the infusion of Aboriginal perspectives into all school structures and activities (e.g., Nick said, 'The rhetoric certainly exists but full commitment to integration still has to be seen'). The teachers spoke about their schools' additive approach of 'introducing initiatives here and there' without the commitment to effectively support and sustain these initiatives on a long-term basis. Ann, for instance, expressed great joy over her school's adoption of the Native Awareness course as an elective open to all students in the school. She, however, expressed regret that only thirty minutes of instructional time per week had been assigned to the course, compared to 50 minutes daily or two or three times per week for other courses. She commented: 'By the time the students settle down or my Native guest presenters arrive, the period is over.'

Lack of sustainable funding for initiatives such as the hiring of Aboriginal community liaison workers or, as mentioned before, honorariums for the services of Aboriginal elders and guest speakers was also identified as an indication of school administrators' lukewarm support for integration. For example, during our interviews, Arnie (the Aboriginal liaison worker) said,

> The position of Aboriginal community liaison officer was created five yeas ago in this school division. There are sixteen schools in the division and only three liaison officers, only three. They are the lowest paid, are given no authority by the school and are forever running around, not providing cultural teaching and information, but dealing with traumas and disciplinary problems among Aboriginal students in the schools ... No wonder the officers quit so often. I am the third one here in only five years.

When a liaison worker was invited into a classroom it was done at the discretion of the teacher. It was the teacher who decided when the liaison worker should visit the class and what to talk about. Arnie's frustration with this approach was evident:

> I have so much more I can teach here – Aboriginal cultural dances, stories, and arts – but I am not given the opportunity. I once asked the principal if I was just a token hire and she said, 'No, we need you.' But I do not feel valued here.

The interest convergence factor in critical race theory, rather than any meaningful commitment to integration, is what emerges from these descriptions of school administrators' lukewarm support for integration. Aboriginal peoples are the fastest growing population in Canada. In human capital terms, therefore, school dropout among them would not only reduce their potential as a tax base, labour pool, and a critical mass with economic clout, but also, they would become an economic burden on the larger society. For these reasons and also because of political pressure from the Aboriginal community and their supporters, schools are under pressure from the White majoritary culture and the federal and provincial governments to integrate Aboriginal perspectives into curricula to enhance the opportunities for academic success among Aboriginal students. The demand on schools to create such opportunities converge with the economic self-interests of White elites who want these opportunities offered but in ways that do not disrupt or dismantle their 'normal' hold over the education system – hence, for example, the token hiring of a limited number of Aboriginal liaison workers, who concurrently serve the school's own interests by being deployed to deal with trauma and disciplinary problems among Aboriginal students that the school cannot deal with. These self-interests of White society and those of the school converge with Aboriginal peoples' desire for the school education of their children to be grounded in Aboriginal cultural realities. Evidently the token approaches to the integration of Aboriginal perspectives, observed in the classrooms and described by the teachers in this study, suggest that this desire will not be quickly fulfilled. In fact, soon after our interviews with the teachers, the Native Awareness course and the position of Aboriginal liaison worker in Ann's school were shut down.

Incompatibility between school structures and some Aboriginal cultural values/practices: The two Aboriginal participants in this study pointed out that schools, as currently structured, posed difficult challenges to the integration of some Aboriginal cultural values and practices into school curricula. They provided three examples of incompatibility between school structures and Aboriginal culture: (a) Incompatibility between schools' rigid approach to dealing with time and Aboriginal people's more flexible view of time; (b) incompatibility between schools' large classes and Aboriginal teaching methods such as the talking circle; and (c) incompatibility between the regimentation of the classroom experience and some Aboriginal peoples' cultural value of 'non-interference' in child-rearing practices in some Aboriginal communities. Ann spoke at length about what she called 'the tyranny of time' and how clock-time controlled everything in Western culture, to the extent where people did not listen to their bodies or their emotional and spiritual needs, and how this contributed to the problem of school attendance and punctuality for some Aboriginal students:

> The way that our school system runs is one of the most oppressive, timed structures that you're going to find ... this is appalling to Aboriginal peoples ... Umm, it is believed by Aboriginal peoples, and even by some Europeans, to be an incredibly oppressive culture in the way we control people through time, and the way we expect people to get up at times when their bodies cannot cope with getting up ... We don't listen to our

physical needs; we don't listen to our spiritual and emotional needs; we don't listen to our bodies ... And so Aboriginal people will not be controlled by time. They will not be, and the other side doesn't get it. Our society is barbaric in the way it runs on time scheduling and I believe it's ill-nurturing to the intellect, to the emotional and spiritual well-being of our people.

So these (Aboriginal) kids have issues to deal with, like a death in the family. They need time to grieve, to recuperate and so they don't show up in school for some time. What happens if you don't show up for Math class every single day? You fall behind and you might as well forget it ... They're too lost and that's considered their fault because they don't show up, and every year we keep flunking them in Grade 9 Math ... and then after three years of doing that, they sit in the halls and do nothing or stop showing up altogether. You want to integrate Aboriginal culture, these are the issues you need to consider.

I asked Ann how she thought the problem of school attendance and punctuality among Aboriginal students could be addressed. She suggested a flexible and modular approach to course scheduling, something she described as successful in a mixed school located in the Greater Winnipeg area, with a high population of Aboriginal students:

I talked with the people from Portage High School (pseudonym) and they have a system ... They run their English, Math, and Social Studies courses as modules for five or six weeks at a time, and they teach each course two hours in the morning and two hours in the afternoon ... same topics are covered each time. They run one course module and then move to another course module. If something happens where you are missing a lot of classes in those weeks, then you don't get those credits, but then there is another starting again – same topics. And if you cannot be there in the morning you can attend in the afternoon ... so you'll have all these chances.

She then went on to propose another flexible alternative to current class scheduling:

Like in my Grade 12 ELA and Native Awareness classes ... you have kids that come every single time; but for others who do not, we can do independent stuff (study). We can say come in and pick up this book and try to read it at home. I mean, one Aboriginal girl in my ELA class, very bright girl, was getting 80%. But what happened with this girl? ... Umm, her boyfriend who was incarcerated was let out, came back, moved into the house, brought his alcohol with him, brought all the trauma back ... and in about a month, her whole studies went whoosh. I kept with her, I kept phoning her. We were so close to graduation; there was only one more book to cover. So she finally came and picked up the book ... and she read it at home, came back and we had a big, long discussion about it, right? So I try to be flexible that way and I know some of the other teachers do, and that's looking at things from an Aboriginal perspective.

We spoke about the Aboriginal cultural value of 'non-interference' (see Chapter 3) in traditional Aboriginal education where adult imposition is minimal and the will and decisions of the child are respected. Formal (Western) schooling, on the other hand, is seen as an imposing and adversarial system where student ideas and behaviours are directly challenged and criticized, often in the public arena of the classroom. According to Ann and Arnie, this drives some Aboriginal students away from the system. Arnie provided an example:

I was in a class a few weeks ago, waiting to speak ... A female student came in and this teacher said, 'Welcome back, tourist.' It was an Aboriginal student, and she turned right round and left ... She was made to feel ashamed by the teacher, without talking to her about whatever issue she was dealing with that had kept her away from school. This was totally disrespectful of that student.

A final example of incompatibility cited was that between school structures such as large classes (over twenty students) with fixed time schedules for each class period (usually 50 or 55 minutes), and the use of Aboriginal teaching methods such as the talking/discussion circle. Ann explained the incompatibility:

I love the talking circle, and so do other teachers who have used it. In the circle you are all equal and no one is in charge or in control of the conversations. You speak when you're ready and you speak for as long as you like without interruption, you are not timed. But how can you have, say, a literature circle with thirty students and only fifty minutes of scheduled class time? Will everyone be able to speak? It's a real challenge ... I have dealt with it by sometimes having an inner circle of speakers and an outer circle of listeners during one lesson and then they change positions during the next class but it's not ideal.

The incompatibilities described in this section echo the concern over authentic portrayal of Aboriginal perspectives expressed by the enrichment teachers in our second study (see Chapter 5) and illustrate clearly that Aboriginal peoples' objective of breaking free from a colonial legacy of education cannot be achieved within the conventional education system. As Schissel and Wotherspoon (2003) have written, education functions not simply as a vehicle by which Aboriginal peoples are able to gain access to opportunities and credentials historically denied them, 'but more importantly, it becomes a means by which their heritage, identities, and future prospects can be linked together in ways that are meaningful to them' (p. 122). To what extent can public schooling realistically foster the cultural identity development of Aboriginal peoples when formal education sometimes blatantly conflicts with the values and practices of the homes and communities of Aboriginal students? Evidently, a range of alternative arrangements is needed with school systems in order to accommodate the developmental and learning needs of diverse students.

Facilitators of Integration

So what did teachers perceive as facilitators of meaningful integration of Aboriginal perspectives in schools and classrooms? Responses to this question were mainly in the form of suggestions for addressing the challenges/impediments which the teachers had earlier identified. Many began by acknowledging some of the initiatives already in place in their schools for implementing the integration of Aboriginal perspectives – initiatives such as the establishment of implementation committees to develop and oversee integration policies and plans, the establishment of Aboriginal curriculum development committees, the hiring of a few Aboriginal community liaison workers by some school divisions, the occasional hosting of Aboriginal cultural events by some schools (e.g., the Pow-wow), and some professional development opportunities for teachers.

The teachers, however, said that much more was needed to facilitate effective integration. For example, they strongly believed that the key to successful integration was the strengthening of what they called *teachers' professional efficacy*, but that this requirement was not being sufficiently addressed by their school administrators. Similar to teacher capacity described in Chapter 6, professional efficacy referred to security in the professional knowledge teachers needed for implementing integration (e.g., knowledge about Aboriginal culture/topics/issues, and knowledge about pedagogical strategies that are effective with particular groups of Aboriginal students). Such professional efficacy, teachers felt, could be achieved through initial teacher education and professional development opportunities for practising teachers. Some of the teachers reported knowing colleagues who wanted to integrate Aboriginal perspectives but could not do so because they did know what to integrate and how to integrate it effectively.

This discussion led us again into the topic of *resource adequacy* in the facilitation of effective integration. Dan, for instance, remarked:

> Right now, I am doing the unit on 'Canadian Government' with my Grade 11 class and I would like to incorporate Native government as much as possible, for example, traditional Aboriginal ways of governing, and where they are currently going with Aboriginal self-government. I have found tons of policy papers on self-government but I still cannot find student-level materials for use on this topic.

From this sample comment, and as highlighted in our second study (see Chapters 5 and 6) it can be seen that teachers placed a high premium on classroom-ready resources for integration into curricula. CAAS (2003), however, has pointed out that simply making resources available to teachers does not mean that they understand the materials or even use them in their classrooms. This reiterates the need for help through *professional development opportunities* for teachers unfamiliar with Aboriginal cultures and histories, so that appropriate materials and the contexts in which to use them can be identified. Unanimously, the teachers in this study perceived this type of professional development as a critical factor in the preparation of teachers for their role as cultural brokers and curriculum integrators.

Sustainable funding that enables teachers to draw on the Aboriginal community as an educational resource, and *respect for and recognition of the expertise* of such resource persons by teachers and school administrators, were cited as potential facilitators of integration, as were support and leadership from school administrators. The teachers fully expected their school divisions and school *principals to act as leaders and catalysts* for integration. As Neil put it, 'They are the school leaders, they are in a strong position to not only recognize how the school system marginalizes certain groups of students but also how to address issues of social justice and inequities in the school system.'

Mentioned by almost all the teachers in the study was the need for *change in school culture* if integration is to succeed. Fullan (1993) observed that curriculum interventions tended to leave the basic policies and practices of schools intact, often ignoring the fact that changes in the core culture of teaching require major transformation in the culture of the school. From the teachers' descriptions of school administrators' lukewarm support for integration, the absence of interest in and enthusiasm for integration among most dominant culture teachers in their schools, the sporadic resource support for integration initiatives, and the additive approach to integration observed among teachers and school administration, it is clear that changes are needed in the cultures of schools if integration is not to remain an empty rhetoric. Bringing about lasting cultural change involves effective school leadership and high quality research aimed at understanding the school contexts where the change is to occur. Sam suggested some directions for this: 'The school leader has to define clearly the values and relationships that need to be developed to facilitate the change.' Leadership also has to recognize the importance of action. As Reeves (2007, p. 30) writes, 'The greatest impediment to meaningful cultural change in the school is the gap between what leaders say they value and what they actually do.' Speeches and announcements are not enough to lead challenging reform efforts. The school leader must be ready to make personal changes in areas such as policy decision-making and resource allocation to back words with action. High quality research is integral to lasting cultural change, for research provides insights into the forces at work within the schools, identify the impediments to change, and utilize the information as the foundation from which discussion and focused change can begin.

Summary

The study reported in this chapter is important because its findings will help policy-makers and educators plan approaches to the integration of Aboriginal perspectives that are informed by teachers' perceptions of such integration. Among the useful insights suggested and replicated in previous studies (see Chapters 5 and 6, for example) are the following:

- To increase the efficacy beliefs and the confidence of teachers for the integration of Aboriginal perspectives, schools and faculties of education should provide opportunities for *all* teachers, non-Aboriginal and Aboriginal alike, to learn about Aboriginal culture/issues/perspectives. This is best done through pre-service teacher education programs, and in schools, through ongoing professional development opportunities for practising teachers and the utilization of the expertise of Aboriginal community members. In both routes, priority should be given to educating teachers about Aboriginal history, issues, pedagogical practices and social interaction patterns for specific groups of Aboriginal students, background knowledge about the particular Aboriginal students in teachers' classrooms, and support systems that increase/enhance Aboriginal student learning in the public school system. Until teachers feel comfortable with their level of knowledge of Aboriginal perspectives, they will not feel confident to implement this reform in their classrooms.
- Schools should provide support that enables practising teachers to take advantage of educational opportunities pertaining to Aboriginal perspectives, for example, sustainable funding that facilitates release time for teachers to attend workshops which typically fall on weekdays when teachers are teaching. This may prove effective in preparing teachers for their role as cultural brokers and curriculum integrators of Aboriginal perspectives.
- Curriculum development units in ministries of education and Aboriginal education agencies should involve teachers in deliberations about integration and work with teachers in respectful ways to implement the integration of Aboriginal perspectives into school curricula. This means encouraging all teachers to enter the process in ways that are comfortable and appropriate for them within their teaching environment, their subject areas, and their skill sets.
- Curriculum development units and schools should provide teachers with easy access to Aboriginal resources that are ready for classroom use. As Aikenhead and Huntley (1999) have noted, teachers who want to help Aboriginal students to succeed in school through the integration of Aboriginal culture/perspectives into the school curriculum must not be undermined by a lack of instructional resources. Resources must be grounded in Aboriginal world-views, flexible enough to meet a variety of teaching and learning styles and situations, and easily integrated into different subject areas. It is recognized that these resource demands are being made within cur-

rent contexts of reduced state funding for education and other social services and, therefore, schools are increasingly finding it difficult to meet new demands. However, the goal to increase educational success for Aboriginal students requires nothing less than new resources and/or the re-allocation of existing resources and services.

- School curricula and textbooks in every subject area must include Aboriginal culture/ content/ issues/ topics/ perspectives, and teachers' pedagogies must integrate these perspectives on a consistent basis. By substantially withholding the cultural knowledge and perspectives of Aboriginal and other ethnic minority students, the curriculum serves to inculcate them into participating in their own oppression.
- High-quality research needs to be conducted on the cultures of schools to know the challenges and resistances to integration, and utilize the data as foundation for policy and practice in the integration of Aboriginal perspectives.
- School principals and school divisions must back their integration rhetoric with action, and they must act as leaders and catalysts for integration.
- Provincial governments must work in concert with faculties of education to put more effort and resources into the training and hiring of Aboriginal teachers. Aboriginal teachers may understand the cultural values of their communities and students, infuse the Eurocentric curriculum with their cultural knowledge, act as cultural brokers and positive role models, and may instill high self-esteem in Aboriginal students. To this effect an aggressive plan to enroll more Aboriginal students in teacher education programs can include strategies such as identifying and tracking Aboriginal students within the secondary school system and providing them with financial incentives to enter teacher education programs.
- Schools must allocate part of their budget to providing and sustaining funding for educational resource persons, such as Aboriginal liaison workers who help parents and community members understand curriculum and school policies and Aboriginal guest teachers and speakers who bring unique Aboriginal knowledge and perspectives to the classroom. Part of the funds can also be used to provide symbolic gifts like tobacco which should be offered to community elders whenever a request is made to visit a school. In Native culture, to offer tobacco is to pay an ultimate respect to that which you are asking.

- The roles, expertise, and authority of Aboriginal elders/experts as resource persons must be recognized and respected by teachers, students, and school principals. To help students to understand and more fully utilize the knowledge and expertise of these community resource persons, teachers should ensure that invited presentations are preceded by an introduction, explanation, and frame of reference that create a context for what is presented. Otherwise, the import would be lost on students. In addition, teachers and students have special responsibility for protecting the Aboriginal knowledge shared with them. Whenever knowledge is shared outside the cultural context where it originates, there is the potential for misunderstanding and misuse. Protection of Indigenous knowledge refers to the appropriate sharing of knowledge in ways that acknowledge that some knowledge is sacred, that is, involving the recognized spiritual entity, the land, and the ancestors. Sacredness should be interpreted in a manner appropriate to the particular context and community. Thus, care should be taken to ensure that cultural information considered to be confidential will be obtained from a person recognized by the community as a knowledge-keeper authorized to disclose that knowledge. Brant Castellano (2000) notes Aboriginal people know that knowledge is power and that power can be used for good or for evil. In passing on knowledge, therefore, the teacher has an obligation to consider whether the learner is ready to use knowledge responsibly. We must also guard against appropriation or misappropriation as we seek to integrate Aboriginal peoples' cultural knowledge into the conventional school system. As Dei and colleagues (2000) warn, 'The process of validating Indigenous knowledges must not lead to Indigenous people losing control and ownership of knowledge' (p. 47). Finally, as a reviewer of this book pointed out and as Smith (1999) reiterates in the context of doing research with and among Indigenous populations, it is important to remember that some insider knowledges and practices are absolutely confidential and sacred, and hence there are ethical limits to the degree to which teachers and researchers can or should pursue community knowledge. As the reviewer wrote, the need to integrate Aboriginal perspectives brings with it the responsibility to so in an ethical way.
- Aboriginal parents must be empowered (e.g., through education) to get involved in their children's education by serving on school com-

mittees and participating in school events and decision making. In this regard their voices and perspectives must be accorded respect and recognition by the school.

- Schools need to consider changes to certain existing school structures such as timetabling and course scheduling. For example, instead of offering five or six subjects per day, schools could try the modular approach suggested by Ann in this study, where only two or three subjects (modules) are taught per term, offered at different times of the day so that if students cannot be in class at a particular time of day, they can have the course at a different time of day. Also, longer class periods (say 75 minutes per period) could be considered so that Aboriginal teaching methods such as the sharing circle, where each student has a comfortable opportunity to speak, can be used.

Concluding Remark

One of the challenges facing the Canadian public education system today is educating diverse students for meaningful and successful participation in the society. This challenge is compounded when there is a wide social-cultural divide between those charged with the responsibility of delivering this education and the students for whom it is intended. This study has explored one of the most controversial responses to this challenge as it affects Aboriginal education, namely, the integration of Aboriginal cultural knowledge and perspectives into the school curriculum, particularly focusing on how classroom teachers perceive integration. The voices of the teachers suggest that integration holds great potential for learning about and from Aboriginal peoples, nurturing the self-esteem and school success of Aboriginal students, and democratizing the educational system. The process, however, is also fraught with enormous challenges. These challenges are not insurmountable if all stakeholders concerned – school administrators, the government, educational researchers, teacher educators, teachers, and the Aboriginal community – play their parts and work together to facilitate the integration process. The findings and recommendations of this study could assist each of these stakeholders in playing their parts meaningfully to address the current inequalities that characterize schooling, inequalities that have, for generations, produced economic, social, and educational inequity for Aboriginal peoples.

QUESTIONS FOR DISCUSSION

1. Summarize in point form the challenges to integration reported by the teachers in this study. In small groups of two or three, choose two of these challenges and discuss them in your group, using the following questions to guide your discussion: Based on your knowledge and experience, would you say that these challenges are real or are they just perceptions? What do you see as the sources of the problems /challenges you chose for your small group discussion? As teachers, are you able to address these challenges? If so, how? If not, where can you turn for help?
2. Do you agree with Tim and James that most (White) teachers are turned off by what they call 'the blame and victimization approach' to professional development workshops on Aboriginal education? Provide reasons for your position on this issue.
3. Should teachers adopt an 'ahistorical' approach to the integration of Aboriginal perspectives in order to achieve social cohesion and move forward or do you agree with the Aboriginal teachers in this study that 'we must return to the past – history – to move forward'?
4. Discuss, first in small groups and then as a whole class, what you see as the advantages and disadvantages of Ann's flexible alternatives to current class scheduling in order to include/accommodate Aboriginal students. Are there other approaches to school and class scheduling that can work for the benefit of all students?
5. As a teacher or prospective teacher, what do you see or know as facilitators and challenges of integration that has not been included in this chapter?

REFERENCES/RECOMMENDED READINGS

Agne, K.J., Greenwood, G., & Miller, D. (1994). Relationship between teacher perceptions and belief systems and teacher effectiveness. *Journal of Research and Development in Education, 27*(1), 141–52
Aikenhead, G.S., & Huntley, B. (1999). Teachers' views on Aboriginal students learning Western science. *Canadian Journal of Native Education, 23*(2), 159–75.
Banks, J.A. (1989). *Multicultural education: Issues and perspectives.* Needham Heights, MA: Allyn & Bacon.
Battiste, M., & Barman, J. (Eds.). (1995). *First Nations education in Canada: The circle unfolds.* Vancouver: University of British Columbia Press.

Brant Castellano, M. (2000). Updating Aboriginal traditions of knowledge. In
G.S. Dei, B.L. Hall, & D.G. Rosenberg (Eds.), *Indigenous knowledge in global
contexts: Multiple readings of our world*, pp. 21–36. Toronto: University of
Toronto Press.

Britzman, D.P., Valles, K.A., Munoz, G.M., & Lamash, L. (1993). Slips that
show and tell: Fashioning multiculture as a problem of representation. In C.
McCarthy & W. Crichlow (Eds.), *Race, identity and representation in education*,
pp. 188–200. New York: Routledge.

Brophy, J., & Good, T. (1970). Teachers' communications of differential
expectations for children's classrrom performance: Some behavioural data.
Journal of educational Psychology, 61(5), 365–74.

Cajete, G.A. (1994). *Look to the mountains: Anthology of Native education.* Skyland, NC: Kivaki Press.

Carson, T.R. (2003). *Negotiating identities: Subjectivities, curriculum change, and
teacher development.* Paper presented at the International Conference on the
Advancement of Curriculum Studies. Shanghai, China.

Coalition for the Advancement of Aboriginal Studies (CAAS) (2003). *Learning
about walking in beauty: Placing Aboriginal perspectives in Canadian classrooms.*
Retrieved 25 June 2009 from www.crr.ca.

Dasenbrock, R.W. (1992). Teaching multicultural literature. In R. Trimmer & T.
Warnock (Eds.), *Understanding others: Culture and cross-cultural studies and the
teaching of literature*, pp. 35–46. Urbana, IL: NCTE.

Day, C., Calderhaed, J., & Denicolo, P. (1993). *Understanding professional development.* London: Falmer Press.

DeCuir, J.T., & Dixon, A.D. (2004). 'So when it comes they aren't surprised that
it's there': Using critical race theory as a tool of analysis of race and racism
in education. *Educational Researcher, 33*(5), 26–31.

Dei, G.S., Hall, B.L., & Rosenberg, D.G. (Eds.). (2000). *Indigenous knowledge in
global contexts: Multiple readings of our world.* Toronto: University of Toronto
Press.

Fullan, M. (1993). *Change forces: Probing the depths of educational reform.* London:
Falmer Press.

– (2001). *Leading in the culture of change.* London: Jossey-Bass.

Goldberg, D.T. (1993). *Racist culture: Philosophy and the politics of meaning.*
Oxford: Blackwell.

Gonzalez, N., Moll, L., & Amanti, C. (2005). *Funds of knowledge: Theorizing practices in households, communities, and classrooms.* Mahwah, NJ: Erlbaum.

Kanu, Y. (1995). The effect of professional development on teacher thinking
and action. *Education 2000: A South Asia Publication, 3*(4), 1–21.

– (2002). In their own voices: First Nations students identify some cultural mediators of their learning in the formal school system. *Alberta Journal of Educational Research, 48*(2), 98–121.

Kirkness, V.J. (1998). Our peoples' education: Cut the shackles, cut the crap, cut the mustard. *Canadian Journal of Native Education, 22*(1), 10–15.

Lincoln, Y., & Guba, E. (1985). *Naturalistic inquiry.* Thousand Oaks: Sage.

Luce, S., & Hoge, R. (1979). Relations among teacher rankings, pupil-teacher interactions and academic achievement. *American Educational Research Journal, 15*(4), 489–500.

McAlpine, L. (2001). Teacher training for the new wilderness: Quantum leaps. In P.K. Binda with Sharilyn Caillou (Eds.), *Aboriginal education in Canada: A study in de-colonization,* pp. 105–19. Mississauga, ON: Canadian Educators Press.

McPherson, S. (2005). Researching Liminal Englishes in ESL classrooms: An interdisciplinary meditation on 'superstition' and the 'strange.' *Journal of Curriculum Theorizing, 21*(1), 39–56.

Monture-Angus, P. (1999). *Journeying forward: Dreaming First Nations independence.* Halifax: Fernwood Publishing.

Reeves, D. (2007). Leading to change: How do you change school culture? *Science in the Spotlight, 64*(4), 92–4.

Rose, J., & Medway, F. (1981b). Teacher locus of control, teacher behaviour and student behavioural determinants of achievement. *Journal of Educational Research, 74*(6), 375–81.

Scheurich, J.J., & Young, M.D. (1997). Coloring epistemology: Are our research epistemologies racially biased? *Educational Researcher, 26*(4), 4–16.

Smith, L.T. (1999). *Decolonizing methodologies: Research and Indigenous peoples.* London & New York: Zed Books.

Starnes, B.A. (2006). Montana's Indian education for all: Toward an education worthy of American ideals. *Phi Delta Kappan, 88*(3), 184–92.

Strike, K.A., & Posner, G.T. (1985). A conceptual change view of learning and understanding. In L.H. West & J.A. Pines (Eds.), *Cognitive structure and conceptual change,* pp. 163–88. San Diego: Academic Press.

8 A Way Forward: Lessons in Implementation

This concluding chapter discusses the broad implications of our three research studies for curriculum and educational policy, practice, and further research. It draws on the lessons and insights gained from the studies to generate curriculum visions/futures and make recommendations for building capacity for the integration of Aboriginal perspectives in classrooms.

My intellectual and political objective in undertaking the studies reported in this book has been to provide a critical and informed perspective on some salient questions and issues surrounding the integration of Aboriginal cultural knowledge and perspectives into school curricula, particularly what to integrate, how to integrate it, the impact of such integration on school success for Aboriginal students, and teachers' perspectives on this integration. Beginning with the premise that people are the experts of their own lives, I interrogated the views and voices of Aboriginal students and public school teachers on these issues as well as assessing the impact of the integration of Aboriginal perspectives on academic achievement, class attendance and participation, and school retention among diverse Aboriginal students. Critical analyses of the data, using an eclectic theoretical approach that helped illuminate the multidimensional nature of school underperformance among Aboriginal students, revealed schools and schooling processes as sites of capital to which some, like Aboriginal students, have unequal access. Although there is intent on the part of the education system to redress some of these inequities, for example, through the integration of Aboriginal perspectives into school curricula, it is impossible to make the necessary changes without the system turning against itself or, as Dei and colleagues put it, 'without dismantling the very structures that allow schools to function' (1997, p. 221). This tension and contradiction became evident throughout our research studies, most notably in the incompatibilities revealed between school structures and some pedagogical practices valued in some Aboriginal communities. As Kawagley (1995, p. 36) observed in his exploration of the relationship between the formal (Western) education system and local and traditional ways of knowing among the Inuit of Alaska, 'The modern public schools were not made to accommodate difference in worldviews but to impose another culture – their own.'

My goal in this chapter is to bury the ghost of imposed curriculum, past and present, which continues to haunt and influence educational practices that produce schooling difficulties for Aboriginal students, and draw on the findings of our research to invoke curriculum theory/ /vision /futures that beckon towards a more livable form of school life for Aboriginal students. In doing so, I stand on the shoulders of a long tradition of critical challenges to past and present educational practices as I grapple with two questions of particular import to this book: Which institutional and curricular contexts best foster the successful integration of Aboriginal perspectives into schooling processes? How might curriculum become affected by what is made possible through this integration? I begin with the premise, based on our research, that the answer to these two questions begins with a radical reconceptualization of curriculum theory.

On the Need for a Reconceptualized Theory of Curriculum

In his introduction to *Curriculum Visions* Noel Gough (Doll & Gough, 2002, p. 15) writes: 'The work of generating futures in curriculum is chiefly concerned with correcting errors (in the broadest understanding of the term) in the past,' and I would add, in the present. The genesis of these errors, I believe, is Western empiricism with its quest for certainty, predictability, and the desire to bring every aspect of the world under human (Western) control. This has created a constricted and unbalanced sense of knowing and being that lies at the heart of modern thinking about curriculum. It has also resulted in authoritarian, unilateral, and imposed control that has taken the shape of structures and hierarchies of knowledge which constricts notions of what it means to know, to do, and to feel. Within these highly controlled structures and hierarchies of knowledge traditional, local, and indigenous ways of knowing and being – for example, through experiential learning, through spirituality, through stories of living and coping, and through numerous other ways articulated by the Aboriginal participants in our research studies – are decentred and marginalized in favour of Western perspectives of what constitutes legitimate and appropriate ways of knowing and being in schools. Students who are 'other' but have managed to succeed within this hiearchicized system have done so at the expense of sacrificing their own cultural inheritance and the rich learning and understanding that go with it. Doll (2002) refers to this restriction and imbalance as the ghost of control in curriculum. He urges us to deploy the formidable 'post' weapon now at our disposal – for example, postmodernism, poststructuralism, postpatriarchy, postcolonialism – to introduce new visions of curriculum that lay to rest the ghost of control and allow curriculum to notice what goes on in its name and what has been lost so that no one ever again gets lost in curriculum's technology, structure, knowledge, and pedagogy.

I want to argue that it is only through authentic encounters with the 'other' – other individuals, communities, and world-views – that we may begin to free ourselves from the ghosts of curriculum control and genuinely hear the voices of non-dominant culture students, like the Aboriginal students in our research, about what constitutes meaningful and empowering learning for them in the formal education system. My argument here resonates with one of the fundamental questions posed by Beyer and Apple (1998) in the interrogation of curriculum for livable forms of life: How must we treat others responsibly and ethically in education?

I support Levinas' (1981) position that an ethical relationship begins when the self encounters the other and recognizes the other's otherness as irreducible to sameness. This encounter has the responsibility to call into question the privileges of the self and to decentre the self to allow the empowerment of the other. It is a reciprocal relationship between two subjects in which no one is an object to be acted upon. Authentic curricular and pedagogical encounters with our students require us, as educators, to step aside and question (and allow students to question) our frames of reference so that spaces can be created for other ways of seeing the world. Such encounters also require us to *listen* and to learn from the manifold funds of knowledge which students bring to the learning situation so that both subjects (the student and the teacher) emerge from the educational encounter with an awareness of their capacity for continuous construction of the world and the awareness that what they are and what they know can never completely

contain what they might be and what they might know. The dislocation involved in this encounter is uncomfortable as we go through the
difficult challenge of questioning our own assumptions and allowing
students to do the same. But it is an important way to begin to develop
ethical ways of being with our students.

In generating a reconceptualized theory of curriculum I want to
invoke four curriculum metaphors which, in my view, will take into
account the voices of our Aboriginal research participants and provide Aboriginal students with curriculum futures that are livable
and imbued with human dignity. Metaphors matter because they
have material effects. According to Norman Fairclough (1992, p. 195)
'When we signify things through one metaphor rather than another,
we are constructing our reality one way rather than another. Metaphors structure the way we think and the way we act, and our systems
of knowledge and beliefs in a pervasive and fundamental way.' My
four curriculum metaphors are curriculum as currere, curriculum as
spiritual journey and transcendence, curriculum as conversation, and
curriculum as community. These metaphors appeal to me personally,
as an educator, because of their potential for evoking meaningful and
empowering learning for students.

Curriculum as Currere

'Curriculum' is defined as 'running, a course, race chariot' and originates from *currere* which means 'to run' and 'to run a course' (Doll,
2002). But there is a distinction between curriculum and currere, one
that became clearer to me after I first read Pinar and Grumet's (1976)
characterization of curriculum both as a noun meaning 'a course of
study' usually prescribed by someone and currere as a verb meaning 'to
run a course.' Hence, it is possible to conceive of curriculum as a noun
where the focus is on the course as material object, and/or curriculum
as a verb which focuses on the running of the course as personal experience. Doll (2002) notes that over the past 400 years curriculum has
been considered almost exclusively as a course to be run and not as the
personal experience of the running. In other words, we have neglected
the personal experiences of the educational journey for students – experiences that are shaped by race, gender, class, sexual orientation, and
other markers of difference. As Doll explains, even though there were
counter-movements to the curriculum-as-sequenced-courses frame,

none began with the personal experience of the individual (the runner) and asked that individual to reflect on what was happening personally as the running (or moving/racing through the curriculum) progressed.

This existential/personal experience of the curriculum is what currere is really all about. The method of currere is devised to disclose and examine such experience 'so that we may see more of it and see more clearly. With such seeing can come deepened understanding of the running and with this can come deepened agency' (Pinar & Grumet, 1976, p. vii). Pinar describes the method of currere as autobiographical, consisting of four steps or moments depicting both temporal and reflective moments in the study of educational experience: the regressive, the progressive, the analytical, and the synthetical (Pinar et al., 1995, p. 520).

In the regressive moment one's lived experience becomes the data source. To generate data, one utilizes the psychoanalytic technique of free-association 'to recall the past, and enlarge, and thereby transform one's memory.' Regression requires one to return to the past, 'to recapture it as it was and as it hovers over the present' (Pinar et al., 1995, p. 520). In the progressive moment one looks toward what is not yet present, what is not yet the case, and imagines possible futures. The analytical moment involves a kind of phenomenological bracketing where one distances oneself from the past and asks: 'How is the future present in the past, the past in the future, and the present in both?' (p. 520). The synthetical moment brings it all together as one reenters the lived present and interrogates its meaning.

In these reflective moments reside opportunities for meaning making, understanding, and the transformation that should accompany the encounter between the student and the curriculum. In a pedagogical sense, it means paying attention to the educational experience of students (e.g., Aboriginal students) and asking them: What does this (topic, classroom activity, experience) mean to you? How does this make you feel? In these probing, personal questions lies the beginning of a dialogic and transformative curriculum which moves experience from being molded and controlled by others to that of reflective dialoguing with self and with others to make sense of experience. It is in this negotiating of passages between ourselves and our students that a new curriculum spirit is born (Doll, 2002). The phenomenological (lived experience) and dialogic nature of this encounter invokes notions of curriculum as a spiritual journey and as conversation.

Curriculum as a Spiritual Journey and Transcendence

Recall the intensely spiritual experience reported by the Aboriginal students as they verbally reflected on their fieldtrips to Aboriginal ceremonies and as they reflected on curriculum topics and classroom activities through reflective journal writing. This experience was made possible by creating the space for these students to draw on their inner and cultural resources to make connections and sense of the educational encounters they had had. Education, I believe, is inherently a spiritual quest in the sense of envisioning it as a journey of continuously transforming the given (e.g., the given curriculum) into new forms of life. Dwayne Huebner (1999), who has spent much of his professional life challenging the dominant scientific language of the curriculum – with its emphasis on efficiency, prediction, and control – and cultivating a spiritual language to talk about education, sees curriculum in terms of 'moreness' and 'beyondness,' more than and beyond the given and the expected so that the educational experience becomes a transcendent journey of continuously entering into newness – new understandings, new awarenesses, and new ways of being.

The meaning of 'spiritual,' in this sense, is imbued with the transformative, transcendent, and creative power of life. As Wang (2002) elaborates in relation to present-day sensibilities, such a meaning of 'spiritual' is no longer trapped by the exclusive and suppressive role of religious dogma which is a source of tremendous fear over the introduction of religious education into schooling. To be spiritual is to identify with more than the present, more than current forms of life, toward a transcendent dimension of human experience (Huebner, 1985).

Like our Aboriginal participants who lamented the absence of the Aboriginal philosophy of 'non-interference' in favour of adult control in the formal schooling of students, I mourn the absence of curricular interactions that help learners participate in the continuous reconstruction of the world. Within the language of normative control there is little room left for anything beyond the given as schooling has become a one-directional process flowing from adult to child, a process which severely limits students' capacity for imagining new possibilities and transcending given forms of life. The conception of curriculum as a spiritual journey in the sense of 'moreness' and beyondness' resonates loudly with what Ann (the Aboriginal teacher in our research) said about the school's relationship with Aboriginal students: 'You know what? I think the school, the school system will give them (Aboriginal students) more by controlling their behaviours less … Schools need to let go, so that Aboriginal students can develop awareness of who they are and what they ought to be' (excerpt from final interview).

Huebner points out that one of the difficulties in seeing education and curriculum as a spiritual journey originates from the language of individualism in notions of the self in Western tradition. This notion of self as an isolated individual – independent, complete, and constant – breeds fear of the stranger and the strange. The stranger is someone alien to us, with unfamiliar language, worldviews, and ways of life. To invite the stranger into our horizon is to risk questioning our own worldviews and forms of life. This fear blocks the possibility of authentic engagement with others for the change and transformation which makes education a spiritual journey. As data from the Aboriginal students in our research show, this concept of the unitary self is not a valued form of life in Aboriginal cultures, where life is embedded in an organic and dynamic interconnectedness with others – other human beings, nature, and the cosmos.

Parker Palmer (1981), in *The Company of Strangers*, suggests that the stranger can serve as a spiritual guide for questioning taken-for-granted views and assumptions, challenging conventional truths, and bringing the promise of new life. Educators can draw on Palmer's notion of the stranger to challenge the language of a unitary, complete self and introduce the notion of stranger into education and curriculum. To dwell in the horizon of the stranger is to regard oneself as incomplete, challenge the 'heimisch' (home, habitual and comfortable ways of thinking and behaving), and open oneself up to new possibilities for learning and developing a new awareness of the world. As Freire (1998, p. 58) writes, 'It is in our incompleteness, of which we are aware, that education as a permanent process is grounded. Men and women are capable of being educated only to the extent that they are capable of seeing themselves as unfinished … It is our awareness of being unfinished that makes us educated.' The 'turning inside out and turning outside in of self' entailing this process helps us better understand ourselves and what we might become. These turnings or critical self-examination, put us in a better position to dialogue with others to mutually construct a new reality marked by mutual transformation. In this sense, education is a spiritual quest for newness and moreness of self, others, and the world. An example of this kind of transformation is the non-Aboriginal student in our research who reported that the negative, stereotypical views he had held about Aboriginal people had changed as a result of our integration of Aboriginal perspectives into his Social Studies lessons. As Huebner (1993) writes, the process of being educated is always a process of 'encountering something that is strange and different, something that is not me' (pp. 407–8).

The meeting of the teacher with students is always a meeting with the stranger. To acknowledge students as stranger is to acknowledge and respect students' otherness – their ways of knowing and being, their difference – and to create room for the teacher's own transformation through encounters with the students. Wang (2002) writes that our very notion of students as 'learners' can sometimes deprive students of their right to participate in the mutual construction of knowledge in this encounter and put students under the control of adults and their established world. In a conception of students as stranger, teaching becomes an invitation for students to participate in a shared construction of a new reality and a joint search for meaning.

Dwelling with the stranger and surrendering part of oneself in order to create a new reality that is informed by mutuality can be overwhelming and even threatening, requiring a community that is supportive and imbued with love, faith, and hope. I will elaborate on this concept of community later in the discussion of my curriculum metaphors. For now I take up that notion of curriculum which makes possible the mutual construction of a new reality, that is, curriculum as conversation.

Curriculum as Conversation

In invoking an image of curriculum as conversation I am attempting to restore a part of ourselves and our being with others that has been lost in what Noel Gough (2002) calls the 'clockwork curriculum' where everything is driven by time and where there is never enough time for anything meaningful. In our research, this loss was lamented by both the non-Aboriginal teacher (Mrs J in School Y) who said she could not find time in the overloaded school schedule to provide the experiential learning which Aboriginal students needed for their personal growth, and the Aboriginal teacher (Ann) who could not use her literature circles to maximum learning effect because there simply was not enough time for every student in the circle to speak. Both teachers appear to be calling for curriculum space that makes possible the creation of knowledge and understanding in the actual lived situation.

In both its common and fairly recent meaning as 'an interchange of thoughts and words' and 'talking with' (*Oxford English Dictionary*) and in its historical meaning as 'to turn oneself about' (Doll, 2002), conversation is the place of learning where we meet with others, exchange ideas, and transform ourselves (turn ourselves about) as our differing views converge on what we are trying to understand. Ellsworth (2005) would describe the process as 'knowledge in the making' which is more life affirming than 'knowledge already made' for impartation to students. Hans-Georg Gadamer (1993/1960) writes that true conversation does not impose prepackaged answers on others as this closes off the possibility of arriving at true understanding. Instead, our task in conversation is not only to speak well but, more importantly, to listen well, to hear back both our own words and those of others and allow ourselves to become transformed. Gadamer writes:

> Conversation is a process of coming to an understanding. Thus it belongs to every true conversation that each person opens himself [sic] to the other, truly accept his point of view as valid, and transposes himself into the other to such an extent that he understands not just the particular individual but what he says. (p. 385)

At the curricular level, I understand Gadamer to mean that genuine understanding can only occur when we transpose ourselves into otherness – for example, the otherness of our students and the otherness of the curriculum materials being studied. Bernstein (1991) explains what hearing the other in true conversation means:

> It means taking our own fallibility seriously, resolving that however much we are committed to our own styles of thinking, we are willing to listen to others without denying or suppressing the otherness of the other. (p. 337)

This call to listen, seen by the Aboriginal students as a requirement for meaningful group work in classrooms, makes conversation more like dialogue where there is genuine interest on the part of both partners to hear the other's voice and a willingness to work together to develop understanding. From dialogue, the subject matter begins to emerge and take on new meanings and novel situations unanticipated by the partners. Aboriginal educators call this 'authentic dialogue' which seeks to understand the other, develops critical consciousness, is transformative, and is useful in helping students make sense of what they encounter.

Conversations also have a way of attending to what Gadamer calls 'the infinity of the unsaid.' These are the sighs, silences, and other bodily expressions which are all elements that should be taken into account for what is implicit and unsaid that may throw light on the topic under consideration. For example, attending to 'the infinity of the unsaid' beckons us to look to silence – a valued aspect of the cultural socialization of many Aboriginal peoples which schooling often marks as lack of knowledge and failure – as containing richness of meaning that pushes conversation beyond centralized control. Within the frenzy of the clockwork curriculum, there is little comfort or patience with silence or the acknowledgement of meaningful silence. It was precisely to counteract this lack of acknowledgement that each lesson in our enriched classrooms began with five minutes of meditational silence, which all the students acknowledged as having a calming effect and 'putting us in the mood for the lesson' (interview excerpt). It was also one of the reasons why the talking/discussion circles were appreciated – no one was forced to speak except if they wanted to.

In my own work as teacher educator and scholar of colour from a formerly colonized country, I have explored and continue to explore ideas of conversation as listening (as explicated by Gadamer and Bernstein) as I have critically engaged with culturally dominant ways of knowing and the vehicles through which this dominance is perpetuated, for example, schools and school curricula. In pursuing this line of work, I have joined a long list of critical educator-scholars for whom the well-trodden path of dominance is no longer tenable because it is a path to nowhere in the immensely complex web of interactions that is the world today. A different world calls for different tools with which to understand it and respond to it. I contend that one such tool is the engagement of curriculum as conversation, for therein lie potentials for encounters that will transform our understanding of curriculum, teaching, and learning.

Curriculum as Community

None of the foregoing three curriculum metaphors/visions is possible without an idea of curriculum as community. Although the meaning of community has expanded to include the ecological and cosmological, the community I have in mind here is the human community. Community is the glue that holds together currere, spiritual journey, and conversation as curriculum futures. Without community these others would be isolated entities without a solid grounding. As Doll (2002) points out, citing Richard Rorty, 'When we give up the notion of an absolute, present reality, then we realize that what is most important to each of us is what we have in common with each other, "they" are really one of us' (p. 50).

Community, with its emphasis on both *care* and *critique*, is what elevates us to something beyond ourselves. Without a community with whom to engage in critical reflection on experience and assumptions, currere becomes nothing more than narcissistic solipsism; the power of the transcendent inherent in the encounter with the stranger is diminished; and the opportunity for co-creation of knowledge and understanding with the other vanishes. Community, in its dual but integrated function of caring and critiquing our basic assumptions, allows the transformative potential of currere, conversation, and newness to emerge.

I wrote earlier in this chapter that the process of encountering the stranger or following the tide of the 'unheimisch' (that which is non-home, uncomfortable, and unfamiliar) can be overpowering, requiring a caring and supportive community in which one can dare to open up, challenge oneself and others, and create/acquire new awareness and understanding. As Huebner (1985) writes, 'We can face the threat of the unknown and of the stranger if we are not alone; if we are in the presence of love which affirms life' (p. 363). A community of love and trust helps us heal and restore unity to what may be disrupted by the stranger (see Wang, 2002). This kind of community seems to be missing in the classrooms of formal schooling. It must be cultivated, however, so that Aboriginal students like Ned and Chris – who said they simply withdraw and shut down in the community of the school classroom – can no longer remain hidden and can speak in the open without fear of criticism or being seen as wrong. This is what the students referred to as a 'nurturing learning environment' (see Chapter 6). It is also this type of community that teachers need to build through supportive networks that will increase their sense of efficacy for integrating Aboriginal perspectives into schools and classrooms.

To think about community in this way is to think relationally, that is, to develop awareness that to understand education is to situate it back into the unequal relations of power in the larger society and the relations of dominance and subordination generated by these relations (see Apple, 2006). Thus instead of simply teaching the curriculum for mastery of subject matter reflected in test scores, curriculum implementation should be an interpretive process attentive to questions such as: Whose knowledge is this curriculum? How did it become 'official

212 Integrating Aboriginal Perspectives into the School Curriculum

knowledge' for all? What is the relationship between this knowledge and who has cultural, social, and economic power in this society? What can we do as critical educators and activists to change these inequalities and help create a more just society through our curriculum and pedagogy? These are serious questions that require serious answers if we care enough about each other as a community and if our goal as educators is to develop critically informed citizens who are able to combine a politics of recognition (identity, representation, positionality of the other) with a politics of wealth redistribution so that the economic and social inequities that have severely limited educational opportunities for Aboriginal students will dissipate. Of course, this makes education quite political, but that's precisely my point.

The curriculum metaphors/futures I have proposed here radically reconceptualize curriculum theory so that curriculum comes to be seen not as 'a thing made' to be transmitted or imposed on others but as an anomalous place of learning – peculiar, abnormal, strange, and difficult, especially when viewed from the perspective of dominant educational discourses and practices – a place where the learning selves (teacher and student) emerge thinking relationally and acknowledging that to be alive is to be continuously in relation with the world, with others, and with readiness to be transformed (see Ellsworth, 2005). Such a reconceptualized theory of curriculum interrupts current colonial relationships which impoverish curriculum and render it morally bankrupt.

Much of the research data I have presented in this book suggest that, if taken to heart, Aboriginal epistemologies and ontologies – distinct in many ways from the Western tradition that drives curriculum thinking – can provide substantial (if anomalous) places of learning that will revitalize curriculum. These places invite the learning self to explore and engage Aboriginal thoughts and beliefs such as the following: that interrelationships are fundamental to sense-making; that knowledge/ curriculum is always knowledge in the making among a community of learners for whom that knowledge is useful; that, as Haig-Brown (2008) concurs, knowledge resides in experience and in life itself and not in codified canons to be transmitted; that community-based knowledge (e.g., as represented by the accumulated knowledge of elders) is vital for the education of youth; that academic/school learning is always mediated and influenced by the learner's cultural socialization processes; that the self is never a free-standing entity, complete, and independent of others; that silence is an important site of learning and not a mark of stupidity; that spirituality is fundamental to some students' educational and personal development; that stories and the storied lives we live are fundamental to our understanding of the sacred curriculum stories that have been constructed for us in the form of answers rather than questions; that knowledge and understanding cannot be compartmentalized without stripping it of its spirit; that learning is a holistic process that takes into account the mental, the emotional, the spiritual, and the physical.

As the reader may notice from the research data on Aboriginal student learning presented in this book, this list is not exhaustive but it captures some of the significant characteristics of Aboriginal thought from which curriculum studies can learn. These characteristics move us beyond the current language of prediction and control in curriculum toward notions of curriculum as currere, spiritual journey and transcendence, conversation, and community as I have expounded. While some of these metaphors are not entirely new in curriculum theorization, their actual implementation at the practical level in schools is still unrealized despite policy demands. Earlier in the book I described some of the challenges and tensions creating the chasm between the demands for and principles of the integration of Aboriginal perspectives and the realities surrounding actual integration.

In the rest of this chapter I will again draw on lessons from our research data to make suggestions / recommendations that may resolve these challenges/tensions and bring Aboriginal perspectives into classrooms. My discussion will focus on four constituencies of salience to the success of the integration of Aboriginal perspectives: teachers and teacher education programs; school contexts; the Aboriginal community; and the larger social, economic, and political contexts of Aboriginal education.

Teachers and Teacher Education Programs

Judging by the curriculum policy frameworks on Aboriginal education emerging across Canada, there is an apparent commitment to closing the achievement gap between Aboriginal students and their mainstream counterparts by calling on school teachers, principals, and administrators to provide learning environments that address the socio-cultural needs of Aboriginal students and their distinct epistemological values and beliefs. The frameworks demand specifically that Aboriginal worldviews, traditions, and perspectives be accounted for in school curricula and teachers' pedagogies, recognizing that a major issue affecting Aboriginal student achievement is a lack of understanding within schools and among teachers and school administrators of First Nations, Inuit, and Métis cultures, histories, and perspectives (see, for example, the Ontario, Manitoba, and Saskatchewan policy frameworks for 2007).

Based on these frameworks it would seem that, theoretically, the principle behind the integration of Aboriginal perspectives is accepted in public educational policy. However, the gap between these theoretical statements and actual practice is as evident today as it was over a decade ago when the Royal Commission on Aboriginal Peoples report was first published. As our research data show, actual implementation is fraught with tensions and challenges ranging from teachers' lack of confidence in their knowledge about Aboriginal histories, cultural values, and issues, to concerns over whether Aboriginal students will perceive mainstream teachers' knowledge of Aboriginal perspectives as legitimate and genuine (see Chapter 5 for a list and descriptions of the challenges/tensions/concerns).

How can teacher education help teachers integrate into their teaching practice a culture, history, and community they do not understand and about whom they know so little? Given the short time available to education faculty members to prepare prospective teachers to acquire a broad array of knowledge and skills for teaching even typical students, policy makers are asking a lot of teacher education programs by demanding that they adequately prepare teachers to meet the challenges of teaching Aboriginal students in public schools. Within its limited time-frame the most effective job teacher education can do consists of the following: First, teacher education should expand prospective teachers' understanding of curriculum to include ideas of curriculum as currere, conversation, community, and spiritual journey and transcendence. Aboriginal perspectives cannot be effectively integrated into classrooms without this expanded understanding, which has the effect of challenging prospective teachers' taken-for-granted notions of curriculum and what it means to be a teacher in a pluralistic, democratic society.

Next, teacher education should help teachers acquire accurate knowledge about Aboriginal peoples and how to infuse that knowledge into school classrooms. Courses like *Aboriginal Studies for Educators*, developed in collaboration with members of university Native Studies departments and other Aboriginal peoples, will provide an important building block for energizing Aboriginal education in schools, class-rooms, and teacher education programs. Some faculties of education are already offering a course or two on Aboriginal history and culture as a graduation requirement for their teacher candidates, but to be effective, Aboriginal perspectives must be integrated into every course throughout the teacher education program. Stand-alone courses are useful for providing knowledge of Aboriginal culture and history, espe-cially the history of pre-contact traditional Aboriginal education versus Aboriginal experiences with education after contact and the history of the appropriation of Aboriginal land, which serve to provide teacher candidates with a clearer and deeper understanding of what is at stake in school and in the broader society for Aboriginal peoples. Howev-er, teacher candidates are often left wondering how and where such knowledge fits into the subject areas they will be teaching, and teacher education should help them make these connections. We also need to infuse more positive messages about Aboriginal people in these cours-es. Often, discussions about the educational needs of Aboriginal stu-dents tend to focus more on the problems they face, including poverty, substance abuse, suicide, teen pregnancy, and less on positives like the resiliency of Aboriginal peoples and the cultural strengths that might be used to support their academic learning. Knowledge that balances the strengths of Aboriginal peoples with the problems they face and an analysis of the social, economic, and political roots of these problems would provide teachers with a much more accurate picture.

Focus should then shift towards helping teachers draw on these expanded understandings and on the research base on Native student learning that has emerged over the last 30 years to improve not only the academic performance of Native students but also the quality of the educational journey/experience (currere) of Native students in public schools. From the research base, including the research presented in this book, we know a lot about how Native students learn, what works for them, and under what conditions (see, e.g., Demmert's 2001 com-prehensive research review of over 100 studies that provide evidence of what works and what does not work to improve academic performance for Native students).

Research (e.g., Stodolsky & Grossman, 2000; Kanu, 2009) has sug-gested that one of the main reasons teachers do not make use of find-ings from such research to change or adapt their practices to meet the learning needs of diverse students, like Aboriginal students, is teach-ers' preoccupation with the narrow goal of transmitting curriculum content for mastery by students instead of using content as a vehicle for achieving broader goals that combine mastery of content with students' personal and social development, and social justice issues. Teacher education can reverse this tendency by socializing teachers into developing a broader vision that encompasses multifaceted teaching goals and beliefs about subject matter and students. An expanded understanding of curriculum, accurate knowledge about Aboriginal peoples, and familiarity with the research base on what works for Native students should serve as the point of departure for learning on the job about how to teach Native students.

Learning on the job means that teachers undertake specific activities in order to become effective educators of Native students. Three such activities, derived from our research findings, are: re-educating yourself, developing a reliable resource pool, and pushing for professional development.

Re-educating yourself: Evidence from our research and from a Student Awareness Study conducted by CAAS in 2002 among post-secondary institutions in eight provinces and one territory across Canada suggests that teachers and students know very little about Aboriginal peoples and what little they know can actually hurt those they teach (see www. Edu.yorku.ca/caas/findings.htm).

Recognizing their own limited and distorted knowledge about Aboriginal peoples and cultures, the Social Studies teachers in the enriched classrooms in our research took steps to re-educate themselves by doing a number of things simultaneously. For example, they availed themselves of the learning opportunities provided by resources such as websites and books designed to convey accurate and culturally specific information about Aboriginal groups; they entered into mentoring relationships with knowledgeable Native colleagues and community members to ensure that what they taught in their classrooms was both accurate and appropriate; and they made concerted effort to know the community of their Aboriginal students by attending workshops and information sessions on Aboriginal issues, attending appropriate cultural and social events, and developing relationships with community leaders. The teachers reported that these efforts paid off by increasing their knowledge, confidence, and efficacy beliefs about their ability to integrate Aboriginal perspectives into their classrooms.

In addition, the teachers surrounded themselves with a support network of colleagues who were also taking steps to teach from an Aboriginal perspective. For example, Social Studies teacher, Mr B (from school X) regularly had lunch with and shared resources with a colleague teaching the Cree language in his school. He also solicited and received support from his department head 'who has been able, somehow, to get the school to fund my attendance at professional development workshops' (interview excerpt). An even bigger pay-off of these 'on-the-job-preparation strategies' (as Mrs J in School Y called them) was their cumulative effect on helping the teachers question their preconceived epistemic and pedagogical values and traditions vis-à-vis those of Aboriginal peoples. As Mrs J put it in an interview, 'The more I have learned new things, the more I have challenged the pre-existing knowledge and beliefs I brought to teaching. It's been uncomfortable but it has changed who I am as a teacher.' I whole-heartedly recommend these on-the-job strategies for teachers interested in becoming effective educators of Native students.

Developing a resource pool: My second recommendation is that teachers should develop their own classroom-ready resources that relate to their curriculum units and the specific students and communities in which they teach. As I suggested earlier in the book, it is incumbent on provincial and territorial governments but also the federal government which is responsible for 'Indians and lands reserved for Indians' (from the Royal Proclamation of 1763) to provide funding for the resources needed to promote Aboriginal school success. Aboriginal organizations and other agencies (e.g., Canadian Race Relations Foundation) working in the interest of racial justice have appealed to the various levels of government for this funding. However, teachers cannot sit back and wait for funding to come through before bringing Aboriginal perspectives to classrooms. As one of the teachers in our study on teachers' perceptions of the integration of Aboriginal perspectives (see Chapter 7) said, 'Some excellent resources have already been developed by Aboriginal educators across the country. We only have to make the time to access and adapt them.' Accessing, validating, and adapting existing materials can be time-consuming as we found out during our research. Reward, however, lies in the increase in students' instrumental motivation, that is, the extent to which they are motivated to engage and complete their school work, which is a prerequisite for achieving academic success. Over time, teachers who create resources for integration into their various curriculum units will have a bank of reliable classroom-ready Aboriginal materials they can use year after year and update as necessary.

In addition to the list of useful resources I have provided in Appendix A to Chapter 6, there are hundreds of websites and books which teachers can access and validate to help them with resource building. To know what is appropriate to access for integration I suggest that teachers consult two documents created by CAAS. The first is the CAAS Learning Circle, which offers detailed insight into the Aboriginal studies content that should be integrated across school curricula in Canada and a framework for how this can be done. The second document is the accompanying Proposed Learning Expectations (PLEx). (These documents are available at www.edu.yorku.ca/caas/LearningCircle&PLEx. doc.) The Learning Circle contains four broad categories/topics placed at cardinal points in the circle, and each category is identified with a season. North, identified with Winter, covers content on the wisdom, understanding, traditions, and world-views of Aboriginal peoples; East, identified with Spring, covers topics on European colonization and its impact, Aboriginal resistance, and survival; South, representing Summer, allows students to understand Aboriginal strength and identity and the diverse Aboriginal Nations, stories, and dynamic cultures; West, depicting Autumn, represents a time of renewal and rebuilding and includes content on Aboriginal peoples' future aspirations and their effort to remove the damaging structures and barriers resulting from colonization. The PLEx serve as an elaboration of the categories/ topics depicted in the Learning Circle.

The Learning Circle and PLEx were created to help educators develop what CAAS calls a classroom pedagogy based on respect and honesty between all the peoples of Canada. Created in active collaboration with Aboriginal teachers and elders and vetted by Aboriginal groups across Canada, these documents are intended to foster the integration of Aboriginal content and perspectives across curricula in Canadian classrooms, rather than compartmentalization of separate study units on Aboriginal peoples. Along with the sample learning outcomes I suggested in Chapter 4, the Learning Circle and PLEx can provide a framework that will help teachers enrich their instruction and enliven the integration of Aboriginal perspectives in their classrooms. Teacher educations programs can also consult these documents to create courses in Aboriginal studies for educators.

Push for professional development: My third recommendation for learning on the job is for teachers to push their school administrators for professional development training that will better prepare teachers to work with Aboriginal students, understand Aboriginal history and cultures, and develop methods and materials that will increase student motivation and academic achievement. Research-based practices that work with Aboriginal students should be sought out by teachers and incorporated into their instructional repertoires. The broader teachers' instructional repertoires, the more able and willing they are to adapt their curricula and pedagogies to meet diverse learning needs.

Overall, our research suggests that when teachers make an effort to educate themselves about Aboriginal peoples and increase their professional efficacy through resource development and professional development training, they are much more likely to increase motivation and academic achievement among Aboriginal students. Success, as Starnes (2006) points out, will not be immediate or consistent, so teachers will need to find a pace that is comfortable, a direction that feels right, and give themselves time: 'Think years instead of months, and months rather than weeks,' Starnes writes. 'We are, after all, trying to change generations of cultural interactions and mistrust. That is slow work' (p. 390).

What Schools Should Do

The self-evaluation and admission of ignorance about Aboriginal peoples among the teachers interviewed for our research suggest that teachers need a lot of help to make them feel confident and comfortable teaching about Aboriginal peoples. The few who are making extra effort on their own to increase their knowledge about Aboriginal peoples, histories, cultures, and issues also expressed the need for support and help. Schools can offer such support and help by doing a number of things.

For a start, schools have to convince themselves about the importance of this work. School principals who show only weak support for the integration of Aboriginal perspectives, who do not back up their rhetoric about integration with action, or who think that integration is only necessary in schools with large populations of Aboriginal students are sending the wrong message to teachers who will pick up on this message and, in turn, develop weak efficacy beliefs about the integration of Aboriginal perspectives in their schools and curricula. With a strong commitment to integration, school boards can push their provincial or territorial and the federal governments for the funding needed for resources and teachers' professional development training, without which teachers will not take the risks necessary to implement integration. Commitment to integration also requires school leaders to undertake professional development activities to educate themselves about Aboriginal peoples and how to implement respectful and culturally appropriate school practices. They should take the time to inform teachers about government policies on Aboriginal education and their implications, if any, for school policies and practices. In addition, some professional development days can be used to bring teachers and Aboriginal educators together to develop materials and bridge the school and the community.

Earlier in the chapter, I mentioned the mentoring of mainstream teachers by knowledgeable and supportive members of the Aboriginal community. Schools should encourage such a mentoring program as part of ongoing support for teachers and other school staff. As evidenced in our interviews with teachers (see Chapter 7), not all teachers know an Aboriginal person or have connections with Aboriginal communities or resources. Developing these connections can be intimidating and often involves extraordinary effort by an individual teacher. Schools should help teachers develop opportunities for this kind of networking by carefully matching teachers with appropriate individuals from the Aboriginal community. Aboriginal mentors can help vet and validate instructional materials and activities, illuminate cultural rules of conduct that may not be clear to school personnel, and protect teachers from controversial issues in the community (see Starnes, 2006). Each school should create a cultural advisory committee consisting of teachers and Aboriginal elders and parents. Such a committee could help the development and screening of Aboriginal curriculum content and learning activities before being implemented in classrooms.

Research (e.g., Kanu, 2009) has shown that school factors such as teachers' workload and the subject department are strong determinants of teachers' willingness and ability to embark on new practices to bring about students' success. The teachers in the regular (non-integrated) classrooms in our research (see Chapter 5) referred to the lack of time, because of a heavy teaching load, to find and adapt Aboriginal curriculum materials for integration in their classrooms. In the light of this finding, schools committed to the integration of Aboriginal perspectives must ensure reduced workloads for teachers to afford them time to pursue what they need to help them with their integration efforts. In addition, members of subject departments must meet regularly to discuss how best they can integrate Aboriginal perspectives into their subject areas and how best to gain access to professional development opportunities for department members. As mentioned earlier, the school as a whole must maintain conversations about effective ways of attending to student diversity.

How the Aboriginal Community Can Help

> Well, the thing about incorporating Aboriginal topics is that I fear I may get something wrong and I'll be judged as another White person intentionally passing on wrong information about Aboriginal people. Even when you think you have read about Aboriginal histories and cultures, it's still difficult to get everything right about each group and you may end up causing harm or controversy. It's safer to avoid Aboriginal topics or just teach what's in the textbook.
>
> Mr J, Social Studies teacher in the regular classroom in School Y

As this excerpt from our teacher interviews shows, many teachers are afraid of taking the risk to integrate Aboriginal perspectives for fear of doing something to offend the Aboriginal community or cause controversy. Even the teachers in the enriched classrooms in our research, who were taking precautions to 'get things right' (e.g., by ensuring that all Aboriginal resources used in their classrooms were screened), and Ann (the Aboriginal teacher in the teachers' perception study reported in Chapter 7) continued to experience anxiety over causing offence and/or controversy.

If the Aboriginal communities see any value at all in the project of integrating Aboriginal perspectives (some may dissent because they see the education system as too corrupt, compromised, and fundamentally destructive) they can help teachers overcome this fear by providing them with accurate and culturally appropriate knowledge about Aboriginal groups. As mentioned earlier, reliable and useful Aboriginal content materials have been developed and more are being developed by Aboriginal educators. The problem, however, as we found out during our research, is that those materials are not getting to teachers or are not available in forms that teachers can readily use or connect with the curriculum units they teach. Nor are the materials getting into faculties of education where they can be used in teacher preparation programs. Two measures, therefore, need to be taken immediately to increase access to these materials. First Aboriginal educators must collaborate with teachers, teacher educators, and curriculum developers to create classroom-ready materials or adapt existing materials so they can support teachers' curriculum units. Second, and in line with CAAS's suggestion for a strategic plan to support the work of Aboriginal educators developing these materials, a system needs to be developed for distributing the materials to schools and faculties of education, and promoting their use through professional development sessions. These measures, along with those I have suggested in the summary section of Chapter 7, will require funding from various levels of government. The Aboriginal community must push for this funding if teachers' fears are to be allayed. Undoubtedly, teachers will make mistakes in their integration efforts, requiring patience from the Aboriginal community, but the biggest mistake of all would be to allow their fears to paralyse them into inaction

Another problem that became apparent during our research among teachers attempting to integrate Aboriginal perspectives into their curriculum units was the lack of or difficulty finding access to Aboriginal resource persons for classroom visits. As Dan said in our interview, it was frustrating that he could not get a resource person he needed for his Social Studies unit on Aboriginal government until four weeks after his request, long after the unit had been completed. Another teacher, Sam, recounted a story about a resource person who failed to show up, even though he had confirmed his visit with the teacher. The Aboriginal community can help by developing a system which will make it easier for classroom educators to access knowledgeable and reliable Aboriginal resource persons. For their part, schools must require their teachers to plan ahead and put in their request for Aboriginal resource persons well ahead of time so that appropriate arrangements can be made for timely classroom visits.

Finally, as I wrote earlier, many Aboriginal elders are quite committed to the idea of tradition being flexible and adaptive to their peoples' needs. However, there are also traditionalists in the Aboriginal communities who see Indigenous knowledge as frozen in some ideal tradition that must be taught to students in pristine forms. To this latter group I say that if Indigenous knowledge is to make a contribution to the development of transformative alternative frameworks for education, we must resist the urge to conceive it as an unchanging and unchanged entity, because tradition is not merely preserved and handed down to subsequent generations. As social and cultural changes occur, so do ways of confronting and organizing experience, and as experiences change so do modes of perception, including perceptions of what a tradition is and means (see Kanu, 2006). Therefore, to remain relevant in the modern world Indigenous knowledge must be constantly questioned and recreated, consistent with Bhabha's third space of enunciation:

> It is that Third Space, though unrepresentable in itself, which constitutes the discursive conditions of enunciation that ensure the meaning and symbols of culture have no primodial unity or fixity; that even the same signs can be appropriated, translated, rehistoricized and read anew. (Bhabha, 1994, p. 37)

As Gadamer argues 'changing the established forms is no less a kind of connection with the tradition than defending the established forms. Tradition exists only in constant alteration' (cited in Hoy, 1982, p. 127). As 'living knowledge,' Indigenous knowledge offers real possibilities for decentring and reframing conventional thinking about curriculum, teaching, and learning. First, however, traditionalists need to read tradition as an open-ended text rather than as a closed entity. They also need to understand that the encounter between Indigenous knowledge and Western Eurocentric school knowledge involves cultural dislocation/ shift on both sides in order to attain mutual accommodation in classrooms. In this sense, encounter with the stranger offers a unique opportunity for critical self-examination which produces a more informed self-understanding and change in perspective.

The Need for Systemic Reform

> Two primary objectives of the residential schools system were to remove and isolate children from the influence of their homes, families, traditions and cultures, and to assimilate them into the dominant culture. These objectives were based on the assumption that Aboriginal cultures and spiritual beliefs were inferior and unequal ...
>
> We now recognize that it was wrong to separate children from rich and vibrant cultures and traditions, that it created a void in many lives and communities, and we apologize for having done this ...
>
> It [the Residential Schools Truth and Reconciliation Commission] will be a positive step in forging a new relationship between Aboriginal peoples and other Canadians, a relationship based on the knowledge of our shared history, a respect for each other and a desire to move forward together with a renewed understanding that strong families, strong com-

munities and vibrant cultures and traditions will contribute to a stronger
Canada for all of us.

Prime Minister Stephen Harper, 11 June 2008

In the foregoing excerpts – taken from Prime Minister Stephen Harper's apology to Canada's Aboriginal peoples for residential schools, delivered in the House of Commons on Wednesday, 11 June 2008 – the federal government of Canada publicly admitted its role in the destruction of Aboriginal cultures and traditions through its assimilationist educational policy, the devastating effect of this policy on Aboriginal peoples, and a desire to move in a new direction by forging a new relationship between Aboriginal peoples and other Canadians, based on respect for each other and each other's cultural traditions. Just as schools have been an endemic part of Canada's assimilationist policy at almost every turn, so can they play a vital role in directing progressive curriculum efforts toward critiquing and reversing the legacies of Canada's colonial educational policy.

As I have indicated throughout, however, schools alone cannot overcome the social and economic disadvantages that contribute to school failure among Aboriginal students, bringing into sharp focus the idea that equality requires holistic and systemic reform. In this regard the federal government should step in very strongly and back its apology and rhetoric of reconciliation and a new relationship with the financial resources needed to address the systemic problems contributing to educational underachievement among Aboriginal students – problems such as chronic poverty, perpetuated by the low participation of Aboriginal families in the labour market; under-resourced secondary schools on many First Nations reserves, which force Aboriginal students to leave their families and home communities to attend school in urban centres; lack of access to affordable, good-quality housing, which causes families to move frequently; poor health resulting from exposure to lead poisoning, smoke, poor nutrition, less than adequate pediatric care; and lack of parenting classes where topics such as the prevention of teen pregnancy and appropriate parenting skills are discussed.

A step in the right direction for addressing these problems and instituting social change was taken in November 2005, when the federal Liberal government, in an agreement known as the Kelowna Accord, pledged $5.1 billion over ten years to close the social and economic gap between Aboriginal peoples and average Canadians by improving education, housing, skills training, economic development, and health care for Aboriginal peoples. This accord, however, was promptly cancelled by Stephen Harper's Conservative government which came to power soon after the pledge was hammered out between Aboriginal leaders and Canada's first ministers. Harper's government refused to recognize the accord, dismissing it as a mere press release because the Liberal government had not provided for the agreement financially, and promising a new approach to improve social services for Aboriginals. The Liberals, however, maintained that the money for the accord had already been earmarked in their budget before they were defeated in the general elections. Needless to say, Aboriginal peoples are outraged by this reversal and as a result, many have expressed serious doubts about the sincerity of Harper's apology and its promise of a new relationship.

One post-apology strategy for redressing some of the inequality and injustice suffered by Aboriginal peoples would be for the Kelowna Accord to be reinstated, because the social and economic benefits accruing from it would have significant educational impact. For example, an increase in access to good-quality stable housing, better health care for Aboriginal peoples, better resourced schools in Aboriginal communities, after-school and summer programs aimed at increasing the academic performance and self-confidence of Aboriginal students, and increased child-tax credits for poor Aboriginal families might all contribute to decreasing the social and economic inequalities that produce the academic achievement gap (see Kanu, 2008).

Future research should especially look into the effectiveness of social and economic reform for the educational success of Aboriginal students. Such research, combined with studies of in-school factors that promote or impede the integration of Aboriginal perspectives and catalysts that encourage teacher transformation toward the integration of Aboriginal perspectives should provide us with a comprehensive picture of the structures that work synergistically to produce school success for Aboriginal students.

Summary

This chapter has discussed, broadly, the implications of the research studies reported in this book for curriculum and educational policy, practice, and future research. Based on the premise that successful integration of Aboriginal perspectives into school curricula requires a reconceptualized theory of curriculum, four curriculum metaphors were propounded as futures in curriculum: curriculum as currere, curriculum as spiritual journey and transcendence, curriculum as conversation, and curriculum as community. Implications were also drawn for a number of constituencies salient to the successful integration of Aboriginal perspectives in schools and classrooms – teachers and teacher education programs, schools, the Aboriginal community, and the larger social, economic, and political contexts of Aboriginal education. The chapter closed with suggestions for future research in three areas: the effects of social and economic reform on school success for Aboriginal students; in-school factors that promote or impede the integration of Aboriginal perspectives; and catalysts that encourage teacher transformation toward the integration of Aboriginal perspectives in classrooms.

QUESTIONS FOR DISCUSSION

1. To what extent do the curriculum metaphors discussed in this chapter expand your understanding of curriculum? What would classroom teaching look like through the lens of each of the four curriculum metaphors?
2. Summarize the in-school factors that best foster the integration of Aboriginal perspectives into schools and schooling processes. Can you think of other equally important in-school factors not mentioned in the chapter?
3. The chapter describes three strategies for learning on the job to integrate Aboriginal perspectives. List and discuss three further strategies you would use on the job to enhance your professional efficacy for integrating Aboriginal perspectives in your classroom.
4. The lead researcher and author of this book would like to describe the work presented in the book as socially relevant research that contributes to social justice. To what extent does the book contribute to social justice or relate to research as a public good that contributes to social redress?

REFERENCES/RECOMMENDED READINGS

Apple, M. (2006). *Educating the right way*. New York: Routledge.
Bernstein, R.J. (1991). *The new constellation: The ethical-political horizons of modernity / postmodernity*. Cambridge, MA: MIT Press.
Beyer, L.E., & Apple, M.W. (Eds.) (1998). *The curriculum: Problems, politics, and possibilities*. New York: State University of New York Press.

Bhabha, H.K. (1994). *The location of culture.* London: Routledge.

Dei, G.S., Mazzuca, J., McIssac, E., & Zine, J. (1997). *Reconstructing dropout: A critical ethnography of the dynamics of Black students' disengagement from school.* Toronto: University of Toronto Press.

Demmert, W. (2001). *Improving academic performance among Native American students: A review of the literature.* Charleston, VA: ERIC Clearinghouse on Rural and Small Schools.

Doll, W. (2002). Ghosts and the curriculum. In W.E. Doll & N. Gough (Eds.), *Curriculum visions,* pp. 22–70. New York: Peter Lang.

Ellsworth, E. (2005). *Places of learning: Media, architecture, pedagogy.* New York: Routledge.

Fairclough, N. (1992). *Discourse and social change.* Cambridge, MA: Polity.

Freire, P. (1998). *Pedagogy of freedom: Ethics, democracy, and civic courage.* Lanham, IN: Rowman & Littlefield.

Gadamer, H-G. (1993/1960). *Truth and method.* New York: Continuum.

Gough, N. (2002). Voicing curriculum visions. In W.E. Doll & N. Gough (Eds.), *Curriculum visions,* pp. 287–99. New York: Peter Lang.

Haig-Brown, C. (2008). Taking Indigenous thought seriously: A rant on globalization with some cautionary notes. *Journal of the Canadian Association for Curriculum Studies, 6*(2), 8–24.

Huebner, D.E. (1985). Spirituality and knowing. In *The lure of the transcendent: Collected essays by Dwayne E. Huebner,* Mahwah, NJ: Erlbaum.

– (1993). Education and spirituality. In *The lure of the transcendent: Collected essays by Dwayne E. Huebner,* pp. 401–16. Mahwah, NJ: Erlbaum.

– (1999). *The lure of the transcendent: Collected essays by Dwayne E. Huebner.* Collected and introduced by William Pinar. Mahwah, NJ: Erlbaum.

Hoy, D. (1982). *The critical circle.* Berkeley, CA: University of California Press.

Kanu, Y. (2006). Re-appropriating tradition in the postcolonial curricular imagination. In Y. Kanu (Ed.), *Curriculum as cultural practice: Postcolonial imaginations,* pp. 203–22. Toronto: University of Toronto Press.

– (2008). Closing the Aboriginal achievement gap: Why school reforms alone are not enough. In A.A. Abdi & G. Richardson (Eds.), *Decolonizing democratic education: Trans-disciplinary dialogues,* pp. 139–49. Rotterdam: Sense Publishers.

– (2009). Changing students, changing teaching: Understanding the dynamics of adaptation to a changing student population. *Journal of Cultural and Pedagogical Inquiry, 1*(1), 22–39.

Kawagley, A.D. (1995). *A Yup:iaq worldview: A pathway to ecology and spirit.* Prospect Heights, IL: Waveland.

Levinas, E. (1981). *Otherwise than being and beyondness.* The Hague: Martinus Nijhoff.

Palmer, P. (1981). *The company of strangers.* New York: Crossroad.

Pinar, W.F., & Grumet, M. (1976). *Toward a poor curriculum.* Dubuque, IA: Kendall/Hunt.

Pinar, W.F., Reynolds, W.M., Slattery, P., & Taubman, P.M. (1995). *Understanding curriculum: An introduction to the study of historical and contemporary curriculum discourses.* New York: Peter Lang.

Spivak, G. (1990). Gayatri Spivak on the politics of the subaltern. *Socialist Review, 20*(3), 85–97.

Starnes, B.A. (2006). What we don't know can hurt them: White teachers, Indian children. *Phi Delta Kappan, 87*(5), 384–92.

Stodolsky, S., & Grossman, P. (2000). Changing students, changing teaching. *Teachers College Record, 102*(1), 125–72.

Wang, H. (2002). The call from the stranger: Dwayne Huebner's vision of curriculum as a spiritual journey. In W.E. Doll & N. Gough (Eds.), *Curriculum visions,* pp. 287–99. New York: Peter Lang.

Index

Deyhle, D., 137

discrimination: of castelike minorities, 43; three forms of structural,
in education, 43–4; perceptions
and responses to, among voluntary immigrant groups, 44–5

Doll, W., 204–5, 209, 210–11; on need
to use 'post' weapon, 203

Doll, W., and N. Gough, 202

dropout. *See* school retention

Eccles, J.S., et al., 152

Edgerton, Susan, 48

efficacy: beliefs, students', 152–3;
beliefs, teachers' concerning
integration, 24–5, 144, 145–6, 177,
180–;1impact of teachers' sense
of, on student achievement, 144,
145–6, 219; strengthening teachers'
professional, 147, 191–2, 194, 219

Eisner, E., 102

elders: as keepers of knowledge, 29,
151; demonstrated understanding
of role of, as learning outcome,
103; as learning resource, 123, 149,
151–3, 156, 196; as teachers, 7, 152

Ellis, J., 79

Ellsworth, E., 209, 212

English-Currie, V., 83

English Language Arts: average
scores among First Nations students in, 20; learning outcomes
concerning Aboriginal cultural
knowledge in, 107–8

Ermine, W., 104

ethnography: avoiding biases in,
xiii; ethnographic data collection
methods, 58–61. *See also* research
studies

Eurocentric: epistemologies, 130–1,

223; perspectives on Aboriginal
peoples and history, 128

Eurocentrism: 15, 16; in education
system, x, 77, 100, 130, 172, 174.
See also colonialism

evaluation. *See* assessment

Eysink, T., et al., 66

Ezeife, A.N., 8, 9, 19, 123

Faulks, K., 11

First Nations: definition of, 28; and
federal government of Canada,
15–16, 20, 28

'First Nations Deficit,' 22

First Nations Education Resource
Centre, 98

First Nations Tribal Councils, 7

Fitznor, L., 150

Flemming, Walter, 69

Forbes, J., 103, 105

Foster, V., 133

Fraser, Nancy, 24, 140–1; on the
'postsocial condition,' 138–9

Freire, P., 207

Friesen, J.W., and V.L. Friesen, 4, 12,
96, 97

Fullan, Michael, 166, 193

Gadamer, Hans-Georg, 89, 223; on
conversation, 209–10; on 'the
infinity of the unsaid,' 209–10

Gaskell, J., and D. Kelly, 16

Gall, M.D., et al., 38

Gay, L.R., and P. Airasian, 38

Gee, J.P., 75

Giles, K.N., 123

Gipps, C.V., 113

Goldberg, D.T., 178

Goddard, R.D., et al., 146

Gonzalez, N., et al., 15, 179

236   Index

poverty, 126–8, 158, 215, 224. *See also*
Aboriginal peoples: socioeconom-
ic conditions of
Proposed Learning Expectations
(PLEx). *See under* Coalition for the
Advancement of Aboriginal Stud-
ies (CAAS)
psychogenesis vs. sociogenesis, 89,
91nn2,3
Pukatawagan: Cree students in, 19

racism: colour blindness, 48–9,
134–5; in the curriculum, 7, 77,
185; demonstrated understanding of the effects of, as learning
outcome, 103; epistemological,
178; as impediment to integration
of Aboriginal perspectives, 136,
176, 185–6; impact on academic
achievement, 24, 42, 134; racist
backlash, 135–6; theories of, and
anti-racism, 22, 40, 47–50
Rahim, L.Z., 54
Ramirez, M., and A. Castenada, 40
recommendations for the successful
integration of Aboriginal perspectives, 193–7, 213–26; need for
systemic reform, 223–5; recommendations for the Aboriginal
community, 221–3; recommendations for schools, 219–21; recommendations concerning teachers
and teacher education programs,
213–19; recommended resources
for educators and curriculum
developers, 160–4, 218
Reeves, D., 193
research studies (comprised in
Integrating Aboriginal Perspectives):
author's personal location in,

xii–xiii, 96, 210; implications of, 25,
201–26; intended audiences, 25;
Manitoba as focus of (generalizability of findings), 25, 26–8, 56–7;
objectives, 4, 56, 201; questions
investigated in, 21, 25, 55–6, 59–60,
98–9, 167, 202; recommendations
based on findings of, 193–7, 213–
26; study concerning integration
of Aboriginal perspectives, 23, 90,
95–164: data collection and analysis, 120–1; definition of 'Aboriginal perspectives,' 23, 30, 95–6;
description of study, 98–102; focus
on Social Studies curriculum, 95;
participants in study, 99–100, 121;
research questions posed, 98–9;
sites of study, 99; study concerning Manitoba teachers' views on
integration, xii, 21, 24–5, 165–97:
data collection and analysis, 168;
findings, 169–93 (*see also* teachers'
views on integration of Aboriginal perspectives); participants in
study, 167–8; research questions
posed, 167; urban focus of, 21;
study concerning students' identification of cultural mediators of
learning, 22, 54–90: data collection
and analysis, 58–61; description
of study, 56; findings, 61–85 (*see
also* cultural mediators of learning
identified by Aboriginal students); participants in study, 56–7;
research methods and procedures,
56–61; research questions posed,
55–6, 59–60; sites of study, 56–7,
58–9; summary, 85–8. *See also* cultural mediators of learning identified by Aboriginal students; data